Monetary Policy and Central Banking in Korea

T0328630

This study is among the first to examine the theory and practice of monetary policy in South Korea. Woosik Moon provides a detailed analysis of the central bank of South Korea, one of the most successful and important economies in Asia. He covers everything from monetary policy to inflation targeting and macroprudential regulation, explaining how these policy tools were used to deal with the aftermath of the 2008 global financial crisis. He then brings his study into our current moment, speculating as to how the use of these policies will change in order to deal with the fallout of the Covid-19 pandemic. This book offers in-depth investigations and the provision of the most up-to-date information about the Bank of Korea's monetary and financial actions, serving as essential reading for central bankers and professionals of financial markets around the world, as well as anyone interested in monetary policy-making.

WOOSIK MOON is Professor of Economics at the Graduate School of International Studies, Seoul National University. He was a member of the Monetary Policy Board of the Bank of Korea from 2012 to 2016.

Monetary Policy and Central Banking in Korea

WOOSIK MOON
Seoul National University

CAMBRIDGE
UNIVERSITY PRESS

Shaftesbury Road, Cambridge CB2 8EA, United Kingdom

One Liberty Plaza, 20th Floor, New York, NY 10006, USA

477 Williamstown Road, Port Melbourne, VIC 3207, Australia

314–321, 3rd Floor, Plot 3, Splendor Forum, Jasola District Centre, New Delhi – 110025, India

103 Penang Road, #05–06/07, Visioncrest Commercial, Singapore 238467

Cambridge University Press is part of Cambridge University Press & Assessment, a department of the University of Cambridge.

We share the University's mission to contribute to society through the pursuit of education, learning and research at the highest international levels of excellence.

www.cambridge.org
Information on this title: www.cambridge.org/9781009094207

DOI: 10.1017/9781009091527

First published 2022
First paperback edition 2024

A catalogue record for this publication is available from the British Library

Library of Congress Cataloging-in-Publication data
Names: Moon, Woosik, 1960– author.
Title: Monetary policy and central banking in Korea / Woosik Moon, Seoul National University.
Description: Cambridge, United Kingdom ; New York, NY : Cambridge University Press, 2022. | Includes bibliographical references and index.
Identifiers: LCCN 2021051454 (print) | LCCN 2021051455 (ebook) | ISBN 9781316514986 (hardback) | ISBN 9781009094207 (paperback) | ISBN 9781009091527 (ebook)
Subjects: LCSH: Monetary policy – Korea (South) | Banks and banking, Central – Korea (South) | Korea (South) – Economic policy. | BISAC: BUSINESS & ECONOMICS / Economics / Macroeconomics
Classification: LCC HG1280.5 .M86 2022 (print) | LCC HG1280.5 (ebook) | DDC 339.5/309515–dc23/eng/20211020
LC record available at https://lccn.loc.gov/2021051454
LC ebook record available at https://lccn.loc.gov/2021051455

ISBN   978-1-316-51498-6   Hardback
ISBN   978-1-009-09420-7   Paperback

To Christian de Boissieu, my teacher at the University of Paris-I, who taught me money and banking.

Contents

Figures

Tables

Boxes

Preface and Acknowledgements

Since the outbreak of the global financial crisis in 2008, monetary policy all around the world has undergone tremendous changes, which have been accompanied by the emergence of new instruments and principles. Many unconventional principles that have emerged because of the unprecedented crisis in 2008 are being established as the new normal. The COVID-19 pandemic is again likely to accelerate this trend. Korea is no exception and thus requires new thinking on its monetary policymaking.

Despite an increasing interest in the topic, not just on the part of the Korean public, but also on the part of international readers, no serious academic work on monetary policy in Korea has been published to date. The only work available is a short brochure published by the Bank of Korea in 2016 under a similar title, 'Monetary Policy in Korea', which leaves out theoretical deliberations as well as topical policy issues and debates. In general, there seem to be very few studies available about the monetary policies of Asian central banks, let alone that of the Bank of Korea. This may be due to the relatively short history of 'independent central banking' in Asia. The market economy has yet to be firmly established in Korea and many parts of Asia. Policymaking in Korea has for a long time been nothing but a bureaucratic and discretionary practice, often lacking democratic principles and theoretical considerations. But, for an independent central bank, monetary policymaking can no longer continue to be formulated in this way. It requires transparent and independent decision-making based upon theoretical knowledge. This explains why there are so few studies on monetary policymaking, despite the strong interest expressed from both academia and professional financial circles.

In the face of this lacuna, it is the intention of this book to conduct a comprehensive examination of the current practice of monetary policymaking in Korea. More precisely, it aims at combining the real practice implemented by the Bank of Korea with the new theoretical principles of monetary policy. And here it cannot be overemphasised that monetary policymaking in Korea has evolved, to a great extent, in tandem with the development of the market economy. The Bank of Korea should, therefore, be a guardian of the market economy against any arbitrary intervention or interference on the part of the government. Based upon this perspective, this book tries to analyse monetary policy and central banking in Korea.

Of necessity, the book also addresses Korean monetary policy and central banking from a comparative perspective. Above all, the Bank of Korea, as well as the Monetary Policy Board as its decision-making body, was modelled on the Federal Reserve System of the United States. Furthermore, many current policy tools and practices were indebted to the policymaking of major central banks such as the Federal Reserve System, the European Central Bank, and the Bank of Japan. The main content of the book will be as follows.

First of all, the volume begins by asking about the goals and objectives of economic and monetary policies in Korea. When it comes to monetary policy, in particular, it seems that many in the Korean public are not clear about its counter-cyclical nature of stabilisation, in that the goal is always to reduce volatility, whether it be inflation or output (employment).

Part II looks at how money and monetary policy affect the Korean economy. The evolution of different monetary and credit instruments is reviewed and the transmission channels through which monetary policy affects price and output in Korea are analysed.

Part III discusses the different aspects of central banking and monetary policy in Korea. As the most important and the longest part of this book, it evaluates and examines the organisation and structure of the Bank of Korea, the strategies and operating principles of its monetary policy, the inflation targeting and interest rate-setting process, as well as the tools and instruments of its monetary policy. This part argues that the traditional view that the interest rate is determined by money supply and demand is no longer valid. Under the current corridor system, the interest rate in Korea is determined by the announcement of the Bank of Korea, as in many other central banks, regardless of the amount of reserve money. Under the zero interest rate lower bound, furthermore, managing yield curves is emerging as a more important future monetary operation for the

Bank of Korea than its current short-term interest rate-setting operation.

Part IV deals with the issue of financial stability, especially macro-prudential policy. Korea was hit twice: first by the 1997 foreign exchange crisis, and then by the global financial crisis of 2008. These crises are not necessarily the result of market failure but are more often due to government failure. This part will examine the respective roles of the Korean government and Bank of Korea in the implementation of macro-prudential policy, given the latter's lack of sufficient policy tools. It will also cover the issue of the recent financial market stabilisation measures introduced to cope with the COVID-19 pandemic.

Finally, Part V briefly touches upon the possible future monetary policy operations and instruments available, given that the Korean economy is expected to record lacklustre economic growth accompanied by deflation. The outbreak of the 2008 global financial crisis and the spread of the COVID-19 virus will lead us to rethink the existing monetary policy framework. Against this backdrop, the Bank of Korea should strengthen its efforts to revamp its existing monetary policy tools and be prepared to manage the yield curve just like the Bank of Japan.

Given the dearth of comparable works on Korean monetary policy, it is my hope that this volume will provide anyone who is interested in monetary policymaking with a valuable in-depth analysis and the most up-to-date information on the Bank of Korea's monetary and financial policies.

This book is a direct development of my work as a member of the Monetary Policy Board. In this regard, I am very grateful to Lee Juyeol and Kim Choongsoo, governors of the Bank of Korea, with whom I had the great pleasure to work. I am also grateful to Jeong Heon Lee, Sunwoo Nam, and Yoonju Shin, who assisted me in accomplishing my work at the Bank of Korea successfully. Their support was essential for me to widen and deepen my knowledge of every task of the Korean central bank, and served as a catalyst for this book. For any and all mistakes and errors in this volume, I assume full responsibility. In closing, I would like to express my special thanks to Hongkee Kim, professor at Hannam University, Yeongseop Rhee, professor at Seoul National University, and Barry Eichengreen, professor at University of California – Berkeley, without whose encouragement I would never have dared to embark upon writing this book. I also wish to thank Seonghoon Cho, professor at Yonsei University, for providing me with the data on the natural rates of interest in Korea. I must also extend my gratitude to my two English language advisors, Frank O'Callaghan and Chris Engert, for their excellent English editing and proofreading, and to Su Gyoung Park, my MA student, for her valuable editorial assistance. This work was supported by the Seoul National University Research Grant in 2021. I am grateful to Seoul National University. Finally, I wish to thank Ransoo Kim, my wife, and Heeyoon, my son, for their consistent support and encouragement.

Abbreviations

ACCL	aggregate credit ceiling loan
ASEAN+3	Brunei, Darussalam, Cambodia, Indonesia, Lao People's Democratic Republic, Malaysia, Myanmar, the Philippines, Singapore, Thailand, and Viet Nam (ASEAN) + the People's Republic of China, Japan, and South Korea
B2B	business to business
B2C	business to consumer
BAI	Board of Audit and Inspection
BILSF	Bank Intermediated Lending Support Facility
BIS	Bank of International Settlements
BoE	Bank of England
BoJ	Bank of Japan
BoK	Bank of Korea
bp	basis points
B/S	balance sheet
CAMEL-R	Capital adequacy, Asset quality, Management, Earnings, Liquidity and Risk-management
CAMELS	Capital adequacy, Asset quality, Management, Earnings, Liquidity and Sensitivity to market risks
CBBLF	Corporate Bond-Backed Lending Facility
CBDC	central bank digital currency
CCyB	counter-cyclical capital buffer
CD	certificate of deposit
CESP	Comprehensive Economic Stabilisation Programme
CET	common equity tier
CIP	covered interest parity
CLS	continuous linked settlement system
CMA	cash management accounts
CMIM	Chiang Mai Initiative Multilateralisation
CNY	Chinese *Yuan* .

COFIX	cost of funds index
DSGE	dynamic stochastic general equilibrium
D-SIB	domestic systemically important banks
D-SIFI	domestic systemically important financial institutions
DSR	debt service ratio
DTI	debt to income
ECB	European Central Bank
ECOS	economic statistics system
ELA	emergency liquidity assistance
EMS	European Monetary System
EONIA	Euro Overnight Index Average
EPB	Economic Planning Board
ETF	exchange-traded funds
EUR	Euro
FCL	flexible credit line
Fed	Federal Reserve
FEEF	Foreign Exchange Equalisation Fund
Fintech	financial technology
FLS	funding for lending scheme
FOMC	Federal Open Market Committee
FRED	Federal Reserve Economic Data
FRS	Federal Reserve System
FSC	Financial Services Commission
FSCMA	Financial Investment Services and Capital Markets Act
FSOC	Financial Services Oversight Committee
FSR	Financial Stability Report
FSS	Financial Supervisory Services
FTA	free trade agreement
FX	foreign exchange
G7	Group of Seven: the seven major advanced economies – Canada, France, Germany, Italy, Japan, the United Kingdom, and the United States of America, plus the European Union
G20	Group of Twenty – comprising Argentina, Australia, Brazil, Canada, China, France, Germany, India, Indonesia, Italy, Japan, Mexico, Russia, Saudi Arabia, South Africa, South Korea, Turkey, the United Kingdom, and the United States, plus the European Union
GATT	General Agreement on Tariffs and Trade

GDP	gross domestic product
GHQ	General Headquarters
HCI	heavy-chemical industry
IMF	International Monetary Fund
IPI	Industrial Production Index
JGBs	Japanese Government Bonds
JPY	Japanese *Yen*
KAMCO	Korea Asset Management Corporation
KDIC	Korea Deposit Insurance Corporation
KFTC	Korea Financial Telecommunications and Clearings Institute
KORIBOR	Korea Inter-Bank Offered Rate
KRW	Korean *Won* (South Korea)
KTB	Korean Treasury Bonds
LCR	liquidity coverage ratio
LIBOR	London Inter-Bank Offered Rate
LOLR	lender of last resort
LTRO	longer-term refinancing operations
LTV	loan to value
MBS	mortgage-backed securities
MCT	M2 + Certificates of Deposit + Money-in-Trusts
MERS	Middle East respiratory syndrome
MFN	most favoured nation
MMDA	money market deposit accounts
MMF	money market fund
MOEF	Ministry of Economy and Finance
MOF	Ministry of Finance
MoFE	Ministry of Finance and Economy
MPB	Monetary Policy Board
MPC	Monetary Policy Committee
MRO	main refinancing operation
MSA	monetary stabilisation account
MSB	monetary stabilisation bond
MSL	macro-prudential stability levy
NDF	non-deliverable forward
NPL	non-performing loan
NSFR	net stable funding ratio
OECD	Organisation for Economic Co-operation and Development

OMO	open market operation
OMT	outright monetary transactions
P-CBOs	primary collateralised bond obligations
PCE	personal consumption expenditure
PF ABCP	project financing asset-backed commercial paper
PLL	precautionary and liquidity line
QE	quantitative easing
QQE	quantitative and qualitative easing
R&D	research and development
RP	re-purchase agreements
SAMP	Systemic Risk Assessment Model for Macro-prudential Policy
SME	small- and medium-sized enterprise
SNA	system of national accounts
SNS	social networking services
SPV	special purpose vehicle
TARP	Troubled Asset Relief Program
TLTRO	targeted longer-term refining operation
WTO	World Trade Organization

PART I

What Is the Goal of Korean Monetary Policy?

1 | *The Goals of Economic and Monetary Policy*

Economic policy refers to the actions of the state in defining its object-ives and using appropriate instruments to achieve them. The objectives of government in this regard are high long-run economic growth, equitable distribution of income and wealth, and stable prices and output. Macroeconomic policies, represented by monetary and fiscal policies, are just those intended to stabilise prices and output. This chapter begins by examining historically how these policy objectives have been addressed by the Korean government and, against this backdrop, looks at the goals of macroeconomic policy, especially mon-etary policy, in Korea.

1.1 The Evolving Goals of Economic Policy in the Korean Economy

As Figure 1.1 shows, economic policy in general pursues three object-ives: (1) high long-term economic growth, (2) equitable distribution of income and wealth, and (3) stable prices and output. They are also the primary concerns listed in Adam Smith's *The Wealth of Nations*, Karl Marx's *Capital*, and John Maynard Keynes' *General Theory*, which John Kenneth Galbraith regarded as the three most important books in the history of economics (Galbraith, 1991: p. 227).

Since the launch of industrialisation in 1960, the Korean government has undergone three distinct phases with different priorities on these objectives. The first phase was the period from 1960 to 1979, under the military government of President Park Chung-Hee, during which the government's primary economic objective was to achieve higher eco-nomic growth. The second phase was the period from 1980 to 1997, during which the government's policy priority shifted to the objective of economic stabilisation. The third phase, from 1998 to the present day, began when Korea was hit by the 1997 Asian currency crisis. During this phase, the redistribution of income and wealth has

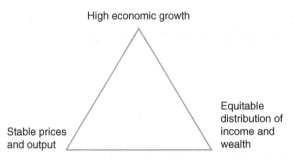

Figure 1.1 The three objectives of economic policy

started to gain importance over other objectives. These three phases are examined in the following three sections.

1.1.1 Growth Period 1960–1979

In order to attain the objective of higher economic growth, the Korean government has consistently intervened in the economy over the last sixty years. The government's actions covered not only trade, industry, competition, and technical policies but also wide-ranging institutional reforms in the quest for efficient resource allocation and in order to cope with market failure. All these actions on the part of the government, which could be described as structural policy today, affected the supply side of the economy, increased its productivity, and ensured its long-term sustainable growth.

Government intervention was particularly notable during the period from 1961 to 1979. Prioritising the enhancement of the long-term economic growth rate over all other goals, the government put two important policies in place. First, the Korean government adopted trade liberalisation policies. Adam Smith had stated, more than 200 years before, that international trade would increase the long-term growth rate of the economy by expanding markets and deepening the division of labour (Smith, 1776). Notwithstanding this, Korea had, for a long time, been obsessed by the then dominant ideology of 'the self-reliant economy', which led to the protection of the domestic economy against the intrusion of foreign economies, thereby opposing and rejecting the liberalisation of trade. The government of the day broke with this ideology and substituted the prevailing 'domestic market first principle' with the 'export-first principle'. Against this backdrop, the government joined the GATT in 1967, which resulted in Korea benefiting enormously from the MFN clause, and the tariff concessions from all GATT member countries. Trade liberalisation was a huge success, as Korea saw its export share increase from 7 per cent of GDP in 1965 to 28 per cent in 1980. Exports have since become the leading engine of economic growth in the country. Trade liberalisation led to financial liberalisation and the entry of Korea into the OECD in 1996. Furthermore, since the 2000s, these liberalisation policies have led Korea to conclude numerous bilateral and multilateral FTAs, including the Korea–EU and the Korea–US FTAs. This has helped Korea to mitigate the impact of the 2008 global financial crisis, as it enabled its exports to continue to grow. As Figure 1.2 shows, exports reached around 45 per cent of GDP in 2010.

Secondly, along with trade liberalisation, the government pushed for the rapid industrialisation of the country, in order to transform the country from a very poor agricultural country suffering from extreme poverty into a modern industrial state. Notably, the government aggressively drove an industrial policy which targeted the HCI. Figure 1.2 shows that the share of fixed investment as a percentage of GDP increased from a mere 15 per cent in 1965 to 32 per cent in 1980, peaking to 37 per cent in 1995. Although the exact costs and benefits of

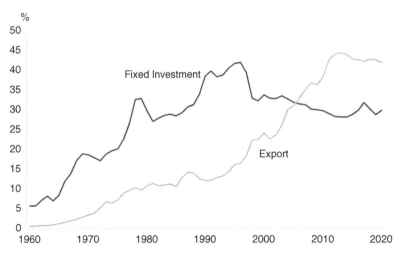

Figure 1.2 The share of exports and investments
Source: ECOS, BoK.

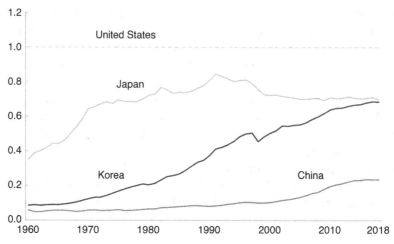

Figure 1.3 Growth in per capita GDP (PPP base and US per capita income = 1)
Source: Madison Project database 2020.

this industrial policy have not been clearly assessed, the policy has generally been considered to have been successful in transforming Korea into an industrial power. As a result, the Korean economy recorded spectacular long-term economic growth throughout this period. After the eruption of the Asian currency crisis in 1997, however, the massive financial and corporate sector restructuring demanded by the IMF made such industrial policy a legacy of the past. About half of the thirty largest Korean business groups went bankrupt or entered restructuring programmes, bringing about a substantial drop in fixed investment. Currently, the share of fixed investment is around 30 per cent of GDP. Nonetheless, the Korean economy continued to grow rapidly following the 1997 Asian currency crisis and has succeeded in catching up with the advanced economies, in particular, Japan. The current per capita income of Korea is around 70 per cent of the corresponding US income (see Figure 1.3).

1.1.2 Stabilisation Period 1980–1997

Unlike growth policy that is a supply-side policy intended to increase the long-term growth rate of the economy, stabilisation policy is a demand management policy through which it is intended to reduce economic fluctuations. All government actions which consist of keeping the inflation rate low and stable, as well as the short-term fluctuations in output and employment small, are elements of macro-economic stabilisation policy (Taylor, 1995). Furthermore, policies to ensure financial stability and to prevent financial crises can be included in this category.

In Korea, as in other countries, the importance of economic stabilisation was highlighted by the emergence of high inflation during the 1970s, when Korea was hit by two oil price shocks. Nonetheless, stabilisation was not a priority under the government of President Park, who did not want to sacrifice growth in favour of economic stabilisation. As a result, Korea suffered continuing budget deficits, high inflation, and increasing current account deficits. The main reasons for this are as follows:

> First, an increase in government spending was required to maintain political unity and social cohesion. Against this backdrop, the Korean government subsidised farmers' incomes by setting a minimum price for rice, the main staple in Korea. Given the meagre budgetary provisions for this task, the budget deficit relating to the purchase and management of rice was largely financed by the Bank of Korea (BoK). The money supply created by monetary financing soared, accounting for 37 per cent of the total increase in money supply during the period 1976–1978.
>
> Second, financial markets were under strong pressure to serve the policy drive for the HCIs, and to provide low interest credit (policy loans) to the targeted industries and companies. The share of policy loans rose to approximately 50 per cent of total commercial bank loans by the end of the 1970s. Thus, monetary policy worked as a simple tool for providing what was called 'growth money'. Clearly, the BoK had no independent competence. The decision-making power in respect of monetary policy was in the hands of the minister of finance. Furthermore, the stabilisation of prices was not handled by the BoK but depended on direct price controls administered by the Economic Planning Board, which subsequently became the Ministry of Economy and Finance through its merger with the Ministry of Finance in 1994.
>
> Third, the balance of payments deteriorated because the excessive investment realised in the corporate sector, particularly in HCIs, outweighed the aggregate savings of Korean households. The rise

in the investment–savings gap and the resulting current account deficit had to be financed by foreign savings. Foreign debt soared, reaching 48 per cent of GDP in 1979, which drove the Korean economy to the edge of bankruptcy (Nam, 1984).

As a result, the Korean government launched the first important stabilisation policy in 1979, titled 'Comprehensive Economic Stabilisation Programme' (CESP), although its full implementation had to be postponed until a change in government leadership had taken place in 1980. It marked a paradigm shift in economic policies because it challenged the then dominant economic framework of the Korean government, which was based upon the drive for the HCIs and the government-led economic development strategy. Furthermore, unlike an ordinary stabilisation programme, consisting of stabilising inflation by implementing fiscal austerity and tight monetary policy, the CESP included much broader objectives, such as making the Korean economy freer and more market friendly through the promotion of market mechanisms, and more open through the enhancement of competition (Cho and Kang, 2013). Inflation dropped substantially, but growth did not, which showed that these two objectives could be compatible. Since the implementation of the CESP, the inflation rate has, to a substantial degree, been contained. Figure 1.4 summarises the performance of the CESP.

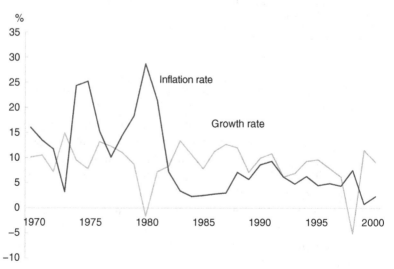

Figure 1.4 Growth and inflation
Source: ECOS, BoK.

1.1.3 The Redistribution Period from 1998 to the Present Day

Redistribution policies for the equitable allocation of income and wealth are without doubt some of the oldest economic policies carried out by any government. In Korea, the equitable distribution of income and wealth had been a crucial national objective since the establishment of the government in 1948 because Korea (South) had to compete with Communist North Korea regarding the superiority of their respective political and economic systems. To this end, government intervention for the attainment of the objective of income and wealth redistribution is clearly laid down in the Korean Constitution. In particular, the first Korean Constitution established in 1948 prescribed a 'mixed economy',[1] specifying income equity as a priority goal over other economic objectives. Praised as an 'East Asian miracle' by the World Bank (1993), the Korean economy had succeeded in combining high and rapid economic growth with an improvement in the distribution of income and the emergence of a middle class. Thus, the Korean government had little reason to emphasise the objective of equitable distribution of income and wealth. The continuation of economic growth was enough.

The currency crisis that erupted in 1997 was a landmark event for the Korean economy because the equitable distribution of income started to deteriorate for the first time since its take-off in 1960. Korean companies had been notorious for their high-gearing ratios, reflecting strong fixed investment demands relative to their international competitors. In particular, big Korean companies, known as '*Chaebols*', were highly criticised for over-investment and often relentless investment, as these investments were regarded as having triggered the currency crisis in Korea in 1997. The occurrence of the crisis changed this behaviour, leading to a massive restructuring of Korean companies and a huge reduction in their fixed investments, which was accompanied by the large-scale shedding of employment and a severe weakening of job-creation capacity. In particular, the massive restructuring of the corporate and financial sectors that ensued in the aftermath of the currency crisis allowed easy lay-offs in Korea, which led to a huge loss of employment and jobs. This drop in fixed investment was the principal cause of the deterioration

---

[1] The advent of communism in the Soviet Union, along with its central planning features, attracted the interest of many intellectuals all over the world, leading many countries to move towards a 'mixed economy' (Tanzi, 1997). Korea was no exception.

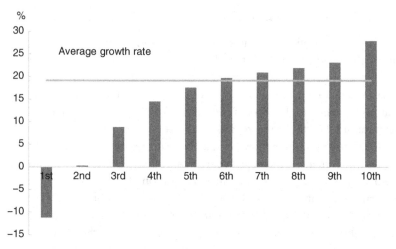

Figure 1.5 Growth rates in real household income by income brackets during the period 1997–2016
Source: Statistic of Korea.

in income distribution in Korea. The consequence of this was not just the increase in the inequality of income distribution, but also the increasing polarisation of Korean society. For an urban household unit comprising more than two people, for example, the first bracket (the bottom 10 per cent of the income bracket) saw its income in 2016 decrease by 11 per cent compared to 1997, while the tenth bracket (the top 10 per cent of the income bracket) increased its income by 27 per cent (see Figure 1.5).

As a consequence, in setting its policy priorities, the Korean government had to take the increasing inequality in income distribution into consideration, by strengthening the social safety net and expanding its expenditure on social protection and security. Against this backdrop, the current government has launched a so-called income-led growth policy, which has led to a spectacular rise in both the minimum wage and social spending, a rapid reduction in working hours, and the strengthening of job protection.

It is, however, notable that this policy has created a trade-off with the objective of economic growth and stabilisation. The 'income-led growth' policy pushed for by the current Korean government, contrary to its supposed complementarity with economic growth and the redistribution of income, has led to a significant decline in fixed investment, thereby damaging the growth potential of the Korean economy.

Furthermore, as the policy has not been managed properly, it has hurt macroeconomic stability.

1.2 Tools of Macroeconomic Stabilisation

Macroeconomic policy is a stabilisation policy intended to manage aggregate demand and thereby to react counter-cyclically to shocks that can affect output, employment, or prices. Monetary and fiscal policies are the two pillars of macroeconomic policy. As discussed earlier, a fully fledged macroeconomic policy was made possible in Korea only after the Comprehensive Economic Stabilisation Programme in 1980.

1.2.1 Fiscal Policy

Fiscal policy stems from the government's fiscal management, through which it collects taxes and makes all the necessary expenditures. But it was only after the establishment of the modern nation state that fiscal policy could be established as an instrument for counter-cyclical stabilisation policies.

In Korea, however, fiscal policy was rarely used for the goal of counter-cyclical stabilisation (see Box 1.1). The Korean government has prioritised fiscal consolidation and sound fiscal principles ever since it implemented fiscal reforms in the early 1980s, which helped to transform a Korean economy with chronic fiscal deficits into an economy with fiscal surpluses. Most fiscal expenditure was just for the long-term economic and development projects, while the fiscal deficit was always regarded as being harmful to the long-term competitiveness of the Korean economy.[2] As a result, fiscal policy was not flexible enough to address short-term economic fluctuations. Counter-cyclical fiscal policy, however, gained prominence in the aftermath of the 1997 currency crisis. Given its weak social safety net, the Korean government had to increase its social expenditure in order to mitigate the impact of the recession by supporting aggregate consumption. Since then, the Korean government has used fiscal policy more counter-cyclically. Fiscal balance went into deficit in the early 2000s and 2008 (see Figure 1.6).

---

[2] Korean government officials were more Classical economists than Keynesian in this respect.

Box 1.1 Co-ordination of Fiscal and Monetary Policies in Korea

Has the Korean government's fiscal policy been sufficiently counter-cyclical? Since 2013, the annual growth rate of the Korean economy has been moving around 3 per cent, which was clearly unsatisfactory to the Korean government, because it saw growth rates of more than 4 per cent as normal. Raising concerns about a possible recession, and with public opinion in its favour, the Korean government continued to put pressure on the BoK, which was responsible for monetary policy, to respond by adopting expansionary monetary policies in tandem with the government with its expansionary fiscal policies. But was the government's fiscal policy sufficiently expansionary over this period?

The government, which tends to put more emphasis on stimulating the economy than the BoK, has argued that its fiscal policy stance was always expansionary. But the evidence suggests otherwise.

In order to assess correctly whether the fiscal policy was expansionary or not, first of all, it is important to look at the receipts side and the expenditure side of the national budget. As shown in Figure B1.1, government revenue has begun to increase sharply above expenditure since 2014. Fiscal revenue is in excess of fiscal spending, indicating that the fiscal stance of the Korean government has been contractionary, rather than expansionary, with the resulting increase in fiscal surpluses.

Against the backdrop of declining economic growth, income taxes, in particular, have surged. The Korean government attempted to boost consumption by increasing household income, which, however, to the contrary, ended up constraining household consumption, due to high income tax rate. Figure B1.1 shows that the share of income tax relative to GDP increased from slightly higher than 3 per cent in 2013 to nearly 4.5 per cent in 2018.

Second, a supplementary budget has been drawn up annually since 2015. However, the supplementary budget, which the government puts forward to the Korean National Assembly as the basis for its expansionary policy programme, has broken with its past norms. In the past, the supplementary budget tended to be financed by additional borrowing, as tax revenue was insufficient, most frequently due to recession. Thus, historically, the

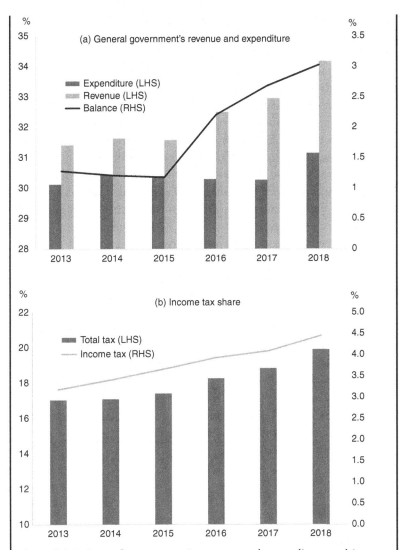

Figure B1.1 General government's revenue and expenditure and income tax share
Source: BoK and Ministry of Economy and Finance.

supplementary budget programme was counter-cyclical. Since 2015, however, it has become more pro-cyclical. The Korean government increased its fiscal spending simply because it had already collected a huge amount of additional tax revenue, which would again suggest that the Korean economy was already in recovery. The extra spending was undertaken to reduce the possibility of increasing fiscal surpluses. Thus, the passing of supplementary budgets is no longer indicative that the government is pre-emptively responding to the economic recession by undertaking expansionary fiscal policies.

Third, the government has repeatedly increased its fiscal spending in the first half of the year, frequently accompanied by a decrease in the second half. While this measure may have helped to increase the economic growth rate for a particular year, it was inevitably offset by a drop in the growth rate for the subsequent year. Thus, this measure, too, which was frequently promoted as a stimulus policy by the Korean government, proved, at best, to be neutral in its overall effect.

It would, therefore, be incorrect to state that the fiscal policy stance of the Korean government was expansionary. On the contrary, it was contractionary. The officials of the Ministry of Economy and Finance, technocrats like the staff of the BoK, probably knew that the Korean economy had recovered since 2013, but they were also well aware that, unless they insisted that they were carrying out expansionary policies, they, too, would be subjected to political interference from the Korean National Assembly. In order to adhere to the long-term fiscal discipline, they may have just resorted to telling the little white lie that their fiscal policy was expansionary.

1.2.2 Monetary Policy

The widespread use of credit and fiat money has led to the managed currency system and the emergence of monetary policy conducted by central banks.[3] Historically, the central bank was the sole issuer of

---

[3] Under a pure gold standard system, for example, monetary policy would be nothing other than the maintenance of convertibility. The central bank would have no policy discretion at all to cope with price or employment instability. This is why J. M. Keynes advocated for the abolition of the gold standard in favour of a managed currency system (Keynes, 1923: p. 65).

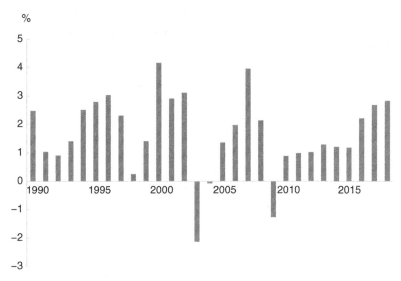

Figure 1.6 Fiscal balance (general government balance as percentage of GDP)
Source: ECOS, BoK.

banknotes, which enabled it to determine the supply of money or the interest rates, and thereby influenced prices and output. Currently, it is the BoK that is responsible for monetary policy in Korea. However, it has not conducted an independent monetary policy, as the government would not be willing to abandon its controlling power over the Korean economy. Until the 1990s, therefore, the goal of the BoK was just to follow and support government policy, rather than to pursue independent stabilisation policies. However, independent monetary policy has been made possible through two developments:

First, fiscal discipline played a very positive role in the implementation of an independent monetary policy, allowing the BoK to be freed from the obligation of supporting the government by monetisation. Fiscal discipline, however, ended up hindering the development of financial markets, particularly the government bond market. The Korean government had little need to issue bonds, which would have rendered the Korean economy more bank-dependent. Only with the increase in the supply of Korean government bonds that were issued to finance the cost of financial restructuring in the after-math of the 1997 currency crisis did financial markets start to develop.

Second, due to strong government control of financial sectors in order to support economic growth, interest rates remained heavily regulated for a long time and financial market development was repressed. With Korea joining the OECD in 1996, however, serious financial liberalisation was pursued. Based upon the Four Stage Liberalisation Plan that proposed gradual liberalisation, by moving from long-term to short-term interest rates, from securities market rates to bank interest rates, and from large-sum to small-sum instruments, all the interest rates were completely liberalised in 1997. Furthermore, the opening of capital markets was achieved, leading to foreign direct investment in the Korean stock and bond markets. It is worth noting that it helped the BoK to shift the instrument of monetary policy from monetary aggregates to interest rates. Currently, the BoK implements its monetary policy by steering short-term interest rates.

Amid the currency crisis that devastated the Korean economy in 1997, the government, under the tutelage of the IMF, had to revise the Bank of Korea Act, thereby allowing the BoK to implement an independent monetary policy. In the light of this, the objective of the BoK changed to the implementation of its sole mandate, that of price stability.

After the 2008 global financial crisis, central banks around the world developed various unconventional monetary instruments and tools as nominal interest rates moved closer to the effective zero lower bound. Here, macro-prudential policy was newly added to the objectives of central banks. Against this backdrop, the Bank of Korea Act was again revised. The BoK, whose role had heretofore been limited to price stability, came to extend its role to financial stability.

1.3 The Goals of Monetary Policy

Figure 1.7 shows that the objectives of monetary policy are to ensure three types of stability: price, output (employment), and financial stability. In the case of the BoK, all these objectives are considered important. Although the stabilisation of output was not specified as explicitly as price and financial stability in the Bank of Korea Act, the BoK aims to attain price stability, reduce economic fluctuations, and prevent financial crises.

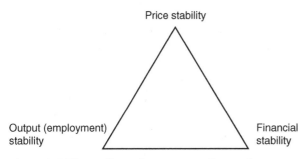

Figure 1.7 Three pillars of monetary policy goals

1.3.1 Price Stability

For every country, price stability is the most important goal of central banks. In Korea, immediately after the 1997 currency crisis, which led to the sixth revision of the Bank of Korea Act, price stability became the sole important goal of the BoK. Prior to this, the goal of the BoK was both to achieve the monetary value of Korean currency, and to maintain a sound financial system and improve its efficiency. But through this revision, the second goal was deleted, and price stability remained the only goal. Furthermore, the BoK introduced, as its framework for achieving the goal of price stability, a strategy of inflation targeting, which had first been introduced in New Zealand in 1990. Inflation targeting is the monetary policy framework or strategy of focusing on inflation itself as the ultimate goal of central banks, aiming to achieve its goal over the mid-term horizon. Currently, the inflation target adopted by the BoK is 2 per cent in the consumer price index. If the actual inflation rate deviates too much above or below this target, then the BoK is expected to take all the necessary actions to reduce the inflation gap.

After the global financial crisis in 2008, however, there was increasing criticism that, despite the sluggish nature of the economic recovery, the BoK adhered strictly to its sole mandate of price stability, neglecting the employment and output stability goal.[4] Against this backdrop, some members of the National Assembly even submitted a proposal

---

[4] It is quite interesting to compare the experience of the BoK with the BoJ. In Korea, the BoK was attacked by politicians for being only concerned with the inflation goal, and not output and employment, whereas, in Japan, politicians were eager

to amend the Bank of Korea Act again, adding the goal of output and employment stability to the goal of price stability, and thus imposing multiple goals on the BoK. However, this attempted change was never realised. One of the proponents' main arguments that the BoK was concerned only with price stability proved to be groundless. The price stability goal specified in the Bank of Korea Act implies that the BoK should, first and foremost, be responsible for price stability, but this does not necessarily mean that it cannot have other goals, such as output and employment stability. Indeed, given that the inflation rates in most countries at the time were below target, central banks also focused on dealing with employment and output stability, even under an inflation targeting system. Inflation targeting everywhere was flexible targeting.

In the case of the BoK, output stability had always been a crucial goal, even though it was not explicitly specified in the Bank of Korea Act. As a matter of fact, there was not a single member of the MPB who overlooked the importance of output stability in the whole history of the BoK. The examination of the minutes of the MPB, made public from 1997 onwards, makes it clear that output stability has always been a primary concern, one which prevailed even over price stability.

Thus, although the BoK has de jure a single goal, it has de facto multiple mandates. The question of whether the BoK should have single or multiple mandates is no longer meaningful. If the BoK has multiple goals, however, it should be careful about achieving goals other than price stability, because these goals can be incompatible with maintaining price stability.

1.3.2 Output and Employment Stability

When inflation remains subdued, inflation targeting is, in practice, inoperative. Instead of price stability, output stability becomes the primary goal. Thus, the focus of monetary policy shifts to reducing the fluctuations in output and employment. But how, then, can output stability be measured?

to introduce inflation targeting as a tool to boost the Japanese economy (see Shirakawa, 2018).

In general, fluctuations in output are represented by the movement of the GDP, unemployment rates, and real interest rates. The MPB assesses how far each of these variables deviates from their targets, such as potential GDP, the natural rate of unemployment, and the natural interest rate, and attempts to reduce these deviations as much as possible through changes in the interest rate or in the quantity of money. Theoretically, determining monetary policy direction should not be affected by the selection of *any* of these variables because they all move in the same direction, although, in practice, they often move *against* each other in opposite directions. Each member of the MPB should, therefore, choose a reference variable that can help capture the business cycle or economic fluctuation as correctly as possible. Currently, the members of the MPB focus their attention on the GDP movement, while variables such as the unemployment rate or the real interest rate are used mainly as supplementary variables to cross-check the output movement.

a) Output Gap

The performance of the Korean economy has been measured by the GDP growth rate. The labour market was not flexible, and, as a consequence, the unemployment rate and other labour market data failed to reflect the underlying economic fluctuations correctly. For the BoK, therefore, the underlying movement of the Korean economy is captured by the extent of the output gap, as emphasised in its Statement on Monetary Policy Decisions. This is the reason why the BoK targets the output gap, although employment stability is more relevant as the goal of the macro-stabilisation policy (Svensson, 2013).

As the Korean economy slows down amid falling inflation rates from 2013, however, there has been a resurgence of the claims that the BoK neglected output stability by adhering excessively to price stability. But this claim is due, among other things, to a misunderstanding of the BoK's mission for output stability. In so far as the GDP movement is concerned, it is important to note that the decline in the growth rate of the Korean economy is derived from the drop in the long-term economic growth rate as well as the increase in the short-term output gap. Basically, the goal of monetary policy is to reduce the output gap, steering the actual growth rate around the potential growth rate, but not to increase the growth rate without any boundaries. If the actual growth rate is too far below or above the potential growth rate, it can jeopardise price stability, creating deflation or inflation, which justifies monetary policy intervention. But monetary policy has little to do with the drop in the potential growth rate, which should be addressed more by the government's structural policy than by the central bank's monetary policy.

To understand output stability in more detail, let us decompose the GDP movement into two parts, the cyclical and trend component, as follows.

$$y_t = (y_t - y_f) + y_f \tag{1}$$

where y_t and y_f are, respectively, the logarithms of y_t, the GDP at time t, and y_f, the potential GDP.

Differentiating both sides of the equation yields:

$$\Delta y_t = \Delta(y_t - y_f) + \Delta y_f \tag{2}$$

Here, $\Delta(y_t - y_f)$ refers to the change in GDP gap because $\Delta(y_t - y_f) = \Delta((Y_t - Y_f)/Y_t)$. Thus, GDP growth rate at a given period t, Δy_t, is the sum of the change in GDP gap and the potential grow rate Δy_f. In general, monetary policy is a short-term counter-cyclical policy to reduce the output gap, while it rarely affects the potential growth rate, which can be addressed more by long-term economic policies, such as structural policy. Thus, as former Chairman of Federal Reserve Board Ben Bernanke stated:

Monetary policy cannot do much about long-run growth. All we can try to do is to try to smooth out periods where the economy is depressed because of lack of demand. (Bernanke, 2012: p. 27)

To be sure, monetary policy is not necessarily limited to affecting the short-term business cycle. It may, to a certain extent, affect the potential growth rate in the case of sustained recession or under-investment. For example, Summers (2014) developed the 'secular stagnation' hypothesis that economic growth would fall in the long run due to so-called hysteresis effect if a short-term recession remained sustained. Inversely, a decline in potential growth could lead to a recession (Gordon, 2015).

The recent lacklustre performance of the Korean economy was not due to an insufficiently accommodative monetary policy, as was claimed by the critics of the BoK. It originated, to a large extent, from

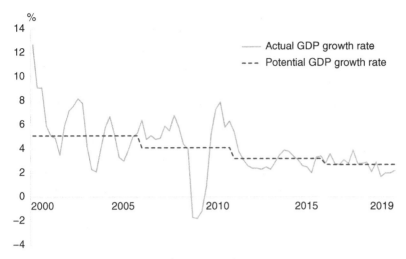

Figure 1.8 Actual and potential GDP growth rate in Korea
Source: ECOS, BoK.

a fall in the potential GDP growth rate, not from the widening GDP gap. Notwithstanding this, the BoK had been regarded as being responsible for the lower growth rate itself, and the MPB had been under severe pressure to adopt an excessively expansionary monetary policy. As Figure 1.8 shows, this was indeed the case for the mid-2010s, when the actual GDP growth rate was not below the potential GDP growth rate. For example, the Korean economy recorded a 3.2 per cent growth rate in 2013 and 2014, which was the midpoint of the estimated range of the potential GDP growth rate of 3.0 to 3.4 per cent. Many of the Korean public thought that this GDP growth rate was still disappointing and insisted on further stimulus, but they failed to recognise that a substantial drop had occurred in the potential GDP growth rate, and therefore monetary policy would not be an appropriate recipe. Furthermore, given that the amplitude of economic fluctuations had been significantly weakened, there was little reason to justify an active monetary policy response.

If the potential GDP growth rate is variable and uncertain in the short term, it is then important for the BoK to estimate it accurately and to know how much the change in GDP is coming from the changes in the potential GDP and GDP gap. But this is not an easy task. There are different ways to measure potential GDP, and often there are quite substantial differences between the thus measured potential GDPs. If this difficulty is considered, targeting the GDP for monetary policy-making can be only a second-best option that arises from the fact that the unemployment rate is not sufficiently sensitive to economic fluctuations in Korea.

Against this background, the BoK decided to publish its potential GDP estimates from 2016 onwards. A priori, there is no way of telling whether the estimates are really accurate or not. But the publication of the estimates can serve to announce the target growth rate or range that the BoK is required to attain. Given the target growth rate or range, the Korean public will clearly understand that the action of the BoK is to reduce the GDP gap, not to increase the growth rate at any cost.

b) Unemployment Gap

The unemployment rate is clearly one of the most widely used target indicators that steer monetary policy in many central banks. The advantage of relying on the unemployment gap is that it can help clarify whether the action of the central bank is to bring the actual unemployment rate to what is called the full employment rate of unemployment or the natural rate of unemployment.[5] Assuming that u_t is the current unemployment rate and u_f the natural unemployment rate, we can decompose u_t as follows:

$$u_t = (u_t - u_f) + u_f \tag{3}$$

Note that the stabilisation of employment is to minimise the fluctuation of the actual unemployment rate around the natural rate of unemployment. Thus, as in the case of the GDP target, the mission of the BoK is to reduce the unemployment gap $(u_t - u_f)$, not the natural rate of unemployment, u_f, itself. In practice, however, the distinction between the reduction of the actual unemployment rate and unemployment gap is not meaningful. The reason is that the natural rate of unemployment is not very variable and is immune to wide measurement errors, at least in the short run, although it can be changed by structural policy, such as labour market reforms in the long run. Because u_f remains constant in the short run, the short-run change in

---

[5] This refers to the minimum unemployment rate that can be achieved without causing an inflation rate increase. Or, according to Mishkin, it is not zero unemployment but the employment rate in which the demand for labour is equal to the supply of labour. Mishkin (2011, p. 318)

the actual unemployment rate thus corresponds entirely to the change in the employment gap as shown:

$$\Delta u_t = \Delta(u_t - u_f) \tag{4}$$

It should be noted that the stabilisation based upon the unemployment gap is equal to the stabilisation based upon the GDP gap if the labour market is flexible enough and Okun's law holds.[6] Given the high degree of labour market rigidity in Korea, however, the unemployment rate or other labour market indicators are not sufficiently sensitive to the movement of the underlying economic fluctuations, and they are rarely affected by monetary policy. Lay-offs have rarely been implemented in Korea, and the institutional and regulatory changes that are currently taking place in Korea tend to strengthen, rather than ease, such rigidity. This is the main reason why the BoK favours the GDP target, despite the fact that labour market developments are always very important concerns that catch the attention of the members of the MPB.

Figure 1.9 shows that, while the natural rate of unemployment in Korea was relatively constant between 3 and 3.5 per cent, the actual unemployment rate also varied little, staying within the narrow band of 3 to 4 per cent over the last twenty years.

c) Interest Rate Gap

Currently, the central banks of all the major economies have interest-oriented monetary policy frameworks. As a result, the natural (or neutral) interest rate is an important concept to predict the stance of monetary policy. The natural interest rate, first defined by the Swedish economist Knut Wicksell, is the interest rate that will prevent cumulative inflation or deflation. More conveniently, it is the interest rate that will prevail at full employment output or potential output while keeping inflation constant. Therefore, if the real interest rate, defined as the interest rate that deducts inflation expectations from the nominal interest rate, matches exactly the natural interest rate, prices will be stable. In contrast, if the real interest rate is higher or lower than the natural interest rate, then deflation or inflation is expected, which will lead the BoK to lower or raise the interest rate. In this regard, there have been several attempts to estimate the (time-varying) natural interest rate in

---

[6] For instance, Okun's law linking unemployment gap to output gap can be described by the equation $(y_t - y_f) = c(u_t - u_f)$ where c is constant.

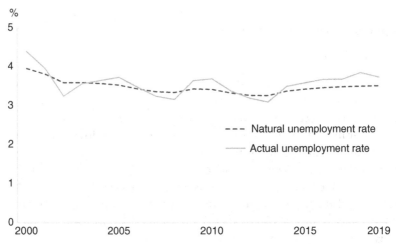

Figure 1.9 Actual and natural unemployment rates in Korea
Source: OECD.

Korea (IMF, 2019, and Cho, 2020, as the most recent study). Figure 1.10 illustrates the movement of the natural interest rates estimated by Cho (2020).[7]

The interest rate gap can be a useful guide for determining what monetary policy stance to adopt. In practice, however, it is not so beneficial because of an associated measurement problem. For instance, Figure 1.10 shows that the monetary policy stance in Korea has almost always been accommodative since the year 2000. It may be close to the truth (Hofmann et al., 2012[8]) but, more importantly, it suggests the possibility of mis-estimations being made. There are, indeed, substantial uncertainties and errors in measuring the natural interest rate, which will critically weaken its use compared to the use of the GDP gap. Given

[7] Using the methodology that Holston et al. (2017) developed for the estimation of the US natural interest rate, Cho calculates two sets of natural rate interest in Korea. The first set uses exactly the same Korean data as the US data, while the second set replaces the policy interest in the United States with the market interest rate in Korea. The latter reflects more closely the Korean economic situation and is reproduced here. See Cho (2020) in more detail.

[8] They show that policy rates have been below the benchmark rate implied by the Taylor rule since the early 2000s in both the advanced and the emerging market economies. This finding that monetary policy has been systematically accommodative globally is termed the 'Global Great Deviation' (Hofmann et al., 2012).

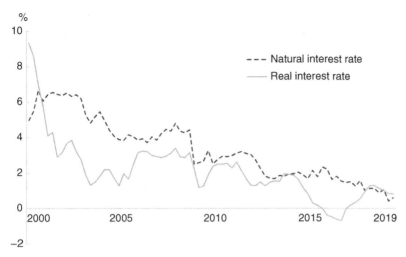

Figure 1.10 Real and natural interest rates in Korea
Source: Cho (2020).

the theoretical one-to-one correspondence between the potential GDP and the natural interest rate, a monetary policy scheme based upon the interest gap is much the same as that based upon the GDP gap, and there is no particular reason to favour the utilisation of the interest gap.

Nonetheless, there was an internal demand for estimating the natural interest rate, because it helps the BoK to derive the Taylor equation and to trace the rule-based benchmark interest rate path reflecting the price and GDP gaps of the Korean economy. Concretely, the Taylor equation which the BoK used was as follows:

$$r_t = r^* + 1.8(\pi_t - \pi^*) + 0.4(y_t - y^*) \tag{5}$$

where r_t and r^* represent, respectively, the current real interest rate and natural (or neutral) interest rate, π_t and π^* the current and target inflation rates, and y_t and y^* the current and potential GDP in logarithms.

However, the reliance on this rule for the determination of monetary policy was never popular in Korea, and the usefulness of the Taylor equation has been constantly questioned. First, given that the information used by the BoK was never made public regarding the natural interest rate, let alone the GDP and price gaps and the parameter values, it seems ironic that the BoK staff had too much discretion in calculating the benchmark interest rate in Korea. The Taylor rule was hardly an appropriate rule for the MPB members.[9] Second, interest rates dropped to near zero levels in the aftermath of the 2008 global financial crisis, which made the existing equation no longer relevant, either in Korea or in the United States (Bernanke, 2015b; Yellen, 2017). The Taylor equation has thus been completely in disuse since 2015.

1.3.3 Financial Stability

Once a financial crisis occurs, central banks or the national governments incur huge costs as the lender of last resort to provide liquidity and financial assistance to financial institutions in distress. In terms of monetary policy perspective, however, the biggest cost from a financial crisis is the drop in output and the increase in unemployment incurred by the national economy. Indeed, it turned out that most of the recessions in OECD countries were accompanied by financial crises (see ECB, 2012: pp. 81–82).

Figure 1.11 estimates the size of the short- and long-term GDP losses that the 2008 global financial crisis caused to the Korean economy.

In the short term, financial crises reduce economic growth while not necessarily affecting potential output. When Korea was hit by the global financial crisis in 2008, real GDP fell below potential GDP from the fourth quarter 2008 until the fourth quarter 2009. The short-term output loss measured by the GDP differences during this period is estimated to reach around 3 per cent of peak GDP in 2007, which is already of a non-negligible magnitude. More serious, however, is the medium- or long-term loss caused by the drop in potential GDP, as emphasised by the IMF (2009a). If, as in Figure 1.11, we assume, for instance, that the pre-crisis trend growth rate recommences four years after the crisis,[10] then the long-term output loss, measured by the sum of all the GDP losses accumulated over the four years following the crisis, is estimated to be around 25 per cent of the 2007 GDP.

Given this huge cost, the need to stem financial crises has drawn attention to the new pillar of economic stabilisation policy. Central banks

---

[9]   Unlike the original Taylor equation, the Taylor equation estimated by the BoK staff allocated a much higher value to the price gap than to the GDP gap, which could provoke the criticism that the BoK staff were too biased towards price stability. But this equation was rarely consulted by the MPB members.

[10]   This assumption is made by Leaven and Valencia (2008).

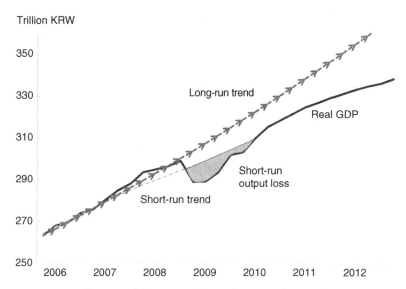

Figure 1.11 Short- and long-term loss of output during the 2008 global financial crisis
Note: The pre-crisis long-term growth rate is calculated as the average of the annual seven-year growth rates three years prior to the 2008 crisis, based upon the IMF (2009a). The estimated growth rate is 4.9 per cent per annum, which is equivalent to around 1.2 per cent on a quarterly basis.
Source: OECD and BoK.

should carry out their monetary and financial policies more counter-cyclically in order to promote the stability of their financial systems as well as targeting output and price stability in the medium- and long-term perspective. A central bank's price and output stability is not separable from financial stability. This is because, among other things, the transmission of the monetary policy conducted by the central bank will always have to be spread through the financial markets, and therefore central banks should always be very careful about maintaining the financial system stable and financial institutions resilient. If the financial system fails to function properly, the transmission channel of monetary policy will not work, harming the effectiveness of monetary policy.

Against this backdrop, the BoK came to revise its Bank of Korea Act once again in December 2011, by taking financial stability as another mandate. Article 1 of the revised Act stipulates that the BoK should consider financial stability when carrying out monetary and credit policies as follows:

Article 1 (purpose) (1) This Act aims to contribute to the sound development of the national economy by establishing the Bank of Korea and promoting price stability through the establishment and execution of efficient monetary and credit policies. (2) The Bank of Korea shall pay attention to financial stability in carrying out monetary and credit policies. (Bank of Korea, 2018)

Furthermore, in Article 96 (Report of the National Assembly, etc.), the BoK is required to submit Financial Stability Reports that assess the stability of Korea's financial system to the National Assembly twice a year.

Is this extension of the BoK's mandate always desirable? This may not be the case. According to Tinbergen's rule, the more diverse the BoK's goals are, the more tools and instruments are needed. Thus, if the BoK is not equipped with the additional policy tools which correspond to its additional goals, it will have only a limited capacity in fulfilling these goals. The evidence so far suggests that monetary policy alone has been less effective in ensuring financial stability in Korea (IMF, 2019). Furthermore, if there are multiple goals, the BoK's responsibility is also likely to be diluted. This is because the policy goals are likely to conflict with each other, which could make it difficult for the BoK to be held accountable. For example, monetary policy of low interest rates, which is intended to ensure the stability of employment and output, can endanger financial stability, and, inversely, monetary policy of raising interest rates too prematurely to contain financial risks can end up damaging the stability of output and employment. These possible incompatibilities between its different goals can blur the responsibility of the BoK.

PART II

How Does Money Affect the Korean Economy?

2 | Money and the Evolution of Monetary Standards

Money refers to a general means of payment used to pay for goods and services and to pay off debts. However, it is difficult to define money accurately because its form has evolved constantly over time and space, along with changes in social customs and technology. This chapter examines the evolution of monetary standards in Korea, through which commodity money is replaced by paper money, and then paper money by electronic and digital payment instruments.

2.1 Commodity Money Standard

The current Korean currency '*won*' derives its name from silver dollar coins, which were the most widely circulated commodity money in Asia. The discovery of silver mines around the world from the sixteenth century led to the creation of diverse silver coins, beginning with the '*thaler*', well known as the origin of the English name 'dollar'. The Portuguese and Spanish governments also minted silver coins and the name 'dollar' was used for Spain's *peso* and Portugal's *real*. Along with the expansion of world trade, these dollars began to circulate widely and became the principal currency in Asia. The currency units, named '*won*' in Korean, '*yuan*' in Chinese, and '*yen*' in Japanese, all originate from the dollar, although the pronunciation of each currency name is slightly different (see Table 2.1).

In China, western silver coins such as Spanish and Mexican dollars were named '*silver yuan*' and were known to circulate widely from the early sixteenth century onwards. A unit of weight called the '*liang*' was used in China, but the traditional silver currencies in *liang* were inconvenient for commercial transactions, with the weight or the purity of the silver contained in the coins showing large differences between regions. In contrast, as the silver *yuan* was standardised both in terms of weight and purity, its use expanded rapidly, replacing traditional Chinese silver currencies denominated in '*liang*'. The Chinese

Table 2.1 *Currency unit names in Korea, China, and Japan*

	China	Japan	Korea
Traditional currency unit (Tael)	*Liang*	*ryo*	*yang*
Modern currency unit (Dollar)	*Yuan*	*yen*	*won*

Source: Moon and Rhee (2012).

government itself began minting *yuan*-denominated silver coins, which were equal in value to Spanish or Mexican dollars. In Japan, Spanish and Mexican silver coins had also been circulating in and around trade ports, but, as their use extended throughout the country, the silver dollar called the '*yen*' was officially adopted as the country's currency unit. Accordingly, Japan's monetary unit was converted from the '*ryo*' (the Japanese pronunciation of the word '*liang*' in Chinese) to the *yen*, and Japan established a currency system that put the *yen* on a par with the US dollar. Unlike China and Japan, the use of silver dollars in Korea fell behind, because foreign trade remained officially banned. With the opening of the Korean economy under the Japan–Korea Treaty of 1876, however, Korea imported many foreign coins. The Japanese brought silver *yen* coins, while the Chinese brought their own silver coins as well as Mexican ones. Some Russian silver *rubles* were also used in the northern border area of Korea. In particular, the silver *yen* coin became the most widely circulated, obtaining the status of legal tender. The inflow of so many foreign coins threw the Korean currency order into confusion. Accordingly, the Korean government decided to adopt a Western-style silver standard, and minted silver coins in '*yang*' (the Korean pronunciation of Chinese '*liang*'), establishing a Mint Office. The silver five-*yang* coin, which had the same value as the Mexican dollar, was minted for use in foreign trade. Finally, the silver dollar standard was officially adopted in 1894, and the use of the silver five-*yang* coin, along with the copper coins in circulation, was legalised (Moon and Rhee, 2012).

Along with the widespread use of commodity money, paper money also emerged. Although it was originally a simple promise to pay, the banknote quickly transformed into fiat money. In Korea, banknotes were almost all fiduciary issue and were widely used as legal tender regardless of their convertibility. The banknote remained the dominant

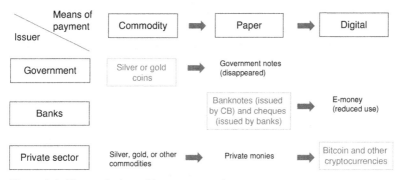

Figure 2.1 The evolution of instruments of payment

form of money, because cheques (US checks) issued by commercial banks were in little use. Subsequent innovations in telecommunications technology brought about the circulation of electronic means of payment. In Korea, in particular, the credit card was developed in place of the cheque. Along with this evolution, the list of issuers of money was extended to the private sector. Figure 2.1 summarises this evolutionary process.

2.2 Paper Money Standard

2.2.1 Banknotes

Historically, the first paper money was government notes issued in China in the early fourteenth century. Similarly, in Korea, the first paper money was issued by the government in the fifteenth century, although it was not circulated widely. No banknotes were issued in Asia, including Korea, until the establishment of modern banks, according to the European model in the nineteenth or early twentieth century.

The banknote was a product of European economic evolution. For instance, the Bank of England (BoE), one of the first central banks in Europe, issued notes by which it promised to pay depositors in commodity money, such as gold, and these notes acquired increased acceptability as a means of payment. A banknote was thus 'a promissory note payable to the bearer on demand' that could be transferable to anyone else. When a bank obtained the banknote-issuing monopoly, it became a central bank, and its banknotes became legal tender.

Table 2.2 *The difference between the government notes and banknotes*

Issuance of government notes		Issuance of banknotes	
Government		**Government**	
Assets	Liabilities	Assets	Liabilities
Tax to collect	Government notes	Tax to collect	Borrowing from central bank
		Central Bank	
		Assets	Liabilities
		Credit to government	Equity
		Credit to private sector	Banknotes

As paper money currently consists only of banknotes, there is no reason to distinguish between government notes and banknotes. Initially, however, the difference was important. Faced with huge government expenditure, such as war expenditure, a government tended to issue notes beyond its capacity to collect taxes. As a result, people had no confidence in government notes, which ended up creating inflation. In contrast, the banknote was regarded as being less inflationary, because it was largely issued in response to private credit.[1] Table 2.2 shows that, as long as central banks restrict their credit to the government, which, in the case of the BoE, was originally limited to the amount of gold subscribed to the bank as equity capital, the issue of banknotes is regulated by private credit, which is self-liquidating and therefore has no over-issue problem.

However, banknote issuance increased in response to central bank credit to government whenever a government had difficulties in financing its expenditure. In many emerging economies, in particular, banknote issuance was possibly the sole instrument with which to cover government deficits. Financial markets were undeveloped and the tax

---

[1] It seems that John Law was the first person who clearly understood the difference between government notes and banknotes (John Law [1705], 1966). The famous polemics between the British Banking and Currency School originated from the failure to distinguish between the two notes (Rist [1940], 1996).

collection infrastructure was extremely inadequate. Thus, the central bank was regarded as an essential institution for supporting the national economy, which ended up overshadowing concerns about price stability.

In Korea, the first central bank was established under the name 'Korea Bank' in 1909. This Korea Bank (known as the Old Bank of Korea) changed its name to the Bank of Chosun, the name of the then ruling dynasty in Korea, after the forced annexation of Korea by Japan in 1910. The Bank of Chosun was an issuing bank, but it did not have a monopoly on the right to issue banknotes. Furthermore, although it was de jure convertible on a par with the banknotes of the Bank of Japan, the banknotes issued by the Bank of Chosun were de facto inconvertible. The credibility of banknotes was based not just upon the credibility of the Bank itself, but also upon the authority of the government, given that the Bank itself had been established by the government. It was akin to an organ of government. This was a huge privilege for the Bank of Chosun, because no other institutions had greater credibility than the government itself in Korea.

Nonetheless, the Bank of Chosun mixed central banking with commercial banking. It not only assumed selected central bank functions, including the issuance of banknotes and the management of the National Treasury, but also carried out some commercial banking business, such as receiving deposits from the private sector and making loans to them. During the Second World War, the Bank of Chosun had to issue a massive volume of banknotes to underwrite Japanese government bonds and support its military spending. Clearly, such moves resulted in serious inflation in Korea when it gained independence from Japanese colonial rule in 1945.

After its liberation, inflation was rampant. In order to stabilise inflation and support economic development, the Korean government decided to create a new central bank, taking over from the Bank of Chosun. The Korean government enacted the Bank of Korea Act in 1950 with the assistance of two American economists, A. I. Bloomfield and J. P. Jensen, who worked at the Federal Reserve Bank of New York. The design of the BoK as Korea's new central bank was therefore strongly influenced by the US Federal Reserve System. The BoK was also granted a legal monopoly right to issue banknotes. All the banknotes were inconvertible legal tender.

When the Korean War (1950–1953) broke out, however, the BoK had to finance the war spending and monetise the large fiscal deficits of

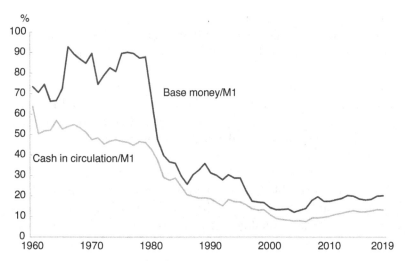

Figure 2.2 Base money and cash relative to narrow money M1 in Korea
Source: ECOS, BoK.

the Korean government. The issuing of banknotes was, in effect, the sole important source of government finance, except for the US government aid. As economic development went on, the monetisation accelerated. As represented by their extremely small volume of demand deposits, the lending power of commercial banks was too weak to support the economic development of the country. The main operation of the BoK was thus to provide what could be termed as *growth money* to the emerging Korean industry in place of commercial banks. In fact, it could be said that the BoK was responsible for the management of aggregate supply, as well as of aggregate demand.

Figure 2.2 shows that the cash (the banknotes and coins in circulation) and the base money (cash plus reserves held by commercial banks), respectively, accounted for 50 per cent and 80 per cent of the M1, narrow money, until the end of 1970s. Price stability naturally emerged as a huge challenge for the government and the BoK, which required commercial banks increasingly to hold a large proportion of their deposits as reserves in order to reduce the circulation of banknotes. Since the 1980s, however, the fiscal austerity imposed by the government under the 'Comprehensive Economic Stabilisation Programme' (CESP) led to the reduction of monetisation. Also, along with the expansion of commercial banks, bank deposits started to substitute banknotes as the main form of money. Reflecting these changes, the share of both base money and cash dropped substantially.

2.2.2 Cheques and Demand Deposits

The advent of bank money originated from the use of cheques. A cheque is a payment order by which the depositor in a bank orders the bank to pay the payee a sum of money. Thus, if the banknote is said to have evolved from the promissory note, the cheque evolved from bills of exchange that order payment to a third party. In the United States and Europe, cheques were developed as substitutes for banknotes, as central banks obtained the monopoly rights over the issuance of banknotes. Commercial banks issued cheques, which circulated widely in parallel with banknotes. Since then, checkable deposits, that is, demand deposits authorising money transfers by cheque, were counted as a general means of payment, called bank money.

In Korea, however, unlike in the United States or in Europe, bank demand deposits were not associated with the issue of cheques. The Korean public had no knowledge of cheques, nor did they keep cheque books. A demand deposit account holder had to visit his or her bank to withdraw cash and to make payments. Nonetheless, such demand deposits were regarded as being equivalent to checkable deposits, which were an important component of the M1. This seems a questionable practice, because demand deposits themselves could not be used directly as a general means of payment. They were more like savings deposits without interest payments. There were only two types of cheques used in Korea: cashier's cheques issued by banks, and commercial cheques issued by companies. Compared to the United States and many advanced European countries where households were using cheques, particularly for high-value transactions, household cheques were not in use in Korea. Although an attempt to introduce household cheques into Korea was made in 1981, their use remained extremely limited, failing to supplant the use of cash. Instead, cashier's cheques issued by banks were extensively used, partly supplementing the absence of household cheques. Demand deposits in Korea did not have the same moneyness as checkable deposits.

Under these circumstances, however, credit cards, which started to be used rapidly after the late 1990s, replaced the function of cheques by means of electronic transfers. Figure 2.3 shows the increase in the use of

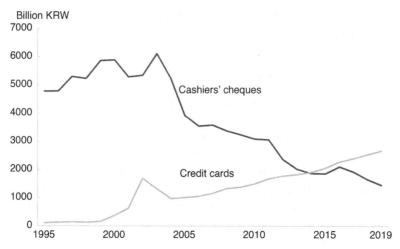

Figure 2.3 Daily average use of cashier's cheques and credit cards
Source: BoK (2020).

credit cards, which almost ended up eclipsing the use of household cheques and cashier's cheques. At the same time, the increased use of Internet and mobile banking has further contributed to accelerating the substitution of cheques.

Thus, it would have been wrong for the BoK to count demand deposits held by households as being equivalent to checkable deposits, at least until the generalised use of credit cards allowed the electronic transfer of payment to come into being. Korea was a cash economy. This might have had two important implications for the conduct of monetary policy in Korea: first, the creation of money through the standard money multiplier did not apply to Korea; second, the officially compiled money stock M1, which was a basic monetary aggregate until the end of 1970s, overestimated, to some extent, the real quantity of money in the Korean economy. For these reasons, it was highly probable that the Korean economy suffered from an unnecessary chronic shortage of money. Credit rationing was very prevalent in the Korean economy and Korean companies were almost always cash constrained.

Eventually, the ongoing financial innovation blurred the distinction between demand and savings deposits. Thus, the BoK compiled the broad money stock, M2, which included not only all demand deposits but also savings and time deposits. Moreover, M2 included the liabilities of non-banking financial institutions as long as they provided investors with payment services similar to bank deposits. Money market funds (MMFs) account for an important fraction of such liabilities in Korea.

2.2.3 Money Market Funds

An MMF is a type of mutual fund that invests in highly liquid short-term money market instruments, such as call loans, CDs, and commercial papers. After their creation in the United States in 1970, MMFs have been widely popular in many other countries including Korea. MMFs collected funds by issuing shares that could be redeemed at fixed book prices, while investing the pooled funds in purchasing short-term securities. Investors in MMFs not only received an income from such investments but could also use cheques based upon the shares that they held. In general, unlike banks, which were required to hold some minimum reserves, MMFs did not need to hold these reserves. Thus, higher interest income could be paid to investors in MMFs, which meant that the investment in the fund was equivalent to a cheque account with interest payments.

With the development of mutual funds, especially MMFs, the difference between banks and such funds has disappeared in Korea as well. The debts of banks and the share of funds both offer the same payment services. Furthermore, the traditional method of dividing the financial system into bank-centred and market-based ones is no longer valid. Just as individuals invest their surplus savings in funds, banks also invest in funds, which, in turn, invest in direct financial markets, such as bonds and stock markets, rather than intermediating their deposits as loans to companies. Against this backdrop, the Korean government wanted to promote capital markets, and passed the FSCMA in 2009. According to this act, a fund is defined as a collective investment scheme in which a pool of money is collected in an investment fund managed by professional fund managers or asset management companies. Unlike in the United States, where separate investment companies were set up to sell shares to investors, however, investment funds in Korea are largely in the form of financial contracts through which the asset management companies collect funds by selling so-called beneficiary certificates.

Mutual funds are also subject to 'fund runs', just like banks are. If investors ask for the redemption of funds due to a sharp rise in interest rates or in credit risk, investment trust companies will sell their held bonds and repay investors at book value, which can end up further increasing interest rates and enlarging the fund losses. This can lead to fund runs by investors. Investors will then rush to obtain the earliest possible redemption before other investors, because the investors who ask for redemptions at later stages will suffer larger losses, given that the fund losses become bigger over time. Such fund runs are the same, in almost every way, as bank runs in respect of deposits. For this reason, the Korean government requires investment trust companies to hold a certain percentage of their assets in cash and other highly liquid assets.[2]

MMFs were first introduced in Korea to support investment trust companies[3] with funding difficulties in 1995. Since then, the MMF market has developed rapidly, thanks to the decrease in interest rates that inversely affected the size of the MMFs. MMFs use an accounting procedure called 'mark to book', which allows investors to be offered a fixed book value. Thus, if interest rates go down (and bond prices go up), investors can make money by buying MMFs, the prices of which will be cheaper than their market prices, thereby reflecting the value of the underlying short-term bonds. Figure 2.4 shows the inverse correlation between the interest rate and the development of the MMF market in Korea. Every time interest rates were cut, there was a surge of investment in MMFs.

Reflecting the lower interest rate trend, MMFs in Korea have reached about KRW100 trillion as of 2019, which is equal in size to the amount of demand deposits. Initially, only asset management companies were allowed to issue beneficiary certificates. Subsequently, banks and securities firms were also allowed to issue similar beneficiary certificates yielding market interest rates, which were respectively called

---

[2] The bankruptcy of Daewoo, the second largest '*chaebol*' in Korea, in 1999, aroused fears about the insolvency of investment trust companies. Concerned investors demanded the wholesale redemption of the outstanding beneficiary certificates that these investment trust companies included in their assets. It was the first fund run in Korea. The crisis was quenched by the government redemption guarantee to the investors of trust companies, which would be analogous to the deposit guarantee to the depositors of banks.

[3] They were renamed as asset management companies after the passage of FSCMA in 2009.

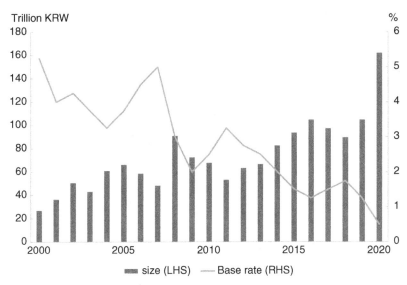

Figure 2.4 The evolution of the MMF market in Korea
Source: Korea Investments Association and BoK.

MMDAs and CMAs. Currently, only the MMDAs dealt with by banks are counted as a part of M1, narrow money, while the MMFs[4] and CMAs handled by asset management companies and securities companies are all counted as belonging to M2, broad money.

2.2.4 Private Monies

Private money is an instrument of exchange created outside the traditional financial sector, although it performs all or part of the functions of money, such as a unit of value, a means of payment, or a store of value. Thus, it operates within a limited exchange network, circulating as a supplementary currency or parallel currency along with legal tender.

Traditionally, the most famous private money in Korea were the bills issued spontaneously by private companies. Private bills and promissory notes were extensively created through inter-firm credits, reflecting the then cash-constrained Korean economic situation. In particular, real bills, created as a result of commercial transactions between firms,

---

[4] It was included in M1, narrow money, until 2007.

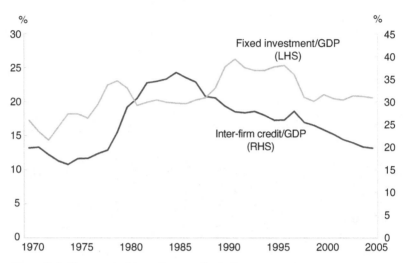

Figure 2.5 The trend of inter-firm credits in Korea
Note: The data after 2005 was compiled as a separate series and is hence omitted here.
Source: ECOS, BoK.

had been in intensive use as private monies, albeit with a limited degree of circulation, and had functioned as a counter-cyclical buffer to business cycles. Figure 2.5 shows the trend of inter-firm credits between Korean companies, which could be derived from the flow of funds accounts statistics.

In the long run, the share of inter-firm credits relative to GDP tends to move in the same direction as the ratio of fixed asset investments to GDP. It is, however, noteworthy that, in the short term, inter-firm credits could substitute for macroeconomic austerity or credit squeezes during periods of recession. During the economic stabilisation period in the early 1980s, for example, inter-firm credits in Korea sharply increased, offsetting, to a substantial degree, the credit squeeze in the loans market.

However, too widespread a use of private bills and notes can result in exacerbating a single bankruptcy into a chain of bankruptcies. For instance, if a company issuing a commercial bill goes bankrupt, then the second party accepting the dishonoured bill will also be likely to go bankrupt, which will put the third company accepting the second party's bill in financial trouble as well. Indeed, chains of bankruptcies have occurred quite frequently in Korea, and these have led to financial mishaps and instability that further amplified economic fluctuations. As a result, various institutional devices were prepared in order to strengthen the regulations on the issuance of bills and enhance the creditworthiness of the companies issuing these bills, at the same time preventing chains of bankruptcies through the provision of guarantees or insurance against the default of bills.[5]

2.3 Development of Electronic Means of Payment

With the development of computer and telecommunications technology, paper-free electronic means of payment are rapidly developing, replacing traditional payment instruments in paper. The widespread use of electronic payment instruments has been made possible through the development of payments and settlements infrastructure, and has often led to the acceleration of financial dis-intermediation, which means it is no longer accurate to define money as a debt of banks or other financial institutions. Electronic payment instruments can be distinguished according to the issuing entity as well.

2.3.1 Central Bank Digital Currency

Against the backdrop of the digitalisation of payment instruments, central banks may consider issuing digital currencies containing electronic information instead of issuing paper money. Central bank digital currency (CBDC) has not yet come into being and different ideas about its concrete form are still under discussion. For instance, if CBDCs are conceived only for wholesale purposes, they will just be similar to bank reserves, with a limited impact on the economy. If the use of CBDCs is generalised even for retail transactions, however, it will have far-reaching consequences on the economy, substituting banknotes and coins, and precipitating the emergence of 'a cashless society'. Some well-known advantages of the CBDCs are as follows:

> First, the creation of CBDCs allows the issuer to economise on the costs linked to the issuing of paper currencies, and, above all, helps to prevent counterfeiting, money laundering, tax evasion, and

[5] This is typically the work of the Korea Credit Guarantee Fund, which was established in 1976.

other illegal transactions. This is because digital currencies are made up of data packages that comprise personal information and identification codes, which makes it possible to trace all the transactions in the economy. However, these advantages do not seem particularly significant in Korea where the use of cash has diminished greatly.

Second, CBDCs can technically enable central banks to conduct a negative interest rate policy, given the problems of cash hoarding outside the banking system. This has led to the interest in 'a cashless society' on the part of many countries with zero or negative interest rates. Korea, however, is not in such a monetary policy environment at this moment.

On the other hand, there are some important hurdles to the introduction of CBDCs. It is claimed that the absence of anonymity in the use of digital currency will severely restrict its circulation. If the use of CBDCs is generalised, the role of commercial banks as financial intermediaries may also be jeopardised, because it extends access to central bank accounts, currently limited to commercial banks, to both private businesses and individuals. Thus, it can be predicted that the issuance of CBDCs will encounter resistance from the existing banks.

Given the increasing volume of online commerce and the use of private digital currencies, however, central banks will face the risk of losing monetary policy control if they do not act. Currently, the BoK does not envisage any imminent introduction of a CBDC. In particular, Article 79 of the Bank of Korea Act prohibits direct transactions between non-bank private sectors and the BoK, which may be a hurdle to the introduction of CBDCs. Under the heading of 'a coinless society', however, the BoK is seeking to replace the use of coins with various electronic and digital media. In contrast to the level of interest in a cashless society, the interest in a coinless society could be universal, and not just limited to Korea. There are two main reasons why the BoK has launched this initiative.

The most important reason relates to the reduction in the social costs and inconvenience associated with the use of coins in diverse economic transactions, as well as the direct cost of minting coins incurred by the BoK. Given Korea's well-developed non-cash payment instruments and methods, such as credit cards and fintech settlements and payments, these gains will be obtained with relatively small implementation costs.

The second reason behind the initiative is to take advantage of the experiment of 'a coinless society' in order to test the possibility of a cashless society. Eliminating coins from circulation has smaller security risks and information-protection costs than eliminating cash, and will make the shift to a cashless society easier. A coinless society would mean that Korea was equipped with the electronic payment infrastructure to allow it to dispense with coins, and this infrastructure could be extended to the realisation of a cashless society.

If a coinless society were established in Korea, it could easily bring about the social environment for negative interest rate policies, and eventually make a quick transition to a cashless society possible (Moon, 2017).

2.3.2 Electronic Means of Payment Issued by Banks and Other Financial Institutions

After being invented in the United States (Mishkin, 2011), credit cards are used worldwide. Given that cash was the dominant instrument for business transactions in Korea, credit cards were introduced as early as 1969 in order to increase the transparency of the business transactions made by many self-employed merchants, and to charge them the appropriate taxes. Credit cards are now the most widely used payment instrument in Korea. The reasons for the rapid expansion of credit card use are as follows:

First, the potential demand for credit cards was strong because, as previously pointed out, cheques were rarely available, and, even after their introduction, Korean households regarded cheques as an inconvenient method of payment. Thus, there was plenty of room for the rapid spread of credit cards in Korea once the convenience of credit cards came to light. The situation in Korea was in sharp contrast with the situation in major industrial countries such as the United States, where cheques were already in widespread use, exhibiting lock-in effects. In these countries, the spread of credit or debit cards was relatively slow, despite the efforts of commercial banks to curb the use of cheques, thereby reducing the cost of processing them.

Second, the Korean government's policy of providing incentives, such as tax deductions to the users of credit cards, which were introduced to help to enhance the transparency of business transactions, played a major role in expanding the use of credit cards. In this regard, too, credit card company law, which allowed consumers to use credit cards even for very small payments, replaced not only the demand for cheques, but also the demand for cash. For example, it is illegal for a merchant in Korea to refuse to accept credit cards or to levy additional charges for using credit cards, no matter how small the payments may be. Anyone who violates this law faces up to one year in prison or a KRW10 million fine. Thus, credit cards are widely used even for very small transactions.

After credit cards, debit cards (check cards) are the second most widely used payment cards. Consumers can use them in any place where credit cards are already accepted, since the payment service is provided through the underlying credit-card network as well as through the debit-card-only network. Banks in Korea have also issued prepaid cards, including K-cash, which are called electronic money (e-money), but they are no longer used.

As a result, Korea could become the first country that successfully switches from a cash economy to a credit economy without using cheques through the development of credit and debit cards only. Figure 2.6 shows the extended use of electronic means of payment in Korea.

Building a robust electronic transfer infrastructure is crucial to support the rapidly expanding use of electronic means of payment. Just as the use of cheques and promissory notes necessitated the emergence of clearing houses as paper-based transfer systems, the widespread use of credit and debit cards in Korea has led to the establishment of electronic payment and settlement systems made possible by the rapid development of telecommunications technology. Payment systems in Korea can generally be divided into three types: (1) the large-value payment and settlement systems used for transactions between financial institutions, (2) the small-value retail-payment systems for diverse transactions between individuals and companies, and (3) the payment systems for international capital transfers. In Korea, the BoK is directly responsible for BoK-Wire, which was established for large-value settlements, while most retail-payment systems are run by the KFTC, established by the BoK jointly with the financial institutions. As well as the traditional cheque-clearing system, the KFTC operates credit-card settlement systems. It also manages the Interbank Shared Network System as a payment and settlement system for Internet, mobile and firm

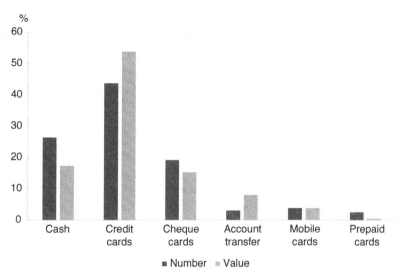

Figure 2.6 Use of different payment instruments in Korea as of 2019
Source: BoK.

banking, and the B2C & B2B e-commerce payment systems. Furthermore, for international capital transfers, Korea has participated in the CLS since 2004, allowing payment versus payment for seventeen foreign currencies including the US dollar (Bank of Korea, 2016). Currently, 98 per cent of all financial transactions in Korea, both in terms of the number of transactions and in terms of value, are carried out by electronic transfer.

2.3.3 Electronic Means of Payment Issued by Non-Bank Private Firms

Among the electronic means of payment offered by non-financial insti-tutions, the most commonly used are prepaid electronic payment instruments, such as public-transportation cards and department-store cards. In Korea, prepaid cards were first introduced in 1994, and were mostly used at petrol stations, department stores, and con-venience stores, but are now expanding into various areas, such as online shopping malls, and restaurants. Among the many prepaid electronic payment instruments issued by specialised electronic pay-ment companies, a public-transportation card, called 'T-money', is particularly famous, expanding its use in diverse transactions including taxis, inter-regional transportation, and various other services.

Moreover, in line with the rapid development of mobile technology and the Fintech boom, mobile telephone companies, SNS providers, and other retail companies are offering various types of new electronic payment instruments and services. Among them, mobile card-payment services by Samsung or by the mobile messenger company Kakao are popular. These services are rapidly increasing their market shares.

2.3.4 *Digital Currency*

Unlike central bank digital currency, private digital currency is endogenously created by a decentralised network of private participants without the intermediary of a central authority. For instance, bitcoin is the most well-known decentralised digital or cryptographic currency. Korea is a very important market for digital currencies such as bitcoin. As of 2020, the Korean currency is one of the most traded currencies behind the US dollar in digital currency transactions.[6]

Digital currencies such as bitcoin are similar to e-money, in that their purchasing power is stored in a digital form, but, unlike e-money, they are denominated in a separate unit of account which is different from legal tender. Thus, it does not need to be linked to any sovereign currency and is itself an autonomous currency. Furthermore, digital currencies supported by decentralised ledger technology are created through a process called mining, like gold mining. Therefore, it is similar in character to commodity money like gold, which is considered as an asset, compared with paper money, which is a liability of banks. It means that the supply of currency is limited, as in the case of gold, and its value changes dependent only on supply and demand. However, high volatility in value has been a factor that has reduced the use of digital currency as a general means of payment (BIS, 2015).

But what is the nature of digital currency? Initially, it was intended to be a network currency, but, once in the real world, high price volatility has made it difficult for it to function as a means of payment. Amid the speculative price increase in 2017, the Korean government decided to regulate digital currencies. Thus, under current Korean law, digital currency is legally neither a currency nor an electronic means of payment. However, it can be regarded as an asset because it is traded with a value. The IMF and BIS (2015) have recommended the use of the term

---

[6] See www.coinhills.com/market/currency.

'crypto-assets', as they believe that bitcoin is an object of real investments even though it lacks the key characteristics of a currency. Against this backdrop, Korea's Supreme Court ruled in 2018 that bitcoin could be confiscated as the proceeds of criminal activity in cases of illegal transactions, judging it to be an intangible asset with a property value.

2.4 Measurement of Money in Korea

Currently, the BoK classifies the quantity of money in Korea, using M1, M2, and L_f or L, based upon the methodology of the IMF manual. As highlighted earlier, M1 is narrow money and M2 is broad money. L_f is the liquidity aggregate of financial institutions, while L is the broadest liquidity aggregate, introduced in 2006. According to the IMF methodology, M1, M2, L_f, and L are defined more precisely as follows:

- M1 = cash + demand deposits + transferable savings deposits;
- M2 = M1 + savings and time deposits + short-term marketable securities, such as CDs and RPs, + yield-based dividend instruments, such as MMFs, CMAs, money-in-trusts, and all other beneficiary certificates;
- L_f = M2 + life insurance and long-term financial products (with maturity longer than two years); and
- L = L_f + all other financial, corporate, and government bonds with relatively low liquidity.

M2, in Korea, is the sum of M1 and all MMFs, CMAs, money-in-trusts, and similar beneficiary certificates, which are under the category of yield-based dividend instruments. It is notable that M2 also contains market instruments, such as CDs and RPs, which have a maturity of less than two years. L_f is the new name given to the previous M3 since 2006. The distinction between M2 and L_f is entirely based upon the term of maturity of the financial instrument with two years as a cut-off. All financial instruments with a maturity under two years are included in M2, otherwise they are included only in L_f. Furthermore, in response to the development of financial markets and liberalisation, there was quite a significant increase in the supply of all the different types of bonds and debentures. Liquidity, L, is the broadest aggregate, which includes not only all financial-sector debt, but also bonds issued by the government and the corporate sectors. Figure 2.7 summarises the composition of money stocks in Korea.

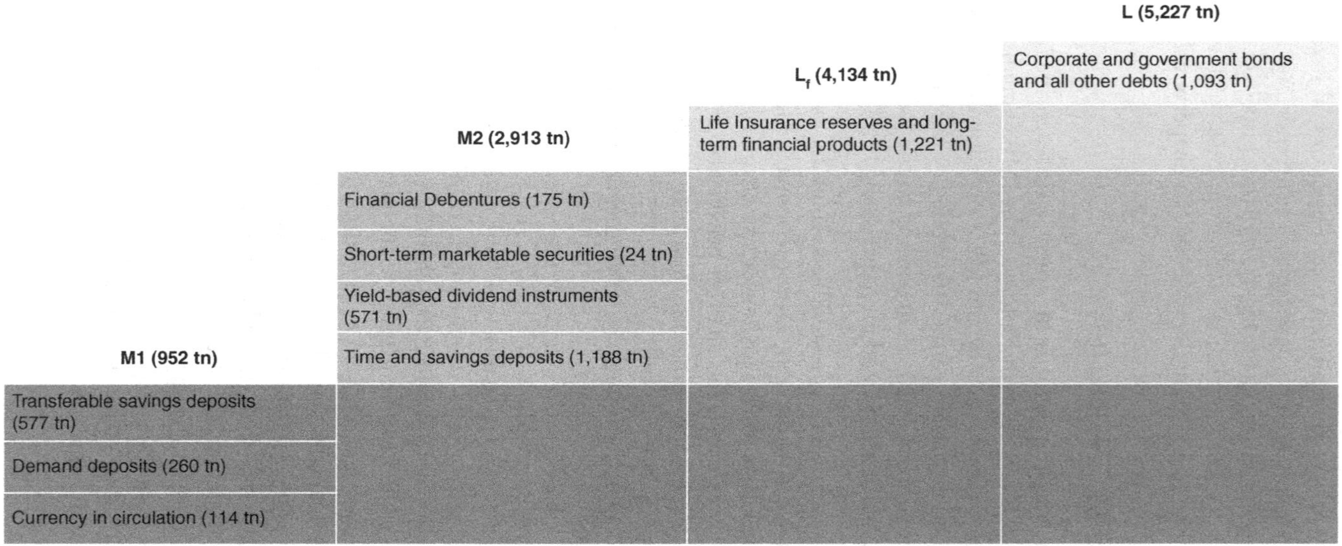

Figure 2.7 Composition of money stocks in Korea as of the end of 2019

Note: Short-term marketable securities include securities, such as CDs and RPs, and yield-based dividend instruments include MMFs, CMAs, money-in-trusts, and all other beneficiary certificates.

Source: ECOS, BoK.

Along with the ongoing financial innovation and rapid technological development, however, these monetary aggregates are losing
importance because of their weakening relationships with the real
economy. Moreover, central banks are not in a position to control
these aggregates. Money supply has been increasingly resilient to
money demand in Korea as well as in other countries. Thus, money
is endogenous and any attempt to control the money supply will be
doomed to fail. In this regard, Knut Wicksell almost one century
ago wrote:

Money becomes constantly resilient, and the supply of money becomes
increasingly dependent on demand. It is no longer possible to talk about
money supply as a variable independent of demand for money. Banks can
always lend money as long as the borrower's credit is guaranteed. ...
Therefore, money supply is subordinate to money demand. (Wicksell
[1901], 1967: p. 110)

Against this backdrop, the BoK shifted its monetary policy framework from monetary targeting operations to interest-based ones from
1997 (see Box 2.1).

Box 2.1 Endogeneity of the Quantity of Money

Until 1997, the BoK had a monetary targeting policy and
announced that it would maintain the growth rate of M2 within the
range of 11.5 to 15.5 per cent. Due to the endogeneity of M2,
however, this commitment could not be realised.

In Korea, money-in-trusts were a very popular financial product
until 1996. Money-in-trusts were originally the long-term and
performance-related debts of banks. Thus, money-in-trusts debts
were not counted as a part of M2, although Korean banks handled
them as though they were ordinary bank deposits. They often had
short maturities and low penalty charges for cancellation of
contract prior to maturity, and some non-specific trusts were fixed
interest rate products. Furthermore, since money-in-trusts products
were not subject to reserve requirements, their yields were higher
than bank deposits. In April 1996, the Korean government suddenly
decided to curb the demand for money-in-trusts, tightening

regulations on the trust system by extending the minimum maturity terms, increasing penalty charges for early cancellation of contracts, and banning non-specific fixed interest rate trusts. This regulation shifted a large portion of the funds from money-in-trusts into bank savings and time deposits. As Figure B2.1 shows, M2 growth started to increase gradually from 14 per cent, and ended up rising to 18.3 per cent, well above the upper bound of the target range of 15.5 per cent (Bank of Korea, 2017c). In sum, although the BoK did not alter its monetary policy stance, monetary growth rose sharply simply by the reform of the trust accounts, which could mislead the public into believing that the BoK was implementing an excessively accommodative monetary policy. Thus, the BoK developed MCT as a new monetary target that was believed to counteract the effects arising from the flows of funds between financial assets. MCT included M2, CDs, and money-in-trusts, and, unlike M2, MCT was considered to be neutral to the movement of funds between money-in-trusts as well as time and savings deposits. Before long, however, another regulatory change made MCT less useful. In 1997, the BoK

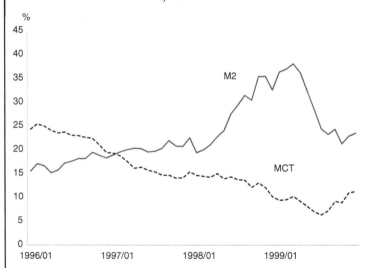

Figure B2.1 Growth rates of M2 and MCT
Source: ECOS, BoK.

imposed a 2 per cent reserve requirement on CDs. Consequently, yields on CDs fell and funds flowed from CDs into short-term commercial bills, which led to further rise in M2 growth rate.

The MCT growth rate continued to drop, making it impossible to maintain the target growth rate. Although there was no change in the monetary policy stance, it looked as if the BoK was implementing an austerity policy. This means that money demand is fundamentally unstable under the circumstance of continuing financial innovation and new financial products, casting the usefulness of the monetary targeting system into doubt.

3 | The Transmission Channels of Money and Credit

How does money affect prices and the real economy? If wages and prices are flexible enough, money can be neutral in the long term and has little impact on business fluctuations. In the short term, however, money can affect national output and employment because wages and prices are rigid. Is this theoretical relationship true for Korea? This chapter looks at the effect of money on prices and on short-term economic fluctuations in Korea. Finally, the chapter examines the relationship between inflation and output in Korea.

3.1 Money and Prices

3.1.1 The Impact of Money on Prices

Inflation refers to a sustained rise in price levels. Thus, a temporary rise in prices does not necessarily mean inflation. A hike in consumption tax, for instance, generates a once-and-for-all rise in prices, but, soon after this rise, inflation falls to zero. In this sense, inflation is only explained by the rise in the quantity of money. As Milton Friedman rightly pointed out, 'inflation is always and everywhere a monetary phenomenon' (Friedman, 1970: p. 181). The relationship between inflation and the growth in money stock is based upon the equation of exchange as follows:

$$M_t V_t = P_t y_t \tag{1}$$

where M_t is the stock of money at a given period t, P_t, the price level, y_t the real national income, and V_t the velocity of money.

The quantity theory of money assumes that the velocity of money, V_t, is constant, and real income, y_t, remains at full-employment level because of wage and price flexibility. Thus, the inflation rate varies in proportion with the growth rate of money. Figure 3.1 shows that this relationship was relatively well held in Korea until the beginning of the

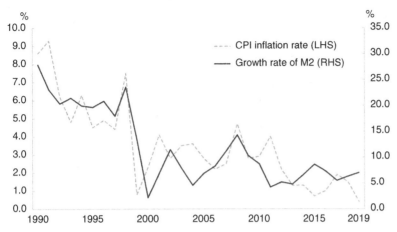

Figure 3.1 The relationship between the growth rate of money (M2) and the CPI inflation rate
Source: ECOS, BoK.

2000s. For this reason, the quantity theory of money remained for quite a long time very popular with many supporters in Korea, especially in the BoK where it was regarded as an inviolable theory which permitted no criticism. Few questioned the view that the best way of fighting against inflation was through the control of the growth rate of money stock. As economic growth slowed down since the 2000s, however, this relationship has substantially weakened.

There are two main factors that contributed to the decrease in the correlation between the inflation rate and growth rate of money in Korea.

First, as in many other countries, Korea experienced a significant increase in the instability of the velocity of money, which was, among others, due to the interest rate liberalisation and rapid financial innovations that started in the 1990s.

Second, the influence of M2 declined sharply as the Korean economy became far more open and global from the 2000s. The WTO membership of China in 2001 and the increasing trade relations between Korea and China have made Korean prices increasingly dependent on Chinese import prices. Korea has also concluded two comprehensive FTAs with the EU and the United States, which took effect in 2011 and 2012, respectively, which also

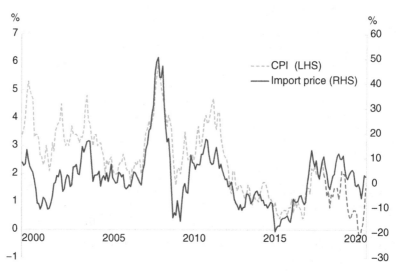

Figure 3.2 CPI and import prices
Source: ECOS, BoK.

contributed to the changing price dynamics in Korea. In a globalised economy, domestic shocks coming from changes in the money stock are quickly absorbed into the adjustment of exports and imports. Inversely, global shocks, such as oil price changes, can exert a much greater impact on inflation dynamics than domestic shocks. Figure 3.2 shows a very close co-movement of the CPI and import prices in Korea, which indicates that inflation in Korea has, to a large extent, been dominated by global factors.

In the aftermath of the 2008 global financial crisis, the BoK continued its easy monetary policy stance, lowering its interest rate to a record low level of around 1 per cent, although, to date, inflation has not surged and low inflation continues to persist in Korea, as in other major advanced economies that actively pursued easy monetary policies including zero or negative interest rates and quantitative easing. In particular, the inflation rate dropped far below its target range from the middle of the 2010s.

Falling prices are raising some concerns about the possible risks of deflation even in Korea. Indeed, Japan suffered from longstanding deflation (see Box 3.1).

Box 3.1 Deflation and Population Decrease

Why doesn't an increase in the quantity of money produce inflation? Japan experienced deflation as its CPI inflation rate fell below zero, amid a continuing economic slowdown, since its bubble burst in 1990. Many critics claimed that the subsequent period of deflation and economic stagnation labelled 'The Lost Two Decades' was due to the mistakes of the BoJ's monetary policy, which was 'too small and too late' (Bernanke 1999; Krugman 1998). Amid lacklustre economic growth and near zero inflation (called Japanification), similar criticisms were levied against the BoK. In this regard, an important question is to see whether Japanese deflation and the resulting recession were really attributable to its lukewarm monetary policy.

Against this backdrop, Masaaki Shirakawa (2012), a former governor of the BoJ, argued that Japan's economic *malaise* was caused by structural problems related to population decrease and aging, rather than its passive monetary policy, as claimed by critics. If Japan's deflation was attributable to a continuously shrinking population, as he convincingly argued, deflation might not be toxic, but, to the contrary, benign for the Japanese economy. Indeed, despite deflation, Japanese economic performance measured by GDP growth rate per capita or per working population was not far behind that of the US economy (Borio et al., 2015; Shirakawa, 2012).

To examine this view in more detail, let us consider the following hypothetical economy with 100 people and 100 kilos of wheat production. Let us assume a closed economy. In fact, Japan was one of the most closed economies among the advanced countries, with its exports barely exceeding 10 per cent of GDP in the 1990s. Let us further assume that the unit price of wheat is one dollar. Suppose now that the population drops to half of the initial level. Then, two adjustment scenarios are possible. The first is that the total supply of wheat remains at 100 kilos. Since fifty people consume 100 kilos of wheat, the unit price of wheat falls to 0.5 dollars as each person buys two kilos of wheat. Thus, the price drops by 50 per cent. The second scenario is that the production of wheat falls from 100 kilos to 50 kilos due to population reduction. Then, because fifty people buy 50 kilos of wheat, the unit price of wheat does not fall, but the growth rate of the economy drops by 50 per cent. Thus, the first scenario with falling prices and increasing real income is preferable to the second scenario with fixed prices and lower real income. Table B3.1 summarises this result.

After all, deflation is not always a bad thing. Deflation can be either good or bad. In countries such as Japan, where the population decrease continues to create pressure for retrenching aggregate demand, deflation can ease the pains of real adjustment, offsetting production declines and increasing per capita income.

Like Japan, Korea is faced with population decline. Will it bring about deflation in Korea as in Japan? Not necessarily, because, unlike Japan, Korea is a very open economy with its export share responsible for around 50 per cent of its GDP. Therefore, the possible decline in domestic aggregate demand can be offset by a rise in foreign demand, which will end up mitigating the deflationary pressure.

Table B3.1 *Hypothetical model economy with a decline in population*

	Initial State	Scenario 1	Scenario 2
Population (Number)	100	50	50
Wheat production (kg)	100	100	50
Wheat consumption (kg)	100	100	50
Per capita consumption	1	2	1
Price (inflation rate)	1	1/2 (−50%)	1 (0%)
Growth rate		0%	−50%

But, given that inflation expectations in Korea still hover at around 2 per cent, it would be more appropriate to say that the Korean economy is faced with disinflation, a slowdown in inflation, and not deflation, a general decline in prices.

3.1.2 Money, Credit, and Asset Price Inflation

Monetary policy can have a greater effect on asset prices than general prices, causing bubbles and collapses in asset markets. The most famous case was probably the Japanese economy in the late 1980s. Despite having an extremely easy monetary policy with interest rates declining to historically low levels, consumer price inflation remained extremely low. In contrast, equity prices tripled, and land prices doubled, ending up with stock market and real estate bubbles. Since the eruption of the 2008 global financial crisis, the advanced economies have again actively implemented expansionary monetary policies, including unprecedented quantitative easing and zero-interest rate policies. Notwithstanding this, inflation has not picked up, but, instead, asset price inflation has been created, with the price of stocks, bonds, and real estate all skyrocketing. Korea is no exception. The CPI continues to remain below target amid the rise in real estate prices. A rise in the quantity of money, instead of being spent on goods and services, as predicted by the quantity theory of money, is being spent to purchase assets, which will lead to asset price inflation and bubbles.

Currently, the consumer price index only covers a small subset of prices in the economy, and cannot fully capture real estate asset inflation. In Korea, a rise in money supply was more correlated with real estate price inflation than with CPI inflation. Figure 3.3 shows the relationship between M2 (broad money) and real estate asset price inflation.

Today, money is almost fiat money created by credit, and thus money and credit are often referred to together. But, strictly speaking, money refers to a liability incurred by banks, while credit represents an asset of

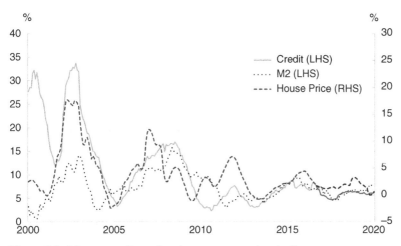

Figure 3.3 Money, credit, and real estate asset prices in Korea
Source: ECOS, BoK.

banks, that is, a loan extended to households or companies. Therefore, apart from monetary aggregates, credit aggregates can be an important indicator for explaining asset prices (Collins et al., 1999). Against this backdrop, Kindleberger and Aliber claim that asset price inflation and bubbles are always the result of the pro-cyclical credit expansions, which they describe as 'fuelling the flames'. For them, axiom number one is 'inflation depends on the growth of money', whereas axiom number two is 'asset price bubbles depend on the growth of credit' (Kindleberger and Aliber, 2005: pp. 55–76). In Korea, as shown in Figure 3.3, private credit had a closer correlation with real estate inflation than M2.

The stability of real estate prices has always been an important political objective of all previous and current Korean governments beyond being a simple economic goal. Real estate is not just a matter of procuring a living space. It is a symbol of economically independent families. It is also a 'safety-net asset', which many Koreans can rely on as a last resort, in order to complement the relatively weak social-welfare system. As a result, there has been a particularly strong desire on the part of Koreans to own their houses at any cost.[1]

Reflecting this situation, MPB members in Korea have always considered the stability of real estate asset inflation as their number-one concern when they take monetary policy deliberations based upon the development of monetary and credit aggregates (see Table 3.1).

Meanwhile, asset inflation begs the question of whether the BoK should target *asset* prices or *consumer* prices. Despite very strong concerns about asset inflation, few actions were taken by the BoK in this regard. The stability of real estate prices in Korea is, above all, the competence of the Ministry of Land, Infrastructure and Transportation, or of the Financial Services Commission, especially if it concerns financial measures that constrain banks by reducing credit for real estate investments. To this end, government officials have deployed all the available regulatory measures, penalties, and tax policies, which seem very arbitrary and are sometimes mixed with the ideologies of the political parties concerned, in order to suppress the demand for real estate assets. This explains the unwillingness of

[1] According to the Housing Survey conducted by the Ministry of Land, Infrastructure and Transport, more than 80 per cent of households surveyed said they would like to own their own homes, showing a strong desire to own a house.

Table 3.1 *Reasons for the concern of the members of the Monetary Policy Board about the trend of money and credit and their frequencies*

Content	Number of persons	Share (%)
Excessive liquidity causes asset inflation, which requires a policy response	56	39.7
Concerns about excessive liquidity	42	29.8
Concerns about inflation	10	7.1
Others	33	23.4
Total	141	100.0

Source: Lee and Kim (2013).

the BoK to be involved in the stabilisation of real estate asset prices, particularly so when this collides with the goal of price or output stability. Against this backdrop, the BoK's approach is currently very cautious, limiting its role to giving early warning signals against real estate bubbles or related excessive credit increases, through its Financial Stability Reports to the National Assembly.

3.2 Money and Real Output

If wages and prices are flexible, labour supply and demand will be equal, and there will be no involuntary unemployment. However, wages and prices are not sufficiently flexible, at least in the short run. Thus, monetary policy can affect national output and employment by redressing the imbalance between aggregate supply and demand. According to a macroeconomic model constructed by the BoK, for instance, a cut in interest rates of 0.25 per cent is estimated to increase the Korean GDP by 0.06 per cent and consumer prices by 0.03 per cent in the first year (Park et al., 2020). The main transmission channels of money and credit policies on aggregate demand are as shown in Sections 3.2.1 to 3.2.3.

3.2.1 *Transmission through Monetary Channels*

a) **The Interest Rate Channel**
Currently, monetary policy in Korea consists of determining not the quantity of money, but the interest rate. Thus, the interest rate transmission channel is presently the most important channel. In general, a cut in

interest rates is supposed to increase investment-expenditure by companies or consumption-spending by households. Theoretically, this should be true. In practice, however, this is not always the case (see Box 3.2). Furthermore, this theoretical effect presupposes a smooth transmission from the BoK's base rate to long-term interest rates. A policy-induced cut in the base rate, for example, lowers short-term money-market interest rates, and this will, in turn, lead to a cut in long-term interest rates, which are by far the most important rates for

---

Box 3.2 Changes in Interest Rate and Income Distribution

An interest rate cut can boost the economy by increasing corporate investment or household consumption. However, in a given period, a rate cut may also have the opposite impact on the real economy due to the transfer of income between debtors and creditors. The mechanism of such income transfers is as follows.

First, an interest rate cut is favourable to companies and unfavourable to households because, according to the flow of funds data in Korea, households are net creditors and companies are net borrowers. Meanwhile, for the household sector as a whole, its financial assets (bank deposits) exceed its liabilities (bank loans) and thus a cut in interest rates reduces the net interest income of the household sector. For example, as of the end of 2014, the interest-bearing debts of the whole household sector were KRW1,162 trillion, while its interest-bearing assets were estimated at KRW1,250 trillion. Thus, a cut in the interest rate led to a net loss of household interest income because interest revenues fell more than the gains from interest-payment reduction. Debt-free households were clearly net losers, while highly debt-ridden households were net gainers. According to the BoK's Financial Stability Report (2014), a 1 percentage point cut in interest rates was estimated to reduce the household net-interest balance by KRW1.4 trillion. Furthermore, a detailed analysis by income group shows that the net balance of interest income was reduced for all income groups from the highest income bracket to the lowest fifth income bracket. This means that, as shown in Figure B3.1, the amount of assets held by debt-free households was larger than the amount of liabilities incurred by debt-ridden households in each income bracket.

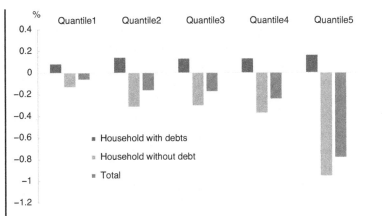

Figure B3.1 Changes in the net balance of interest income with a 1 percentage point interest rate cut by income group and by net debt position in Korea
Source: BoK (2014).

Meanwhile, the fall in the net balance of interest income may be smaller, because the household financial assets are mostly fixed-rate bank deposits, while its financial liabilities are variable-rate loans. The drop in the net balance, however, will be far larger, if a cut in interest rates induces households to borrow more, thereby resulting in an increase in interest costs.

Thus, a cut in interest rates can lead to a fall – rather than a rise – in consumption. In August 2014, the BoK cut its key interest rate by 0.25 per cent, lowering it to 2.25 per cent. However, considering that Korean companies at that time were reluctant to invest, and were stuck in a liquidity trap, despite the large size of their internal profits, such a cut was not effective enough to boost the Korean economy, as was commonly anticipated. The cut in interest rates merely transferred income from households to businesses by increasing corporate profits and decreasing household interest income, without any increase in corporate investment or aggregate demand. The net effect was rather contractionary, which was the opposite of the Korean government's intention to boost consumption. It only contributed to the deepening of household-debt problems, together with the real estate market deregulation policy simultaneously taking place. From 2014 to the present day, the increase in Korean household debt has been around 40 per cent.

the investment and consumption plans of companies and households. Thus, the effectiveness of monetary policy depends on the extent to which short-term rates influence long-term interest rates. Thus, for each interest rate adjustment, the BoK closely monitors the movement of the different short- and long-term interest rates. Given that the current short-term interest rates are only one of the many factors that determine long-term interest rates, there is no guarantee of a smooth spillover from short-term interest rates to long-term interest rates. In general, when financial markets are functioning normally, it often happens that all interest rates move in the same direction, but when financial markets are under stress, some interest rates move in different directions from others. However, as Table 3.2 shows, as far as the Korean economy is concerned, the transmission from base rate through short-term market rates to long-term interest rates (for instance, three-year and ten-year government bond yields) has been very smooth to date. It has also affected lending and deposit rates as expected.

Furthermore, a change in the short-term policy rates may have a disparate effect on government bonds and risky corporate bonds, depending on the degree of risk-taking. In this regard, the BoK carefully monitors the yield gap between safe low-yield government bonds and risky high-yield corporate bonds. And here it would seem that the yields on government bonds and corporate bonds in Korea have been diverging more and more from each other after the 2008 global financial crisis.

b) The Asset Price Channel

A change in interest rates can also influence national output or unemployment through a change in stock prices. For instance, if interest rates decline, the present value of future profits from stocks rises, which leads to a rise in stock prices. An increase in stock prices increases the market value of companies relative to the replacement cost of their physical capital such as machinery and factories, which is called Tobin's q ratio, and thereby can increase the investment expenditure of companies. A cut in interest rates, however, does not necessarily lead to an increase in share prices in Korea, because share prices are affected by many other factors including the overall economic conditions. Furthermore, because the Korean stock market is dominated by a high proportion of foreign investors, domestic share price movements

Table 3.2 *Spillover from short-term policy rate cuts to long-term market interest rates*[1] (*unit: bp*)

Period	Base rate cuts	Decline in market rates[2]			Decline in loan and deposit rates[3]	
		91-day CDs	3-year government bonds	10-year government bonds	Loan rates	Deposit rates
Feb. 2001–Sep. 2001	125	253	205	64	134	223
May 2003–Nov. 2004	100	137	150	135	96	89
Oct. 2008–Feb. 2009	325	332	208	94	181	294
Jul. 2012–May 2013	75	85	51	44	114	98
Aug. 2014–Jun. 2016	125	129	153	189	117	125

Note 1: Extent of changes from two months before the first base rate cut through the month following the last base rate cut;

Note 2: Based upon the monthly average; and

Note 3: Based upon new transactions.

Source: BoK (2017b).

may be more sensitive to foreign stock market movements, such as the movement of the US Dow Jones, than to changes in domestic monetary policy.

A cut in interest rates also increases demand for real estate, which leads to a rise in real estate prices. The effects of interest rate cuts through changes in real estate prices in Korea are likely to be far more important than through changes in share prices (BoK, 2017c). This may be due to the relatively small Korean stock market. Furthermore, Koreans hold more assets in the form of real estate than in financial assets and shares, as shown in Figure 3.4.

A rise in real estate prices has three important transmission channels in Korea:

First, it boosts household consumption through an increase in the value of real estate (so-called wealth effect).

Second, a rise in real estate prices increases the value of collateral. Banks in Korea rarely provide unsecured loans and thus having real estate collateral has always been an important precondition for obtaining bank loans. Thus, increases in collateral value enable companies and households to increase their investments or

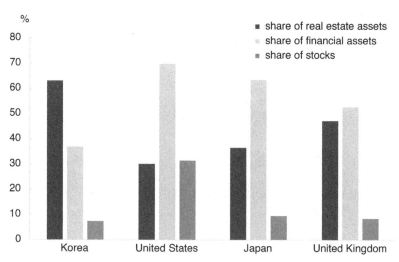

Figure 3.4 The share of real estate assets, financial assets, and stocks held by households
Source: BoK (2017b).

consumption spending, a mechanism which is called a financial accelerator (Bernanke, Gertler and Gilchrist, 1996; Kiyotaki and Moore, 1997). This channel had played a key role in stimulating the economy in Korea, but its effect was partly offset by the stronger regulations which the Korean government introduced to stabilise house prices and stem housing speculation, such as the hike in the LTV ratio for mortgage loans.

Third, the real estate market contains many self-employed businesses in Korea and a rise in real asset prices is often accompanied by a corresponding rise in real estate transactions, which generates a non-negligible number of jobs and incomes.

c) The Exchange Rate Channel

In an open economy, if the domestic interest rate rises above its foreign counterparts, the domestic currency will likely appreciate against foreign currencies, due to increased capital inflows. Inversely, if the domestic interest rate decreases relative to foreign interest rates, the domestic currency depreciates. The consequent exchange rate movements will, in turn, affect the export and import sectors, and, therefore, the real economy. The effects can be particularly important for Korea, given its export-oriented structure with its export share peaking around 45 per cent of GDP. Figure 3.5 shows the relationship between the movement of Korea and US interest rate differentials and the *won–dollar* exchange rate.

Any consistently negative relationship between the interest rate differential and exchange rate movement is not confirmed in Korea. This is, first and foremost, because capital movement in Korea was more affected by the changes in global risk aversion than by the interest rate differential. In particular, the risk-on and risk-off alteration by global investors had a dominant impact on the movement of the Korean *won* until 2010 when Korea had low sovereign credit ratings. It is also due to the opposite impact of interest rate changes on bond-market investors and stock-market investors. A cut in the interest spread, for instance, causes a capital outflow for bonds investors, exerting depreciation pressure on the Korean *won*. But it can simultaneously boost the stock market and consequently bring about capital inflows in the form of equity investment, offsetting the capital outflows in the bond market. The relatively high share of foreign investors in the Korean

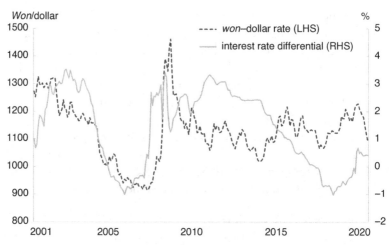

Figure 3.5 Interest rate differential[1] and exchange rate movement
Note 1: refers to the difference between three-month CD rate in Korea and three-month US LIBOR.
Source: ECOS, BoK.

stock market has left the relationship between the exchange rate and interest rate differentials looking very ambiguous and unpredictable.

Although the exchange rate channel remains important for the Korean economy, the BoK has never sacrificed its monetary operation of inflation targeting in favour of exchange rate targeting. This was because the Ministry of Economy and Finance had ultimate responsibility for the exchange rate policy. Furthermore, when the need arose to affect the exchange rate, the instrument used was direct intervention on the FX market, not interest rate changes. Thus, the impact of monetary policy on the exchange rate has been, at best, indirect, through its impact on the stability of prices or output, with which the BoK was primarily concerned.

3.2.2 Transmission through the Credit Channel

The transmission of monetary policy through credit focuses, among other things, on the financial intermediation of banks. Many small- and medium-sized companies and individuals find it difficult to raise funds directly from markets. There is no funding unless they borrow from a bank. Thus, Bernanke (1993, 2007) stresses that monetary policy affects the economy by influencing the availability of bank loans and lending conditions. According to his view, which is called the credit view of the money-transmission mechanism, credit channels are further divided into bank lending and B/S adjustment channels, depending on the supply of, and demand for, credit.

First, an adjustment of the base rate influences a bank's lending behaviour (the bank lending channel). A cut in interest rates decreases the riskiness of loans or the likelihood of default by households or companies. This will induce banks to increase their loans to promote more investment by companies and more consumption by households.

Second, changes in interest rates also affect the net worth of households and firms (B/S channel). A cut in interest rates, for example, increases the net worth of firms, leading to higher collateral values, and thus an increase in the ability to borrow.

Credit was a central transmission channel of monetary policy in Korea because Korea was a bank-oriented economy. Korean companies relied heavily on bank loans, which ended up creating predatory lending practices (see Box 3.3). After experiencing massive restructuring during the 1997 currency crisis, however, big Korean companies have drastically reduced their reliance on Korean banks, which has contributed to transforming Korea from a bank-oriented economy to a financial market-centred economy. Thus, although the credit channel remains active, its effect has become much smaller than before (Bank of Korea, 2017c).

3.2.3 The Expectations Channel

Monetary policy can affect long-term interest rates and thereby also effect aggregate output and employment changes in at least two ways. First, as outlined earlier, central banks can alter current short-term interest rates. By itself, however, this has only minor direct influence on long-term interest rates, which will be more affected by all future short-term interest rates. Consequently, central banks try to influence public expectations for the future path of short-term interest rates. Currently, expectations play a prominent role in the decision-making and behaviour of economic agents. Against this backdrop, monetary

Box 3.3 Bank or Pawnshop?

Before the 1997 currency crisis, Korean banks did not have a credit risk management system, which involved the examination and evaluation of the risks associated with loans, given the historical practice of collateralised loans. Against a backdrop of chronic excess demand for investment, banks exercised a monopoly power over many SMEs, unilaterally imposing loan terms excessively favourable to themselves. For instance, banks required SMEs to provide collateral far in excess of the amount of their loan. Moreover, when borrowers could not repay on time, banks forced them to pay a penalty at exorbitant interest rates, which were two or three times higher than the normal loan rates. As a result, banks received high returns on their loans to SMEs without having to bear any credit risk. In other words, the banks always earned a profit, irrespective of the default of their borrowers. From this viewpoint, Korean banks might not be different at all from pawnbrokers. Consequently, for Korean banks, the loans granted to SMEs were much more profitable than those to large companies, given the excessive collateral provided by SMEs. As shown in Table B3.2, for example, Korea had a strictly compartmentalised financial system in which regional banks lent principally to SMEs, while national banks provided a relatively greater number of loans to big companies. Profitability, represented by the loan-to-deposit margin was therefore significantly higher for regional banks which lent to SMEs than for national banks which lent to big companies. In general, high loan-to-deposit margins should have reflected legitimate compensation to banks for bearing higher credit risks, but even the default ratios represented by NPL ratios were far smaller for regional banks than for national banks. Thus, the high profit margins realised by regional banks were proof that Korean banks abused their monopolistic bargaining power vis-à-vis SMEs.

Notwithstanding this, many Korean banks lent excessively to big Korean companies, partly under government direction and with implicit loan guarantees. When Korea was hit by the currency crisis in 1997, these banks almost all went bankrupt. Since then, Korean banks have taken mortgage banking as their main business. Table B3.3 shows that loans to individual households in Korea were more profitable and safer than the corporate loans until the early 2000s. The current problem of excessive household debt in the Korean economy is a natural outcome.

Table B3.2 *NPLs and loan-deposit margins (%)*

		1987	1989	1990	1991	1992
Share of loans to	National Bank	34.5	38.4	50.3	51.9	52.3
SMEs	Regional Bank	80.0	84.8	86.0	87.1	86.9
NPL ratio	National Bank	5.46	3.19	2.21	1.90	1.80
	Regional Bank	4.87	2.40	1.42	1.00	0.90
Loan-deposit	National Bank	2.45	4.34	4.25	1.78	1.79
margin	Regional Bank	4.31	6.01	5.79	3.79	3.99

Source: Bank Management Statistics, FSS.

Table B3.3 *Interest rates and delinquency rates for households and corporations*

	Interest rates (%)		Delinquency rates (%)	
	Household loans	Corporate loans	Household loans	Corporate loans
1998	15.21	15.20	7.1	8.9
1999	10.85	8.91	3.2	4.4
2000	9.88	8.18	2.4	3.4
2001	8.20	7.49	1.3	2.1
2002	6.92	6.50	1.5	2.0
2003	6.50	6.17	1.8	2.1
2004	5.88	5.92	1.8	2.1

Source: ECOS, BoK.

policy has shifted its focus to influencing the expectations of economic agents in the desired direction. As Woodford (2005) pointed out, the core of monetary policy is, after all, to manage expectations.

To see the role of expectations in more detail, let us consider the relationship between national output and interest rate, which is commonly called IS (or Euler) equation (see, for instance, Clarida et al., 1999):

$$y_t = Ey_{t+1} - \phi(i_t - E\pi_{t+1}) + e_t \text{ with } \phi' \geq 0 \qquad (2)$$

where y_t and Ey_{t+1} are current and expected real output in period t, i_t the nominal interest rate, $E\pi_{t+1}$ the expected inflation rate, and e_t external shock with zero mean.

This equation can be solved by iteration as follows:

$$y_t = E\sum_{j=0}^{\infty}\{-\phi(i_{t+j} - \pi_{t+j+1}) + e_{t+j}\} \text{ with } \phi' \geq 0 \qquad (2')$$

Thus, current real output is affected by the path of all current and expected future inflation rates as well as by the path of current and future interest rates. Let us suppose that short-term interest rates are given. Then, central banks can attain their objective of economic stability through the management of expectations of future inflations. As Marvin King, former governor of the BoE, put it, letting 'the market do the work for us' is more important for central banks than a simple change in policy rates, and, in this regard, 'the practical effect of monetary policy stems from the monetary policy framework that controls inflation expectations rather than from the monthly policy rate decision' (King, 2005: p. 229). Against this backdrop, the inflation-targeting system, which the BoK introduced as a monetary policy framework in 1999, has played a key role in anchoring the inflation expectations of the Korean public.

Second, given future inflationary expectations, central banks can change the expectations of future short-term interest rates, and thereby those of long-term interest rates, which are the average of current and future short-term interest rates. In this regard, the effectiveness of monetary policy depends on how effectively central banks can communicate with the financial markets on the future direction of short-term interest rates. For example, if central banks send a signal to the market that the interest rate will remain low for a considerable period of time, long-term market interest rates will remain low, which will probably boost corporate investment and household consumption. After the 2008 global financial crisis, managing the expectations of future interest rates through communication has emerged as particularly important, because central banks were unable to lower the interest rate below zero. This led to the development of a monetary instrument called 'forward guidance' by many central banks. However, managing expectations in this way is not an easy task. Diverging movements between short- and long-term rates, referred to as the 'Greenspan's conundrum', were not rare. This phenomenon has become frequent in Korea. For instance, when the BoK cut its base rate, hoping to boost the Korean economy in early 2013, this generated an opposite rise in both future short-term interest rates and long-term market rates (see Box 3.4).

Box 3.4 Base Rate Adjustment and 'Taper Tantrum'

The year 2013 was a tumultuous year for the BoK as well as for global financial markets. Since early 2013, financial markets had been anticipating a base-rate cut due to a slowdown in the Korean economy following the launch of QQE in Japan, and the consequent depreciation of the Japanese *yen* vis-à-vis the Korean *won*. This expectation translated into a massive buying of Korean government bonds by foreign investors, which brought down the three-year Korean government bond yield to a record low rate of 2.44 per cent on 2 May 2013, before the base rate was actually cut. The long-term bond yield fell 30 base points below the base rate, which was 2.75 per cent, accentuating the inverted spread between the base rate and the three-year government bond yield that emerged from 6 February of the same year. On 9 May 2013, the BoK lowered its base rate further by 25 bp from 2.75 per cent to 2.5 per cent, against the backdrop of the downside growth risks amid the slow recovery of the global economy. As a result, the spread inversion was resolved.

On the other hand, the US Treasury bond yield rose by more than 100 bp from May to the end of August 2013, starting with the ten-year US Treasury bond yield soaring 31 bp for five days during 20–24 June, following Federal Reserve Chairman Bernanke's remarks on 19 June that the FOMC might proceed to taper off QE. The likelihood of an early exit from QE in the United States triggered world wide shocks called 'taper tantrums' in Korea and in many of the other emerging economies, leading to sudden surges in their market interest rates and sharp depreciations of their currencies. The extent of the taper tantrum was relatively weak in Korea compared to other emerging economies, but, nevertheless, the three-year Korean government bond yield rose rapidly to a yearly high of 3.12 per cent on 24 June, although it fell again to 2.88 per cent at the end of August. This rise in the long-term government bond yield completely nullified the effect of the cut in the base rate by the BoK. This is a good example of how difficult it is for the BoK to manage the future interest rate expectations of the market. In Korea, in particular, bond market investment by foreign investors increased sharply after the 2008 global financial crisis, which led to the intensifying of the synchronisation of the Korean financial market with the US financial market, and increasing the correlation between the Korean and the US long-term interest rates (Bank of Korea, 2013: pp. 79–93).

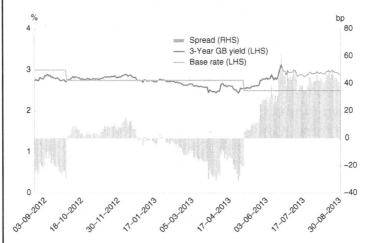

Figure B3.2 Short- and long-term interest rates during the Taper Tantrum
Source: ECOS, BoK.

3.3 The Relationship between Inflation and Output Fluctuation

In the long run, prices and wages are completely flexible. In the short run, however, they are fixed, and the effect of monetary policy is reflected in the fluctuations in output and employment. In moving from short-run equilibrium to long-run equilibrium, prices and wages change slowly, along with output and employment. The relationship between the inflation rate and the adjustments in output and employment is captured by what is referred to as the Phillips curve. The Phillips curve has been one of the most important relationships for many central banks, including the BoK, because, given the dual stabilisation of price and output, they rely on this curve to know how much their inflation target is related to their output and employment targets. Basically, it refers to a trade-off between inflation and unemployment as follows:

$$\pi_t = \pi_t^e - a(u_t - u_n) \tag{3}$$

where π_t and π_t^e represent the actual and the expected inflations in the period t, u_t and u_n the actual and the natural unemployment rates, and a is a positive coefficient.

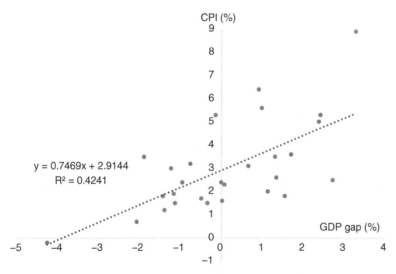

Figure 3.6 Phillips curve represented by the inflation and output gap in Korea (1991–2019)
Note: The output gap in 1998 reached 9 per cent of potential GDP, reflecting the shock of the 1997 currency crisis. This datum was thus removed as an outlier. Inflation was measured by the core CPI that removes the shocks coming from supply side, such as low oil prices, from the overall CPI inflation.
Source: BoK and OECD.

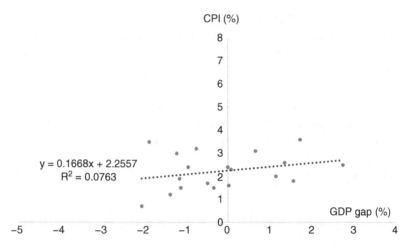

Figure 3.7 Flattened Phillips curve in Korea (2000–2019) .
Source: BoK and OECD.

Thus, given the expected inflation rate, the higher the unemployment rate compared to the natural unemployment rate, the lower the inflation rate. Figure 3.6 shows that, over the period 1990–2019, there was a robust correlation between inflation and the output gap in Korea. It is noteworthy that the output gap was used as a proxy for the unemployment gap, and thus its relationship with the inflation rate turned positive.

Meanwhile, the continuing low inflation phenomenon in Korea, which began in the early 2000s, has significantly weakened the correlation between inflation and the output gap as in other major industrialised countries.[2] As a result, the coefficient α in the Phillips curve has dropped substantially. Figure 3.7 illustrates this.

The flattened curve may have new implications for the inflation-targeting system which the BoK has adopted since 1999. Under the traditional Phillips curve, achieving the target inflation rate was tantamount to achieving the unemployment goal at the same time. If the Phillips curve becomes flat at low inflation rates, however, it can push the BoK into being more active in stimulating the Korean

---

[2] See IMF (2013) for the flattening Phillips curve as a global phenomenon.

economy without necessarily risking inflation.[3] But, at the same time, this creates new risks by inviting more political interference not only from the government but also from the National Assembly, thus threatening the hard-won independence of the BoK.

---

[3] The Phillips curve itself may not be broken, as Gordon (2013) pointed out, when the supply factors are taken into account. But when the trade-off between the CPI target and unemployment breaks, there is little reason to insist on continuing the inflation targeting strategy.

PART III

How Is Monetary Policy Conducted in Korea?

4 | The Organisation and Functions of the Bank of Korea

Currently, monetary policy in Korea is implemented by, and is the responsibility of, the BoK. More precisely, it is the MPB, an autonomous administrative agency modelled after the Board of Governors of the FRS in the United States, which determines monetary policy through collective decisions. This monetary policy system was only established when the BoK became independent in 1998. This chapter looks at the history, organisation, and decision-making structure of the BoK and its relationship with the Korean government.

4.1 A Short History of the Bank of Korea

4.1.1 The Foundation of the BoK

After its liberation from Japanese colonial rule in 1945, Korea suffered from rampant inflation, a dysfunctional financial system, and social and political unrest. The Korean government's top policy priority was to rebuild the country's currency system, and, to this end, it decided to create a new central bank and to reform its banking sector. Against this backdrop, the National Assembly passed the Bank of Korea Act in 1950, along with the General Banking Act. It should be noted that Arthur I. Bloomfield and John P. Jensen, two experts from the Federal Reserve Bank of New York, played a key role in drafting these acts. Especially dispatched by the Board of Governors of the FRS to support the establishment of the BoK, they submitted to the Korean government a 'Recommendation regarding Central Banking Reform in Korea', which contained a draft Bank of Korea Act and Banking Act. Given their background, it is not surprising that their proposal contained the idea of setting up an independent governing agency, the MPB, similar to the Board of Governors in the United States, as the highest decision-making body of the BoK. The establishment of the MPB, which exercised extremely wide powers over all money, credit, and FX policies, as well as over the general management of the BoK was the biggest innovation in the financial history of Korea, because it meant that Korea was subject to a continental European law system under which policy competences were considered to belong exclusively to a function of the government, such as to the Ministry of Finance. Furthermore, given the historical subservience of the BoK to the Korean government, the recommendation attempted to divide the powers and competences, and thus to 'democratise' the policymaking of the BoK, as Bloomfield and Jensen explicitly stated with regard to their mission.

A third purpose has been to free the Bank as far as possible from political pressures and arbitrary interferences, which have plagued it all too frequently in the past, by putting the management and operations of the Bank under the control of a seven-man group representatives of different interests. (Bloomfield and Jensen, 1950: p. 74)

In contrast to the FRS, which was originally formed to place the private banking sector under government control (Johnson, 2010; Rowe, 1965), the plan for the establishment of the BoK was precisely to free it from government control and for it to represent private interests. Thus, the initial conditions for the establishment of the two central banks were completely the opposite.

Notwithstanding this, given the economic situation of the Korean economy at the time, which was 'so heavily dominated and controlled by the Government' that 'it was rather difficult . . . to locate segments of the economy that were completely freed of Government control', they had to make compromises, and recommended the appointment of only three out of the seven members of the MPB from the private sector, thereby giving the majority vote to the members coming from the government sector (Bloomfield and Jensen, 1950). Against the same backdrop, they also added a clause to their final draft of the Bank of Korea Act, which stated that the minister of finance was to chair the MPB. Later, this clause, which was ambiguously drafted in their recommendation, turned out to be one of the most controversial issues in the long battle for central bank independence led by the BoK against the Ministry of Finance.

As the MPB was an independent administrative agency, like the Board of Governors of the FRS, it also had the right to regulate and supervise banks within its competences, which enabled the BoK to exercise comprehensive powers over financial and FX matters as well as monetary issues, albeit under the auspices of the MPB. As a former minister of the economy and finance acknowledged, the Bank of Korea Act not only proposed the constitution of the Bank, but also provided the central bank system of Korea with three pillars: (1) the MPB as the decision-making body, (2) the BoK as the executive body, and (3) the Department of Bank Supervision and Examination as the regulatory and supervisory body (Kang, 2005).

However, this view was disputed by BoK staff, who claimed that the MPB was an internal board of the BoK. This explains why there have been persistent controversies and confusion about the role and organisation of the BoK, and, in particular, about the MPB. There are two reasons for this:

> First, there was a power struggle between the government officials and the BoK staff. This led both of them to interpret the role of the newly established MPB to their own advantage, ignoring the fact that its structure was modelled after the Board of the Governors of the FRS. They were even unwilling to grant separate powers to the newly created organ, which was neither a ministry nor a bank. Bloomfield and Jensen had hoped that the BoK staff would work as the staff in the MPB. This was the reason why they had organised the Research Department of the BoK to be directly subordinate to the MPB, bypassing the governor of the BoK (Alacevich and Asso, 2009). However, the staff of the BoK continued to consider themselves as belonging to the BoK, rather than the MPB. They did not accept the supremacy of the MPB over the governor of the BoK as long as the chairman of the MPB was the minister of finance, which resulted in the failure of collaboration between them and Board members. Furthermore, the members of the MPB were not full-time members. This, again, critically weakened the independent function of the MPB, which the staff of the BoK took over on their behalf.
>
> Second, there was also a deliberate attempt, perhaps disseminated by the BoK staff themselves, to blur the differences between the MPB of the BoK and the Policy Board of the BoJ. Like Korea, the Japanese government, which was under the influence of the US military government (GHQ) in the aftermath of the Second World War, set up a Policy Board, following the model of the FRS.

However, unable to harmonise the Policy Board with the Japanese legal system, the Japanese government eventually incorporated the new institution within the internal governing body of the BoJ (BoJ, 1985). In the case of Korea, in contrast, the MPB was, from its inception, an institution *external* to the BoK, and therefore much closer to the Board of Governors of the FRS. However, the staff of the BoK refused to accept the view that the MPB had been established separately from the BoK, and insisted that the MPB was an internal organ within the BoK, like its Japanese counterpart. This was probably because they refused to acknowledge Bloomfield and Jensen's compromise, which allowed the minister of finance to chair the MPB, and therefore wanted to replace him with the governor of the BoK by making the MPB an internal board subsidiary to the BoK. But they failed to recognise that, once the MPB became an internal organ of the BoK, it would no longer assert the right to keep the regulatory competence and the Department of Bank Supervision and Examination within the BoK. In 1998, the BoK finally succeeded in making the governor of the BoK the chairman of the MPB, but it had to pay a price for it: detached from the tutelage of the BoK, the Department of Bank Supervision and Examination was placed under the control of the Ministry of Finance.[1]

4.1.2 *The Subservient Bank of Korea under the Tutelage of Government*

The first important revision to the Bank of Korea Act was made in 1962, after the establishment of a military government under the late President Park Chung-Hee. The government was quick to adopt national economic planning, and, to this end, put the financial system under its control. Korea was then almost a command economy.

Against this backdrop, the self-evident aim of the BoK was to provide financial support to government-led growth policies, including economic development plans, which resulted in the removal of the autonomy of the BoK and the furthering of government interference in

---

[1] See Chapter 11 regarding the reorganisation of regulatory and supervisory institutions in Korea.

financial and monetary affairs. Some key points of this legislative revision were as follows:

First, and most importantly, the initiative of formulating a broad range of monetary, credit, and FX policies shifted from the MPB to the Korean government. To modernise the industrial sector and enhance its international competitiveness, the government set up the EPB in 1961. The EPB (1961–1994) was a super-ministry, with its minister serving as a deputy prime minister, and was responsible for all domestic economic policies including price controls, development planning, and budgeting. Since the minister of the EPB was deputy prime minister, and had budgetary control over all the other ministries, it had sufficient institutional power to carry out its functions of planning and policy co-ordination. Along with the EPB, the Ministry of Finance assumed a major role in deciding money, credit, and FX policies until 1994, when the EPB and MOF were merged to form the MOEF. The role of the MPB was, therefore, relegated to simply ratifying the policies decided by the Ministry of Finance and its name was also changed to the Monetary Policy Management Board. Against this backdrop, the minister of finance, as the final decision-maker, obtained the right to revoke policies decided on by the MPB. In particular, the competence for FX policies was completely transferred to the Ministry of Finance. Given the primary goal of the Korean government was rapid industrialisation, monetary and financial policies in Korea could not be separable from industrial policies, not to mention macroeconomic stabilisation policies. To mobilise financial savings as much as possible and to channel them to strategic sectors, such as export industries, the Ministry of Finance carried out interest rate controls, preferential policy lending, selectively allocating FX reserves, and putting all financial institutions under its strong scrutiny, similar to the financial controls imposed during the war. Against this backdrop, the BoK's main instrument was to rely on credit rationing and selective credit in order to stem inflation, on the one hand, and to support industry, on the other hand. Not surprisingly, the two objectives proved difficult to harmonise.

Second, coupled with the revision of the Bank of Korea Act, the number of MPB members increased from seven to nine, and the number of government-recommended members increased from two (excluding the minister of finance and governor of the BoK, ex officio members) to five, while the number of members recommended by private organisations was reduced from three to two. This change was designed to strengthen the government control over the MPB. Furthermore, the Ministry of Finance acquired the right to examine the BoK's workings, its budget, and closing statements, which further reduced the autonomy of the BoK.

Third, the amended Bank of Korea Act established the grounds for the BoK's direct subscription to government-guaranteed securities.

Through this revision, the Ministry of Finance obtained complete control of the BoK, nullifying the independent decision-making power of the MPB. This situation continued until the 1980s, during which time the framework of the Bank of Korea Act remained almost intact, except for minor revisions. In retrospect, it meant that, despite the attempt to democratise the Korean economy and decentralise state power by Bloomfield and Jensen, the Korean economy slid back to the wartime Japanese system of the state monopoly of economic power.[2]

Amid the liberalisation of the Korean economy triggered by the democratisation movement in 1987, however, there were continuing efforts to amend the Bank of Korea Act in order to make it more independent. In effect, the independence of the BoK was considered to be a symbol of democracy. Notwithstanding this, all these efforts failed because the acute differences in views that existed between the Ministry of Finance and the BoK over the central bank's neutrality and autonomy could not be resolved. What was particularly at stake was the issue of who should serve as chairman of the MPB. Clearly, the BoK wanted its governor to replace the minister of finance and chair the MPB, with which the Ministry of Finance did not agree. In its turn, the Ministry of Finance wanted to place the supervisory functions of commercial banks under its auspices and thus separate the Department of Bank Supervision and Examination from the BoK, to which the BoK was strongly opposed.

The revision of the Bank of Korea Act became a thorny public issue again in 1997, when the Financial Reform Committee, belatedly set up by President Kim Young-Sam, submitted a proposal on reorganising the central banking and financial supervisory systems, with the aim of harmonising both of these opposing viewpoints. However, the

---

[2] Indeed, similar reforms were made by the US government in respect of the BoJ, where the power of the Ministry of Finance remained unchanged.

proposal was too ambitious to achieve a compromise between the BoK and the Ministry of Finance, and eventually no change was made to the Bank of Korea Act. However, the eruption of a currency crisis in 1997 changed the stand-off, as Korea had to apply for a rescue package from the IMF. The memorandum of understanding signed between the Korean government and the IMF called for the passage, by the end of 1997, of thirteen financial bills, including an amendment of the Bank of Korea Act, which was pending in the National Assembly at the time. At the end of December 1997, the new Bank of Korea Act, along with the other financial bills required, were passed by the National Assembly.

4.1.3 The Independent Bank of Korea in the Aftermath of Currency Crisis

The 1997 Bank of Korea Act, the sixth re-drafting of the original act, reflected the most comprehensive change in its scope since its first revision, ranging from the composition and organisation of the MPB to the goals of monetary and credit policy. The key points of this sixth amendment can be summarised as follows:

> First, the goals and objectives of the BoK were modified, with particular emphasis on its neutrality and autonomy. In particular, the objectives of the bank were changed from stabilising monetary value and maintaining the soundness of the banking and credit system to the single objective of maintaining price stability. The revised Bank of Korea Act explicitly highlighted the independence of the BoK in its formulation and implementation of monetary and credit policies. The amended Bank of Korea Act also required that any request by the minister of economy and finance to revoke the decisions of the MPB be publicly announced in a prompt manner.
> Second, the BoK's policymaking body was reorganised. Specifically, all members of the MPB became full-time members, and the composition of the board was also modified. The minister of economy and finance was excluded from participating in the board meetings, and the position of chairman, previously held by the minister of economy and finance, was transferred to the governor of the BoK. Moreover, the total number of board members was reduced from nine to seven and the number of members recommended by the government was reduced from five to two.

Third, the BoK's bank supervisory function was separated and transferred to the new financial supervisory authority. The FSC was set
up as a separate administrative agency, placing the bank's regulatory and supervisory role and other non-bank regulatory and
supervisory functions under a single umbrella.

Fourth, the new Bank of Korea Act changed the operational framework of monetary and credit policies. It stipulated that the BoK
should adopt a framework of inflation targeting, and, to this end,
decide a target inflation rate in consultation with the government.
The revised Bank of Korea Act also clarified the legal grounds of
the payment and settlement system operated by the BoK, specifying that the BoK should be responsible for the operation and
management of the payment and settlement systems.

Fifth, along with strengthened independence, the accountability of the
BoK was also strengthened. In addition, the BoK had to prepare a
report at least once a year on the implementation of its monetary and
credit policies and submit this to the National Assembly.

Then, in 2011, the Bank of Korea Act was again revised to reflect the
incorporation of macro-prudential policies in its mandate, along with
price stability. Thus, Article 1 of the 2011 Bank of Korea Act stipulates
that, in carrying out its monetary and credit policies, the BoK should pay
attention to financial stability. This revision was in tandem with the
movement towards strengthening the financial stability function of central
banks, led by many major countries in order to overcome the global
financial crisis and prevent a repetition of the financial crisis in the future.

Table 4.1 summarises the major changes and revisions made to the
Bank of Korea Act over the last seventy years.

4.2 The Roles and Functions of the Bank of Korea

4.2.1 *Conventional Function as a Bank*

A central bank is, above all, a bank, and, as a bank, the functions of the
BoK are as follows:

First, just like every other central bank that starts its business by
issuing banknotes and then gradually acquires the right to monopolise their issue, the BoK has the monopoly right to issue banknotes
and coins within Korea. The MPB determines their dimensions,
designs, and denominations, subject to government approval.

Table 4.1 *Changes in the main features of the Bank of Korea*

	From the founding of the BoK in 1950 to 1962	From second Revision in 1962 to 1997	From the sixth Revision in 1997 to date
Priority of the government	Stabilising the currency value	Economic development	Price stability and growth
Goals of the BoK	1. Maintaining stable value of money. 2. Development of national economy and efficient resources allocation through the soundness of banking and credit system. 3. Managing foreign reserves to achieve normal international trade and balance of payments.	1. Maintaining stable value of money. 2. Development of national economy and efficient resources allocation through the soundness of banking and credit system.	1. Sound development of the national economy by pursuing price stability. 2. Paying attention to financial stability (newly added in the revision of 2011).
Monetary policy strategy and leadership	Credit rationing decided by the MPB.	Credit rationing and monetary targeting largely determined by the government.	Inflation targeting led by the MPB.
Name of the MPB	MPB.	Monetary Policy Management Board.	MPB.
Chairman of the MPB	Minister of finance.	Minister of finance.	Governor of the BoK.

Table 4.1 (*cont.*)

	From the founding of the BoK in 1950 to 1962	From second Revision in 1962 to 1997	From the sixth Revision in 1997 to date
Number and terms of the MPB members	Seven part-time members with four-year term.	Nine part-time members with three-year term.	Seven full-time members with four-year term (with the exception of the deputy governor who has only a three-year term).
Competence of the BoK	All monetary, financial, and FX affairs were assumed by the powerful board composed of government officials and people from the private sector.	FX operation was transferred to the Ministry of Finance.	Bank supervision operation was also transferred to the newly established FSC.
Independence of the BoK	Political neutrality and autonomy emphasised.	Subject to complete government control.	Independence regained (the government has the right to recommend two MPB members).

Second, the BoK plays a role as the government's bank. As the fiscal agent of the government, the BoK carries out various kinds of business for the government in accordance with the Bank of Korea Act and other relevant laws. For instance, the bank handles the receipt of national revenues and the disbursement of national expenditure as the depositary of the government. The government maintains a current deposit account with the bank, to which taxes and all other government revenues are committed. The BoK can also extend credit to the government on overdraft or in other forms, and directly subscribe to government bond issues. However, to prevent monetary expansion resulting from excessive government borrowing from the BoK, the Bank of Korea Act requires it to limit the credit extended to government. Specifically, the BoK's credit to the government and subscriptions to government bonds, combined with government's borrowings from financial institutions and elsewhere, cannot exceed a ceiling set by the National Assembly. Furthermore, the BoK supports government debt management. Under the National Government Bond Act, the Ministry of Economy and Finance issues government bonds. Under its direction, the BoK currently conducts the issuance and redemption of Korea Treasury Bonds.

Third, the BoK is a bankers' bank. In a country, such as the United States where there was no central bank until the early twentieth century, the role of the bankers' bank was assumed by a clearing house or large private banks, which would cause a conflict of interest between their private and public activities (Goodhart, 2010). This, however, was exceptional, in the sense that it would apply only to the US economy, with its unit bank system in which the failure of banks was more frequent than in other countries. In Korea, the BoK is a special judicial person without capital and is therefore banned from profit-making activities.[3] Serving as a bankers' bank, the BoK currently receives deposits from banks, maintains current accounts for them, and uses their reserves in

---

[3] When the BoK was founded in 1950, it was completely owned by the government with its paid-in capital of KRW1.5 billion. However, along with the revision of the Bank of Korea Act in 1962, it was converted into a special judicial person without capital.

their BoK accounts to clear cheques and to settle interbank accounts. It also grants credit to banks by re-discounting commercial bills or by extending them loans against eligible collateral with maturities of up to one year. In particular, as the lender of last resort, the BoK can extend loans to banks in liquidity difficulties, when no other lender is prepared to do so in times of financial crisis.

4.2.2 Role as Monetary Policy Authority

Irrespective of whether central banks start their business as a bank of government or as a bankers' bank, they have transformed themselves into public institutions that carry out government economic policies. For many industrialised countries, it was the outbreak of the Great Depression in the 1930s that rendered it normal for governments to intervene in the operation of central banks. The goal of central banks has been transformed into carrying out the national policy objectives aimed at stabilising not only prices but also employment and output.[4]

After the Second World War, Korea and many other emerging economies established central banks as they became independent nations. Against this backdrop, the BoK was not just a central bank conducting stabilisation policies aimed at managing aggregate demand, it also had to assume the function of supporting the general economic policy of the government. Especially when the government pursued its industrialisation policy, the BoK had to provide financial support to a government that was facing a shortage of fiscal revenue, which led to the chronic monetisation of fiscal deficits and the consequent inflation until the early 1980s. The role of the BoK was therefore broader, as it had to try to enhance the long-term growth rate of the economy through aggregate supply policy. This explains why, despite the intentions of Bloomfield and Jensen to the contrary, the BoK was not able to be an institution that was independent from a government that never thought of delegating power in its pursuit of economic policies. Price and output stability as the primary goals of the central bank could be

---

[4] This position is especially highlighted by the Radcliffe Report. 'It is no longer appropriate to impose clear tasks on monetary authorities that can be clearly distinguished from other government policies' (Radcliffe Committee, 1959: p. 17).

effective only when the Korean economy achieved a certain degree of economic development, freeing itself from the chronic shortage of aggregate supply. Only from the year 1998 *circa* has the BoK been able to perform such stabilisation policy properly. Currently, the most important mission of the BoK in its implementation of monetary policy is that of price stability. To this end, the BoK adopted an inflation targeting system in 1998, thereby changing its operational framework from the management of monetary aggregates to the setting of interest rates.

As far as monetary policy is concerned, it is no longer the bank, but the decision-making process that has become the primary focus of attention. In this regard, most central banks currently establish monetary policy committees or governing boards to make decisions on monetary policy. In Korea, the MPB was designed as an independent administrative agency, as already pointed out (see Box 4.1). Thus, the efficiency of monetary policy depends on the role and the structure of the MPB. Although the MPB was designed to exercise wide powers in the management of the BoK as well as in the conduct of monetary policy, it was, however, barely operational, with its autonomy continually being encroached by the BoK and the Ministry of Finance. Under these circumstances, the MPB members were only marginally exercising their expertise and skills. The MPB was just a 'Yes Board', similarly to the 'Sleeping Board' in Japan, in the sense that any agenda submitted for the deliberation of the MPB was always invariably approved.

It was only in 1998 that the MPB was awarded autonomy in respect of monetary and credit policy along with the appointment of the full-time board members. Notwithstanding this, the MPB members currently do not participate in the internal management of the BoK, except for those matters specifically stipulated in the Bank of Korea Act, such as the BoK's budget, and organisational changes. This may be because, among other things, the BoK staff were still reluctant to accept the comprehensive authority of the MPB to supervise the bank's operations and management. The full independence of the MPB, be it internal or external, is still threatened, not necessarily by external political pressure, but rather by the internal suspicion of the BoK staff, who have historically encroached on the rights of the MPB members to decide monetary and credit policies independently.

Box 4.1 Comparison of the Governing Board and Monetary Policy Committee

The governing board is the most basic decision-making unit of central banks and has full responsibility for their management and operation. Thus, for most central banks, the role, composition, and responsibility of the governing board are specified by law. In the case of the United States, for instance, the Board of Governors of the FRS was set up as an independent administration agency composed of seven members, set apart from the Federal Reserve Banks of the twelve districts, which had their own board of directors. It is thus an external organisation to the Federal Reserve Banks, with its own staff. The Board of Governors, however, controls the Federal Reserve Banks by appointing three out of the nine directors of the Reserve Banks. The Board of Governors is responsible for various monetary policy decisions, including the determination of policy rates as well as decision-making related to the management of the FRS. At the same time, the increase in the importance of professional and technical expertise in the decision-making of monetary and financial policies has led some central banks to operate independent monetary policy committees by separating policymaking tasks from the central bank's management work. For example, the FRS carries out its interest rate-setting monetary policy through the FOMC. All seven governors are members of the FOMC and make decisions on the conduct of open market operations. The FOMC is composed of twelve members with five presidents of the Reserve Banks as well as the seven governors.

Central banking in Korea, as in the United States, originally had a dual structure composed of the MPB and the BoK, although they are regarded as a single organisation by the general public. The MPB, as pointed out, is an independent administration agency and is, therefore, external to the BoK. It is responsible not only for the internal management of the BOK – albeit not active – but also for monetary and credit policies. Thus, unlike the Board of Governors of the FRS, the MPB itself is simultaneously a governing board *and* a monetary policy committee setting interest rates. There is no separate monetary policy committee like the FOMC in Korea.

In Japan, the Policy Board, as the highest decision-making body in the BoJ, was introduced in 1949 by J. M. Dodge, financial advisor to the US military government (GHQ) established in Japan in the aftermath of the Second World War. Modelled after the FRS, the

Policy Board was considered important to enhance the autonomy of the BoJ and to reduce interference by the minister of finance (Bank of Japan, 1985). But, unlike in Korea, the Policy Board was installed as an internal organ of the BoJ, because of the incompatibility of the independent administration agency with the then prevailing Japanese continental European law system. The Policy Board was, however, inactive in policymaking, as its nickname the 'Sleeping Board' suggested. In 1998, the Bank of Japan Act was revised and the Policy Board, again like the MPB in Korea, acquired the competence to carry out independent monetary policy. As a result, the Policy Board is currently implementing all important monetary policy decisions, as well as the management of the bank, including the supervision of the staff of the BoJ.

In many countries, the governing board is an internal organisation of central banks. In the United Kingdom and many continental European countries, among others, central banks have an internal governing board. In the United Kingdom, for instance, the BoE is governed by a board called 'the Court', composed of thirteen directors including the governor, the three deputy governors and nine non-executive directors. In contrast, the MPC is just the BoE's technical committee, which focuses solely on interest rate-setting monetary policy, and therefore has nothing to do with the internal management of the bank. The MPC members are separate from the board members. This has long been regarded as an ideal system by many BoK staff, who do not want to be controlled by the MPB. However, if this were the case, the current BoK would be illegitimately run as it would not have a governing board in place. Table B4.1 summarises the features of different central banks regarding their governance and monetary policymaking structures.

Table B4.1 *International comparison of the governance and monetary policymaking structure of central banks*

	Board as external to the Bank	Board as internal organ of the Bank
Monetary policy decision separated	FRS (Board of Governors/FOMC)	BoE (Court/MPC)
Monetary policy decision integrated	BoK (MPB)	BoJ (Policy Board)

4.2.3 Role as Supervisory Authority

The BoK also has a mandate for supervising financial systems and maintaining financial stability. The role of the BoK as a financial supervisory body covers three areas:

> First, the BoK was responsible for maintaining a sound banking system, and, in this regard, it established the Department of Bank Supervision and Examination, which conducted regulatory and supervisory operations under the guidance of the MPB. It is noteworthy that the department in charge of the regulation and supervision of banks was under the direct tutelage of the MPB as an independent administration agency, and not under the direction of the governor of the BoK. Indeed, financial regulation and supervision was not the proper and legitimate function of the BoK, but, rather, of the government. Along with the sixth amendment of the Bank of Korea Act in 1997, this regulatory and supervisory function was transferred from the BoK to the newly organised Financial Supervisory Commission (now the FSC), which was separated from the Ministry of Finance, and to the Financial Supervisory Service (now called FSS), which annexed the Department of Bank Supervision and Examination.
>
> Maintaining financial stability is inseparable from the monetary and credit policy of the central bank, and is intrinsically part of central bank policy. The BoK, therefore, continues to assume the financial stability function, albeit to a limited extent and with a reduced competence. For instance, the BoK can request the FSS to conduct independent or joint examinations of financial institutions when deemed necessary for the implementation of its monetary and credit policies. The BoK may also require the FSS to take the necessary corrective measures against financial institutions upon the basis of the findings of such examinations. In addition, the BoK may directly check the operation and status of the assets of financial institutions to which it has extended emergency credit. Finally, as the importance of macro-prudential policies has grown globally in the aftermath of the 2008 global financial crisis, the Bank of Korea Act was revised again to strengthen the bank's responsibility for the financial stability and macro-prudential policy. For instance, Article 1 of the newly amended Bank of Korea Act stipulates that 'the Bank

of Korea shall pay attention to financial stability in carrying out its monetary and credit policies'.

Second, operating safe and effective payment and settlement systems is crucial not only for the efficient allocation of resources and the promotion of economic growth, but also for financial stability. Accordingly, the BoK is operating and overseeing the payment and settlement systems for the Korean economy, and its role in ensuring the security and efficiency of such payment and settlement systems is gaining in importance. Currently, the BoK operates BoK Wire+, the large-value payment system, and provides intraday overdrafts to financial institutions temporarily short of settlement funds. The BoK also oversees the various individual settlement systems, monitors and assesses them, and recommends any necessary improvements to the system's operators.

Third, the BoK oversaw the formulation and execution of foreign exchange policies and managed the FX until the early 1960s. With the enactment of the Foreign Exchange Control Act in 1961 and the subsequent revision of the Bank of Korea Act in 1962, however, FX policy formulation was transferred to the government. Notwithstanding this, in consultation with the government, the BoK continues to maintain responsibility for the stabilisation intervention of FX markets, the managing of foreign reserves, the formulation of prudential regulations on the FX businesses of banks, and of the handling of the overall management of the FX market. In addition, the BoK acts as an agent for the government in managing the 'Foreign Exchange Stabilisation Fund', which was founded in 1967 with the objective of stabilising the FX market. The BoK represents the Korean government in all dealings and transactions with the international financial institutions of which Korea is a member.

4.3 The Structure and Quality of the Monetary Policy Board

Currently, monetary policy relies on collective decisions made by the policy committee members. A collective decision by a committee is superior to individual decision-making. The committee may create what is called 'collective intelligence' by sharing the knowledge and forecasts of all its members. Collective intelligence means the intellectual ability of a large number of diverse and independent agents co-operating and competing with each other, which is known to yield better judgements than those made by a few experts or individuals (Surowiecki, 2004; Wooley et al., 2010). The committee can also help to remove noise from signals. That is to say, if decisions are taken by a majority, the committee is more likely to pick the best option than any of its individual members (Blinder and Morgan, 2005). Thus, a committee is more than just the sum of its parts (Sibert, 2006). However, collective decisions by a committee can sometimes be costly. Individuals can be free-riders, not devoting their full efforts to improving the collective performance. There are cases in which a committee strives too hard for consensus, and a particularly harmful form of group polarisation, called 'group think', can occur, as committee members stop considering the alternatives (Janis, 1973). The benefits and costs of committee decision-making will depend on the structure of the policy committee. Against this backdrop, Blinder (2008) examines the different factors of policy committees, such as the method of consensus-achieving among the policy committee members, the leadership, the voting methods, and the committee size. It is based upon these factors that the performance of the MPB in Korea can be assessed, although it should be stated that such assessments are somewhat subjective, given the importance of the personal characteristics of the governor of the BoK in decision-making.[5]

4.3.1 The Quality of Decisions

First, leadership qualities seem to be the most important factor in determining the performance of the MPB in Korea. The governor of the BoK has a very dominant power within the MPB. The governor chooses the deputy governor who, serving as a member of the MPB, practically always votes in accordance with the governor. The governor is therefore likely to rule an MPB with only seven members. Among the five external members, there are also one or two members who will always side with the governor. This means that, in order to counteract

---

[5] This is based on the author's personal experience as a member of the MPB and is, therefore, highly dependent on the personal characteristics of the two governors with whom the author worked.

the vote of the governor, at least four outside members have to vote against the governor at the same time, which is very unlikely because they are rarely of the same opinion. Furthermore, the BoK staff habitually support the governor, while other MPB members do not have their own staff. Consequently, the governor's view is almost always dominant. To date, there seem to have been only one or two cases in which the governor's view has failed to dominate the MPB since 1998.

However, if the governor plays too dominant a role in the committee, there is a high risk of falling into 'group think'. In particular, the more uncertain the policymaking environment, the more important it is that the decisions reflect the various opinions of the MPB members. Nonetheless, if correct decision-making is difficult, MPB members are likely to side with the majority view in order to lessen the risk of their misjudgement, thereby increasing the chance of 'group think' and 'herding'. Furthermore, only the dissenting MPB members are required to make their views immediately public under their own names, while the members voting with the majority view are not required to do so, which makes dissent more difficult and less frequent. In addition, dissenters are required to explain why they disagree with the majority view, which is also, almost invariably, the governor's view, as their transcripts are sent immediately to the government. While such a system can easily lead to consensus by imposing asymmetric pressure on the dissenting members, it is likely to cause serious harm to the credibility and neutrality of the MPB. The pressure will be particularly strong when the dissenters express hawkish views, which will very likely contradict the government's policy stance, not to mention the governor's view. One possible solution might be to make the decisions of all MPB members immediately public under their own names.

Second, consensus-seeking is an important feature in Korea. Blinder (2008) distinguishes between individualistic and collegial committees. In the case of an individualistic committee such as the BoE's MPC, the members of the committee do not strive to reach agreement with their colleagues; members express their opinions independently using their own judgement, and decisions are made by majority vote. Thus, various views can be reflected in policy decisions. In contrast, under a collegial committee, members make a concerted effort to reach agreement with collective responsibility. The European Central Bank's Governing Council, for instance, is regarded as a genuine collegial committee. Meanwhile, the FOMC in the United States is considered as a mixed committee in which members are free to express their opinions, while the chairman can exercise strong leadership (Blinder, 2008). The MPB in Korea is also considered to be a mixed committee. Clearly, this description may be too mechanical because efforts in consensus-building may be preferred to simple voting, depending on the personal characteristics of the governor. Consensus-seeking in Korea may facilitate the sharing of responsibilities but it may also deter a free and frank exchange of views between the members of the MPB, where dissenting views are rarely respected.

It is very difficult to assess, a priori, what kinds of committee arrangements can deliver a better performance in Korea. However, in order to draw the benefits from 'collective intelligence', individualistic committees would seem to be more desirable than collegial committees. In Korean social culture, freely expressing individual judgements is still not very common, and expressing a dissenting opinion which runs contrary to the view of the governor of the BoK is especially challenging. Age-based seniority plays a role as well. All these factors prevent differences in opinions from being transformed into collective intelligence and thus hamper the proper working of the MPB. Thus, collegiality is likely to do more harm than good, and will lead to a rather conformist MPB. Clearly, an individualistic committee could increase the risk of causing confusion in the markets when very different opinions prevail among the members. But, given the small number of dissenters, this risk does not seem to be great in Korea.

Third, the question of voting arrangements, be they by majority or by unanimous vote, is of little significance in the current Korean context. Currently, majority voting is rather well established in Korea. It is questionable whether unanimous voting is even necessary under the current Korean operation of the MPB in which diversity of views does not frequently occur, and the market seeks out the reasoning behind the diverse views of each individual MPB member. The governor of the BoK might prefer unanimous voting, but it would only end up strengthening the dominance of the governor's views within the MPB.

The extent of agreement can, however, be flexible, depending on the content of the policy decisions. For example, MPB members seek to obtain unanimous agreement on important decisions other than interest rate-setting monetary policy, such as macro-prudential policy measures and the provision of emergency liquidity to the banking system during financial turmoil, because these issues often involve highly confrontational sectoral interests and the division of the views of the MPB members may result in political interferences.

4.3.2 The Quality of the MPB Members

In general, 'collective intelligence' has little to do with the capabilities of the members in their collection of data and analysis of information (Wooley et al., 2010). In practice, however, the number of members in the MPB in Korea is relatively small, such that the selection of capable MPB members can critically determine the performance of monetary policy.

Against this backdrop, the Bank of Korea Act stipulates that the appointed MPB members must have abundant experience or outstanding knowledge in finance, the economy, or industry. Notwithstanding this, democratic representation that favours the diversity of the MPB members is also an important principle. Currently, however, there is increasing consensus among the Korean public that MPB members should be appointed based upon their professional expertise rather than because of the diversity of the sectors of the economy from which they come. Table 4.2 shows the background of the MPB members over the last twenty years.

Among MPB members, the governor is an ex officio member and is appointed by the President of the Republic of Korea, following hearings by the National Assembly. The governor serves as the chairman of the MPB. Among the six governors appointed since 1997, three came from academic circles while the remaining three were ex-BoK staff. Clearly, they should be equipped not only with professional expertise, but also be politically neutral and free from private sector interests, which explains why neither career government officials nor private business leaders have ever been appointed. In general, there seems to be an increasing consensus that experts from academic circles and BoK staff should alternate as governors.

The deputy governor is also an ex officio member, appointed by the President on the recommendation of the governor. This change was introduced in 2003 to strengthen the governor's decision-making powers within the MPB and to assist the governor's internal management of the BoK, especially in cases where the governor comes from academic circles. To date, the deputy governors have all been internal BoK staff, promoted for their technical and professional expertise, and,

Table 4.2 *MPB members according to their background and their recommendation institution during the period 1998–2020*

Recommended by	Ex-government officials	Ex-BoK staff	From academic circles	From banks and industry
Governor (ex officio)[1]		3	3	
Deputy Governor (ex officio)		6		
Ministry of Economy and Finance	4		4	
BoK	1	2	4	
Financial Supervisory Board	2	1	3	1
Chamber of Commerce	1	1	4	1
Banking/Securities Companies' Association	4	1	2	2
Total	12	14	20	4

Note: The current governor, who is serving two terms, is counted twice.
Source: Author's compilation

as stated earlier, they rarely express dissent in relation to the governor's opinion, which results in constraining the input of his technical expertise in the decisions of the MPB.

In contrast, all other external members are appointed by the President on the recommendations of five institutions, which include the BoK, two governmental bodies (the Ministry of Economy and Finance, and the FSC), and two private institutions (the Chamber of Commerce, and the Bankers Association). This system was originally intended to reflect the diverse interests of the recommending institutions involved, but, because Korea was not a pluralistic society, and power was concentrated in the hands of government, the recommendations, particularly by private institutions, did not accommodate the principle of democratic representation. Thus, the appointments were largely made based upon the technical quality of the candidate members.

The largest number of external members of the MPB comes from academic circles, which reflects the increasing importance of technical knowledge and expertise in monetary policy and central banking. Given the heavy interference in and dominance by the government over the private sector, the government seems to have a large pool of highly talented experts as well. In particular, ex-government officials have unparalleled technical expertise in policymaking, which other members from the private sector could not easily emulate. Compared to former government officials, it seems that there was little room for members with a career in private banking or business to contribute to the performance of the MPB. This explains why private institutions, such as the Chamber of Commerce or the Bankers Association, have recommended only a small number of career bankers or business leaders as members of the MPB. Former BoK staff tend to be preferred in their stead for their professional expertise.

In brief, technical and professional expertise remains the single most important quality in Korea. An emphasis on diversity can increase the risk of political appointments and the entanglement of the MPB with the politics of bargaining and compromise, given the relatively short history of independent central banking in Korea. Currently, members of the MPB are largely appointed for their technical expertise and are required to be politically neutral (see Article 19 of the Bank of Korea Act). For these reasons, the MPB is regarded as one of the few politically neutral public institutions in Korea.

4.4 Independence and Accountability

4.4.1 Independence

A central bank's independence can be defined as the extent to which the central bank is free to set and enforce monetary targets without interference from government.

Traditionally, central bank independence was important from the perspective of the separation of the power to print money and the power to spend it. However, because the BoK has the role of the government bank, the monetary policy of the BoK cannot be separable from the government's fiscal policy. Indeed, if government can rely on central bank credit for its budget deficit, it is equivalent to the government printing the money directly without budgetary constraints, which could end up damaging the private sector's confidence in the national currency.[6] From this perspective, the BoK, or, more precisely, the MPB, may not be completely independent. There remain some legal provisions that can restrict and threaten their independent implementation of monetary policy, such as direct credit to the government or the direct acquisition of government bonds by the BoK. For example, Article 75 of the Bank of Korea Act stipulates that the government can receive a loan or another form of credit from the BoK and that the BoK can underwrite government bonds directly from the government. In addition, Article 76 stipulates that the bank can directly underwrite bonds guaranteed by the government. Notwithstanding this, the BoK has remained independent because government finances have been relatively sound to date. In particular, since the early 1980s, when the 'Comprehensive Stabilisation Package' was successful in consolidating the government's fiscal position, there has been little need for monetary financing of the government deficit by the BoK. In contrast, many

---

[6] The first proposal for central bank independence goes back to the plan to set up a banknote-issuing Commission proposed by D. Ricardo (Ricardo, 1824). Concerned about the abuse of the issuance of banknotes by government, he said, 'It can't be safe for the government to issue banknotes. It is almost certain that the government will abuse it', proposing the setting-up of a third-party organisation independent of the government to take charge of the issue. 'The committee I propose should not lend money to the government at any time and under any circumstances. However, if there is too much money that the government wants to raise, the committee can buy government bonds from the open market and, on the other hand, sell them in the open market if it needs to reduce its holdings of government bonds'.

central banks in advanced economies, albeit independent, came to support government spending through the QE (see Box 4.2).

Box 4.2 Quantitative Easing and Hidden Budgets

In general, interest payments on outstanding government bonds reduce government revenue. However, the government's interest burden is limited to the interest paid on the government bonds held by the private sector, and do not apply to those held by the central bank, because the interest income which the central bank earns from its government bonds is transferred back to the government. The transfer of central bank profits to government, that is, seigniorage, stems from the fact that the government grants the exclusive right to issue banknotes to the central bank. Thus, only the net interest resulting from the consolidation of the accounts of the central bank and the government will be counted as the government's interest burden. This can be understood with the aid of Table B4.2.

Thus, the central bank's interest income is hidden government revenue. After the 2008 global financial crisis, many central banks which conducted massive purchases of government bonds ended up with a huge increase in their interest income, which is concomitantly an increase in government revenue.

In the case of the US Federal Reserve System, for example, about US$80 billion of its retained earnings was transferred to the Department of the Treasury in 2017, which accounted for about 2.3 per cent of the US federal government's fiscal revenue, which totalled US$3.4 trillion in 2017. The same is true of the BoJ. At the end of 2017, the BoJ transferred a total of JPY 851.6 billion, including its corporate taxes to the Ministry of Finance, which was equivalent to about 1.3 per cent of Japan's JPY 63 trillion fiscal revenue for the same year.

In the case of Korea, Article 99 of the Bank of Korea Act requires the BoK to retain 30 per cent of its net profits, which is obtained after paying its corporate taxes to the government, as a precautionary reserve, and to transfer only the remainder to the government's coffer. As of 2017, the BoK earned about KRW5.3 trillion in pre-tax profits from which it paid KRW1.3 trillion in

Table B4.2 *Consolidated balance sheet of central bank and government*

Government Account			Central Bank Account			Consolidated Account	
Assets	Liabilities		Assets	Liabilities		Assets	Liabilities
Future tax revenue	Government bonds held by private sector		Government bonds	Currency		Future tax revenue	Currency
Central bank deposits	Government bonds held by central bank		Other assets	Government deposits		Other assets	Government bonds held by private sector
Other assets				Commercial bank deposits			Commercial bank deposits

corporate taxes, and transferred KRW2.7 trillion to the government. Thus, the BoK contributed a total of KRW4 trillion to the general budget of the Korean government. The amount was equivalent to about 1 per cent of Korea's fiscal revenue of KRW414.3 trillion in 2017. However, most of the assets held by the BoK were foreign assets, not government bonds, and the money issued was again absorbed into the BoK through the issuance of MSBs, which was issued by the BoK itself. Thus, its profits did not come from direct seigniorage, but rather from the interest differential obtained after deducting the interest expenses for the outstanding MSBs from the interest proceeds resulting from the investment in foreign assets. It means that, even though it has recorded a profit, the BoK could be likely to incur a big loss any time domestic interest rates become higher than foreign interest rates.

Central bank independence in Korea, however, was only established in 1998 along with the sixth revision of the Bank of Korea Act. The main change in the independence of the BoK can be examined from the institutional, organisational, financial, and instrumental aspects of decision-making (Merch, 2017). It cannot be over-emphasised here that this independence specifically concerns the MPB in particular, rather than the BoK in general.

First, in respect of the institutional arrangements to stem the government's influence in its decision-making, the MPB has gained substantial independence. As well as maintaining price stability, which was established as the BoK's sole goal, the governor of the BoK has also substituted for the minister of economy and finance in chairing the MPB. Although the deputy minister of economy and finance could participate in the MPB, he had no voting rights and has rarely participated in the MPB meetings. Thus, there is little room for the government to interfere in monetary policy decisions. Furthermore, the minister of economy and finance's right to inspect the operation and management of the BoK was abolished in 1998. In general, current Korean government officials are very careful not to be involved in the polemics surrounding central bank independence, which is still a politically sensitive issue in Korea, given its relative short history of democracy. The MPB has increasingly been taking over the management of the BoK in place of the government.

Second, organisation independence is the equivalent of protecting its top people. In so far as independence is concerned, the MPB members, along with the governor of the BoK, were all granted full autonomy of decision-making through the guarantee of their terms in office. Their terms in office were fully secured. In the case of the governor, the term had been notoriously short in the past, whereas, after 1998, the legal term has been properly guaranteed. There were fourteen governors during the period 1962–1998, which means that their average term was only 2.5 years. Among them, there was only one governor who served two terms, that is to say, eight years. From 1998 to date, in contrast, there have been five governors who completed their four-year terms, while the current governor is serving a second term. Similarly, prior to 1997, a large number of the external members of the MPB had had to resign or quit their membership early, despite their right to complete their three-year terms without being dismissed against their will. Since 1998, their term of office has been almost completely protected (see Table 4.3).

Currently, MPB members serve four years, with the exception of the deputy governor, who has a three-year term. However, given the

Table 4.3 *Employment status of the MPB external members (unit: number of persons)*

	1962 (May)–1998 (March)	1998 (April)–2020 (April)
Completed the full term	32	25
Resigned after the term extended	7	0
Resigned	31	4
Resigned due to the change in the Bank of Korea Act	7	1
Fulfilled only the term left after the resignation of a member	1	3
Total number of MPB members	78	33

Source: Author's compilation

increasing complexity of the economic and financial worlds, the four-year term of the board members would seem to be too short. A longer term of office is necessary because decisions in monetary policy and other areas require more and more technical and professional knowledge and sufficient time and experience to understand central bank affairs.

Third, financial independence has increased, as the scope of the budget, which is required to be approved by the Ministry of Economy and Finance in the wake of the seventh revision of the Bank of Korea Act in 2003, was limited to the payroll expense budget of the BoK. However, the biggest new threat seems to be interference from the Board of Audit and Inspection (BAI), a governmental organisation which is responsible for the audit and inspection of the accounts of all governmental organisations and administrative bodies. The BoK is subject to examination and inspection by the BAI, not to mention the National Assembly. Although the BAI was originally responsible only for the examination of the financial operations of governmental bodies, its power has become too over-stretched to cover all their detailed operations and management interventions. Thus, the BAI inspects each task performed by the BoK and every duty of the BoK staff. In Korea, there is a deep-rooted ideology that the government should control everything. Against this backdrop, the possibility that the over-stretched BAI might exceed its competence and abuse its position is the greatest threat and risk to the independence of the BoK.

Fourth, the instrumental power to choose autonomously the instruments and tools of monetary policy has also been increasingly in the hands of the MPB. Notwithstanding this, MPB competence has remained very much restricted because of the hidden conflict between the MPB and BoK, as had been the case between the Board of Governors of the FRS and Regional Federal Banks in the United States prior to the passage of the Banking Act in 1935. This was, above all, due to the fact that all the governors of the BoK considered themselves as representing more the BoK than the MPB. Given that the chair of the MPB was for a long time occupied by the minister of finance, the BoK staff also regarded the MPB as being suspiciously close to the government, and thus they could not accept the supremacy of the MPB over the BoK, which often resulted in encroachment upon the power of the MPB by the BoK. As for the MPB, it could not implement its own mandate without the co-operation of the BoK staff because, unlike the Board of Governors in the United States, it did not have its own support staff. The MPB was a bodiless decision-making head. For these reasons, even many Korean economists have mistakenly regarded the MPB as *belonging* to the BoK, rather than the inverse, which allowed the dissemination of a great deal of – and possibly intentional – confusion. In part, the BoK staff had been propagating this view in order to win the battle for independence over the Ministry of Finance. In part, they might have wanted to exercise greater power themselves in place of the MPB. Or else, they might have had no personal interest in being responsible to the MPB, given that the power of appointment and promotion of the BoK staff was entirely concentrated in the hands of the governor. But the reluctance of the BoK staff to accept the authority of the MPB might have led to hampering the implementation of active and unconventional monetary policies. A proper recognition of the role of the MPB in the management and conduct of monetary policy by the BoK therefore seems essential for full instrumental independence.

In brief, the independence of the BoK has substantially improved since 1998. This independence has allowed the BoK to compete with the government for the more effective implementation of the stabilisation policy, which seems a major achievement in an economy like Korea's, where government power has been always preponderant. However, as interference from the executive branch of government recedes, interference from the National Assembly is rapidly increasing. This can be even more dangerous to the independence of the BoK because it reflects more short-term *partisan* interests than long-term *national* interests. To protect it from this interference, the BoK needs to strengthen its transparency and communications drastically.

4.4.2 Accountability

Despite its independence, the interaction of the central bank with the government will be inevitable if it is to fulfil its responsibilities as a public institution. Thus, unless independence is infringed upon, the central bank needs to collaborate with the government, because, as the former chairman of the Federal Reserve Board, W. M. Martin, emphasised, 'independence is not from the government but within the government' (Axilrod, 2011: pp. 17–18).

Formal interaction between the BoK and the government is not yet common. Partly because of the long dispute and rivalry between the BoK and the Ministry of Finance regarding central bank independence, there are currently no formal established meetings between the governor of the BoK and government officials. Similarly, there are no such formal meetings between the members of MPB and the government officials. However, informal meetings have often been held, especially between the governor, the minister of economy and finance, and the chairman of the FSC. Meanwhile, the deputy governor participates on the Financial Supervisory Board as an ex officio member and holds many formal and informal meetings with the government. However, he does not represent the MPB.

There are at least three areas in which the BoK and the MPB need to interact with government to fulfil their legal mandates and strengthen their accountability.

First, closer information exchange on general economic conditions and outlook is important. Both the MPB and the government make public their own economic outlooks, but they are often different from each other. The government tends to lag behind in its outlook of the Korean economy. For instance, in circumstances in which the MPB anticipates economic recovery sufficiently quickly from a recession, the government still continues to adhere to its own pessimistic outlook, and pushes for additional stimulus, hoping that the MPB will take the necessary steps towards stimulating the economy in accordance with the government's outlook. Inversely, in circumstances in which the MPB warns about forthcoming recession, the government tends not to trust the economic assessment of the MPB and adhere to a more optimistic outlook. Thus, to attain the best configuration of monetary and fiscal policies, the government needs to respect the assessments of the MPB, particularly with regard to the outlook of the Korean economy.

Second, along with the emergence of financial stability as an additional objective of the BoK, the need for close interaction and cooperation with the government in respect of financial stability and crisis prevention has increased. Since the global financial crisis, the BoK has moved beyond its traditional realm of price stability to managing financial stability, which, no doubt, has distributional and fiscal consequences. Furthermore, along with increasing income inequality, financial inclusion has emerged as a new agenda. Calls for such financial inclusion have always been paramount in Korea.

Third, increasing international economic linkages and the resulting policy co-ordination call for a joint response between the BoK and the government. This need for international policy co-ordination is particularly important given that Korea is an open economy with a big export sector. Currently, the governor of the BoK attends the G20 meetings of finance ministers and central bank governors, which naturally increases opportunities for information exchange or policy co-ordination over economic policies at the global level.

To the extent that the BoK has been accountable to the government, it is also increasingly accountable to the National Assembly, in order to address the democratic deficit regarding policymaking by the non-elected members of the MPB. Ever since its foundation, Korea has been a country well known for having strong presidential powers and broad government intervention. When the BoK was subservient and the minister of finance controlled the BoK's monetary policy and management through the MPB, the government was principally accountable to the National Assembly on behalf of the BoK. However, along with its increasing independence, the BoK has to explain its monetary policy directly to the National Assembly. Against this backdrop, the BoK, under the responsibility of the MPB, submits to the National Assembly two official reports, the Monetary Policy Report, and the Financial Stability Report, which are published twice a year. Furthermore, the governor of the BoK attends various meetings of the National Assembly, including its audit and briefing meetings, where it must not only provide an analysis of the general economic situation both in Korea and abroad, but also explain the reasoning underlying the decisions of the MPB, along with outlining the overall management work of the BoK. Currently, such responsibilities are not extended to the external members of the MPB, although they are likely to be in the future.

It should not be forgotten that the independence of the central bank in Korea has always been associated with the issue of choosing the market economy over a government-controlled economy. When the BoK was created in 1950, Korea was not a market economy at all, and when it gained some independence in 1998, the market economy was still not completely established. Therefore, the BoK should be the guardian of the market economy against any and all arbitrary intervention or interference on the part of the government in the economy. Indeed, this may be the biggest responsibility of the BoK as the central bank of an emerging economy. The reports and explanations of the BoK to the National Assembly should highlight this point.

5 | The Monetary Policy Strategies of the Bank of Korea

To carry out monetary policy properly, central banks prepare a strategy through which they attain their goals. Initially, the BoK set its priority on stabilising exchange rates and maintaining a balance of payments surplus, but this goal was gradually overshadowed by the goal of price and output stability. Accordingly, the BoK shifted its strategy from exchange rate and monetary targeting to inflation targeting. This chapter examines the historical development of the monetary policy strategies in Korea, and the current monetary policy framework adopted by the BoK.

5.1 Monetary Policy Strategy prior to the Currency Crisis

Central banks are required to attain a variety of goals, such as exchange rate stability, growth, employment and price stability, and even financial stability. To attain these goals, central banks use various tools and instruments, including foreign exchange market intervention, open market operations, and standing facilities. However, because the transmission process of monetary policy is very uncertain and volatile, central banks need a strategy or a frame on how to link the monetary policy tools and instruments at their disposition to their final goals. Historically, the BoK first adopted a strategy of targeting exchange rates and monetary and credit aggregates.

5.1.1 Exchange Rate Targeting

Prior to the adoption of a floating exchange rate system in 1997, the goal of the BoK was to maintain the stable value of money, which meant attaining external as well as internal stability. Thus, the BoK was concerned with securing exchange rate stability as well as price stability. However, against the backdrop of the export-led growth strategy adopted by the government, price stability was not given precedence over exchange rate stability. It is notable that it was the Ministry of Economy and Finance that had the principal power in deciding on the level of the exchange rate. The MPB lost its competence in respect of the exchange rate policy after the revision of the Bank of Korea Act in 1962. Thus, although the BoK was responsible for the carrying out of all FX-related transactions and operations, the Ministry of Economy and Finance was ultimately responsible for exchange rate policy as the decision-making body. Worried about the harmful effects of exchange rate volatility on exports, the Ministry of Economy and Finance pegged the exchange rates of the Korean *won* to the US dollar, while adjusting them to maintain export competitiveness and a balance of payment surplus in the Korean economy.

Against this backdrop, the Korean government took the real effective exchange rate as the intermediate target. To steer the exchange rate to the target rate, it relied on two instruments: exchange controls and FX market intervention.

At the early stage of economic development, the interbank foreign exchange market was undeveloped in Korea because the Korean government had set up a FX concentration system through which the BoK monopolised all purchases and sales of foreign currencies. This system gave the BoK the capacity to fix exchange rates at the desired level simply by decree. As a matter of fact, the BoK carried out quite frequent exchange rate realignments. It is important to note that Korea was a developing economy with domestic investment exceeding domestic saving. As a result, the Korean economy was under constant inflationary pressure, running chronic current account deficits. The rising inflation gap and the consequent current account deficits led to shortages of foreign reserves, necessitating rather systemic devaluations to raise the real effective exchange rate of the Korean *won*. Along with the heavy devaluation of the Korean *won* against the US dollar in 1980, the government decided to introduce exchange flexibility through a multiple currency basket peg, which allowed the exchange rate of the Korean *won* to vary according to the movement of the basket of currencies of its major trading partners.

The Plaza Accord and the subsequent extensive appreciation of the JPY against the US dollar in 1985 brought about a sudden depreciation of the Korean *won*, helping the Korean economy to record its first current account surplus. Confident about the economic strength of the country, the government decided to relax FX regulations, in particular the FX concentration system, to promote the development of an interbank foreign exchange market. This led to the adoption of the Market Average Exchange Rate System in 1990, under which the exchange rate of the Korean *won* was determined by market forces in the interbank exchange market. The BoK was merely one of the many market participants, so it could influence the exchange rate only through trading with other participants in the FX market. The exchange rate of the Korean *won* fluctuated, depending on market forces, albeit within the upper and lower limits set daily from the target market-average rate. The daily fluctuation limits were continuously widened. Amid improving current account balances and increasing capital inflows, the Korean *won* rapidly appreciated. Stabilising the real effective exchange rate of the Korean *won* emerged as the urgent task of the government, and, to this end, the BoK started so-called leaning against the wind market interventions. However, these market interventions were often ineffective (Rhee and Song, 1996). Moreover, the goal of these interventions was incompatible with internal price stability. Given that concerns about internal price stability outweighed concerns about external stability, a substantial appreciation of the Korean *won* went unabated until the outbreak of the 1997 currency crisis.

Figure 5.1 shows the movements of the real effective exchange rate and the current account balance in Korea. It is notable that, until the end of the 1990s, their relationship was very close, highlighting the importance of the real effective exchange rate as a target variable that steers the movement of current account. However, the market intervention by the Korean government and the BoK was not very successful in stabilising the fluctuation of the real effective exchange rate. In particular, large and sustained appreciation of the real effective exchange rate in the early 1990s turned the current account of the Korean economy from a surplus to a deficit, which was considered as a factor which triggered the currency crisis in 1997.

When Korea was hit by the currency crisis in 1997, the government officially moved to a free-floating exchange rate system, abolishing its real effective exchange rate targeting system. This allowed the BoK to pursue an autonomous monetary policy by adopting inflation targeting, similarly to the practice of the BoE, which decided to exit from the EMS and to introduce inflation targeting in the early 1990s. Notwithstanding this, real effective exchange rate targeting was not completely abandoned

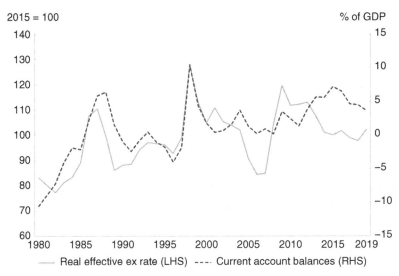

Figure 5.1 Real effective exchange rate and current account balances
Source: Statistics Korea and BoK.

(Eichengreen, 2004). Firmly believing that the excessive appreciation of the real effective exchange rate of the Korean *won* was an important cause of the 1997 currency crisis, government officials made strenuous efforts to avoid such appreciations, which led to interventions, often stealthy, until the heavy depreciation of the Korean *won* triggered by the capital outflow of the 2008 global financial crisis rendered them unnecessary.

In the meantime, the usefulness of the real effective exchange rate as an exchange rate target has diminished. Capital market liberalisation and increasing short-term capital movements since the year 2000 have caused wide fluctuations of nominal exchange rates, weakening the relationship between real effective exchange rates and the current account (see Figure 5.1). Against this backdrop, the goal of the FX interventions by the BoK changed towards smoothing excessive exchange rate volatility, instead of aiming at maintaining the export competitiveness of Korean industry.

5.1.2 Monetary Targeting

The BoK's proper conduct of monetary policy was subordinated to that of the exchange rate policy by the Korean government for a long time.

However, as the government put an emphasis on price stability and allowed wider flexibility in the movement of the exchange rate from the 1980s, the BoK had greater autonomy in designing its own monetary policy. While maintaining exchange rate targeting, the BoK decided to introduce a monetary targeting strategy, following the example of the FRS in the United States and the Bundesbank in Germany. This monetary targeting strategy had three features: (1) reliance on a monetary aggregate as an intermediate target to carry out monetary policy, (2) the announcement of targets, and (3) an accountability mechanism to preclude large and systematic deviations from the monetary targets set (Mishkin, 2001).

The BoK adopted such a strategy in 1979, setting the growth rate of M2 as an intermediate target. Until then, different monetary and credit aggregates, such as reserve money, domestic credit, and M1, were informally targeted. But no public announcements on their target growth rates were made, and the commitment to the targets was not strong. Only from 1979 did the BoK annually announce the growth rate of M2 as a target to anchor inflationary expectations, and this time it was fully committed to meeting this target.

However, the monetary targeting strategy adopted by the BoK could not be assimilated to those used in the United States and in Germany.

First, it is questionable whether the monetary targeting strategy adopted by the BoK was sufficiently successful to anchor inflationary expectations in Korea. According to the equation of exchange examined in Chapter 3, the target growth rate of M2 is determined as the sum of the inflation rate and output growth rate less the trend change in the velocity of money. In the case of Germany, for example, the Bundesbank announced its target inflation rate based upon the long-term potential growth rate. In the case of Korea, the BoK did not make precise information on the target inflation rate and target GDP growth rate public, although the target growth rate of the M2 was announced. Furthermore, the target inflation rate was not set independently by the BoK, because central bank independence had not yet been secured in Korea. Notwithstanding this, the BoK was obsessed with a monetary targeting strategy.

Second, interest rates were regulated in Korea until the early 1990s, and thus the main instrument for the control of the money supply was credit rationing. Amid chronic excess demand for money, the

BoK controlled both interest rates and the supply of reserve money, even when it conducted open market operations. Thus, unlike in the United States and Germany, where monetary targeting strategies could be used as a means to steer interest rates to the desired level, based upon the trade-off relationship between reserve money and short-term market rates (S. Axilrod, 2011: p. 109; Clarida and Gerler, 1997), changes in the growth rate of reserve money had little relationship with changes in interest rates in Korea. The transmission channel of monetary policy through interest rate changes was absent or, at best, weak in Korea.

Nonetheless, Figure 5.2 shows that the actual growth rate of M2 followed the targets relatively well. It is important to note that the substantial reduction in the growth rate of M2 in the early 1980s was the first important step towards price stability. The growth rate of M2 remained subdued thereafter, which probably contributed to a drop in the inflation rate.

This monetary targeting strategy was abandoned in 1997 along with the transition to a floating exchange rate system. Compared to the FRS

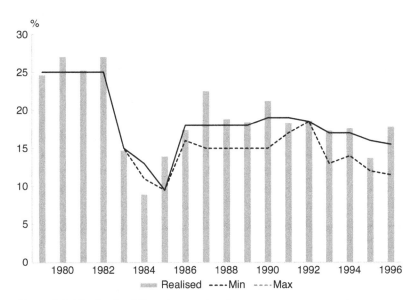

Figure 5.2 The Bank of Korea's actual and target monetary growth rates
Source: BoK.

in the United States, the BoK maintained a monetary targeting strategy for a much longer period. This was because, among other things, the stable relationship between monetary aggregates and inflation was maintained longer in Korea than in the United States and other advanced economies. In Korea, financial innovation progressed at a relatively slow pace, while interest rate liberalisation took time. Thus, M2 continued to be highly correlated with prices until the end of the 1990s. However, from the mid-1990s, unstable movements in the demand for money began to appear, along with the creation of new financial products and the change in government regulation. Also, monetary targeting strategy assumes that a central bank can exogenously control the reserves and thereby control the quantity of money in the economy. But the causality could also be the opposite, going from the quantity of money to the reserves. This endogeneity of money supply was particularly the case when the BoK shifted its monetary policy regime to interest rate targeting from reserve targeting in 1997 (Jo et al., 2018).

Another reason for the long sustenance of monetary targeting was the BoK's tenacious attachment to it. Considering that controlling M2 required technical operations that only the BoK staff could handle on their own, without much interference from the Ministry of Finance, they would have wanted to be independent, at least operationally. Thus, a monetary targeting strategy remained a sacrosanct dogma inside the BoK for a long time, which would translate into its extremely strict policy of keeping the growth rate of M2 within its target range.[1]

5.2 Inflation Targeting Strategy

Inflation targeting is a monetary policy strategy or framework under which central banks announce target inflation rates and try to meet the targets over the medium term.[2] Generally speaking, inflation targeting is composed of three elements (see Figure 5.3): (1) the setting of price stability as a primary goal of the central bank, (2) the announcement of the target, and (3) the accountability of the central bank for its performance.

---

[1] According to Mishkin (2011), and Bernanke and Mishkin (1992), for instance, these central banks neither maintained a strictly tight monetary policy, nor did they think that the monetary growth target should be strictly adhered to.

[2] For a general assessment and review of inflation targeting, see Svensson (2011, 2013).

Figure 5.3 Three elements of inflation targeting

Unfortunately, there is no rigorous underlying economic theory about how inflation targeting centred on these three elements can stabilise the inflation rate.[3] However, some important implications can be drawn from the works of Kahneman and Tversky (1974), Kydland and Prescott (1977), and Barro and Gordon (1983). Investigating the mechanism of decision-making under conditions of uncertainty – in particular, the relationship between uncertainty and anchoring – Kahneman and Tversky argue that explicitly announcing the target is an important element of anchoring.[4] Furthermore, the greater the uncertainties, the stronger the effects of anchoring. On the other hand, according to Kydland and Prescott, and Barro and Gordon, strong commitment to the goal is paramount in stemming time-inconsistent actions and forging credibility. It goes without saying that, if a central bank is not credible, the announcement of the target will have little impact in anchoring inflationary expectations.

Inflation targeting was first introduced in Korea after the 1997 currency crisis as a part of the conditionality attached to the stand-by loans granted to the Korean government by the IMF. It led to the sixth revision of the Bank of Korea Act in 1997, which stipulated that the BoK should determine the annual inflation target in consultation with the government and render this target public. Initially, however, inflation targeting coexisted with monetary targeting. Because the goal of the monetary policy was to replenish foreign reserves and to overcome the crisis as soon as possible, the BoK established a ceiling on the growth rate of reserve money in order to limit the growth rate of the moncy supply M3, and to reduce aggregate demand. The inflation

---

[3] For instance, the first country to adopt inflation targeting, New Zealand, did so on political grounds, rather than on economic logic. See Svensson (2011).

[4] From this perspective, the implicit target system, as was the case for the United States before 2012, was not as effective as the explicit target system that most inflation targeting countries have adopted.

targeting system became fully operational only from 2001 onwards, as consultation with the IMF was no longer necessary.

According to the recommendations of the IMF, the BoK also had to make a dramatic increase in the call rate. This policy, which the IMF considered essential to bring stability to the FX rate, eventually ended up exacerbating the crisis rather than stabilising the market. The BoK pushed up the overnight call rate to the upper legal limit of 25 per cent, as specified by the Korean Usury Law. Then, as this upper limit was raised to 40 per cent, the BoK raised the overnight call rate again above 30 per cent. Accordingly, the yields on corporate bonds and bank loans and deposit rates all rose sharply. These absurdly high interest rates were the principal cause of the economic *malaise* in Korea. It was no longer the quantity of money, but the level of interest rates that emerged as the subject of public debate in Korea.

Against this backdrop, the BoK exercised its newly acquired policy of independence, by shifting its monetary policy strategy to targeting call rates, even though monetary targeting was still its existing monetary policy framework. It began to present the operational direction of interest rates in its Direction of Monetary Policy, the text of which was decided at the monthly interest rate-setting meeting of the MPB, from July 1998. As the FX market quickly regained stability, the BoK continued to ease its tight monetary policy. As a result, the overnight call rate and other interest rates showed immediate declines. In particular, the BoK announced a cut in the call rate in September 1998, making use of the interest rate as its official operating target. This was a fundamental new departure in that a specific interest rate target was announced. Given that the overnight call rate closely tracked the interest rate in the open market offered by the BoK, this measure represented a big step towards a monetary policy operation employing the overnight call rate as an operating target. From early 1999, the overnight call rate was firmly established as the operating target of the monetary policy. Furthermore, a specific figure for the overnight call rate began to be suggested as a target rate from May 1999 onwards. The MPB started to make statements on the level of the call rate, stating, for instance, that 'the call rate will remain at the present level', which substituted the hitherto vague statements, such as 'the downward stability of the call rate will be induced'. As the extent of the adjustments of the call rate target was explicitly announced, a framework of monetary operations through which the call rate is targeted as the policy rate and open market operations are conducted for steering the call rate became the norm. The call rate target functioned as the policy rate until 2008 when it was replaced by the BoK base rate target.

5.3 Determination of Monetary Policy Direction under Inflation Targeting

Currently, the MPB decides on Korean monetary policy through its policy rate-setting meetings, called 'meetings for the determination of monetary policy direction', which were held monthly until 2016. The MPB decided, in 2016, to reduce the number of these meetings to eight times a year, that is, about every six weeks.[5] The lessening of the frequency of the policy rate-setting meetings was made in order to give working-level BoK staff and the members of the MPB sufficient time to identify and cope with changes that would have a lasting impact on the economy because of the monetary policy time lag. A month was too short a time period to grasp significant changes in the economy fully, especially in February, when Korea has a Lunar New Year, or in September during its mid-autumn holidays, when collecting the necessary data was difficult. Another underlying reason for the change was the need to adjust the schedule of the meetings in Korea to coincide with those of the other major central banks in order to facilitate global monetary policy coordination. At the same time, the meetings' schedule was adjusted to coincide with the announcement of economic forecasts, which are made four times a year in January, April, July, and October. It allowed the MPB to decide on monetary policy direction consistently, based on economic forecasts and their interim checks on the transmission channels of monetary policy. In addition, the four meetings left over from the previous monthly monetary policy meetings were substituted with meetings to examine financial stability. This change was a part of the response to the revision of the Bank of Korea Act in 2011, which required the BoK to include financial stability as well as price stability in its mandate.

---

[5] Since the early 1980s, the US Fed decided to hold eight policy rate-setting meetings a year, while the European Central Bank has reduced its policy rate-setting meetings to eight from twelve times a year since 2014. The BoJ and the BoE also have reduced the number of their policy rate-setting meetings to eight since 2015 and 2016.

The detailed decision-making process in the policy rate-setting meetings of the MPB is divided into three steps: (1) examination of economic outlook, (2) deliberation and base rate setting, and, finally, (3) the announcement of decisions and their communication.

5.3.1 The Examination of the Economic Outlook

According to its annual schedule which is released in advance, when the MPB holds a policy rate-setting meeting, it also has a further meeting called 'the economic outlook briefing meeting', which is held one day ahead of the policy rate-setting meeting. The economic outlook briefing meeting is important in the sense that the MPB members discuss the economic outlook of the Korean economy in depth with the BoK staff, framing their views on monetary policy direction. In this meeting, the BoK staff brief the MPB members on both the domestic and the international economic outlook, domestic financial market trends, and FX and international financial market trends. The MPB members prepare themselves in advance to participate actively in discussions on major issues, including holding an informal preliminary meeting with a limited number of the BoK staff a week in advance. Through this meeting, the MPB members try to identify the current status of the economy and to predict its future direction.

First, to assess the current economic status correctly, the MPB members examine various economic indicators provided by the BoK staff on production and output, inflation, unemployment, and financial conditions. In this regard, output data such as GDP are the most important variable for assessing the prevailing economic conditions (see Box 5.1), while inflation data are losing importance, reflecting the sustained low level of inflation in Korea. Unemployment data, although recently increasing in importance, are relatively unimportant because of rigidity of the labour market in Korea. Finally, monetary aggregates, which were highly important indicators in the past, have largely lost their importance. This is due not just to the unstable demand for money and the abandonment of the monetary targeting system, but also to the significant reduction of the risk of inflation under the recent low inflation conditions in Korea. Instead, it is the trend on various interest rates that has become all-important. Furthermore, the estimates on the potential output or the natural rate of unemployment provided by the BoK staff are very important reference variables for checking on the extent of prevailing economic slack or tightness.

Box 5.1 Industrial Production Index Versus Gross Domestic Product

Over the period 2013–2015, not only did the gap between the growth rates of GDP and the IPI increase, but they also moved in opposite directions to each other. This posed a question regarding the effectiveness of the IPI for the MPB members. Figure B5.1 shows the gap between the growth rates of the two indices, which grew enormously from 2012 to 2015.

Basically, GDP is compiled by the BoK for the purpose of measuring the income that all economic units generate by their economic activities during a given period of time, while the IPI is compiled by the Korea Statistical Office to measure upon a monthly basis the output of the diverse sectors covering mining, manufacturing, electricity and gas, water supplies, and so on, with a view to tracing the short-term real economic trend. The main differences between these two indices are as follows.

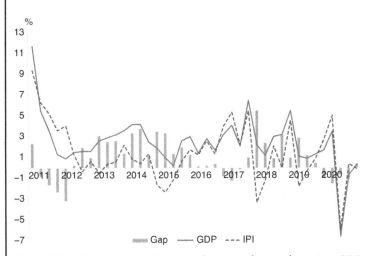

Figure B5.1 Gap between the growth rates of manufacturing GDP and IPI
Source: ECOS, BoK.

First, GDP traces output on a value-added basis, while the IPI is measured on a total output basis, including all intermediary inputs. Thus, if the intermediate inputs required to produce a given quantity of output decreases due to technological developments or falling raw material prices, the GDP growth rate measured in value-added terms may exceed the IPI total output growth rate.

Second, GDP is based upon value, reflecting changes both in quantity and quality, while the IPI is compiled mostly upon a quantity basis. In other words, GDP reflects the price changes caused by improvements in quality by dividing the nominal value by the price index for production items with significant quality improvements, such as mobile phones and automobiles, while the IPI captures only the quantitative changes, such as number of products produced, because their sales value data cannot be monthly obtained. Thus, a wide gap can exist between the two indicators. In 2014, the shipment of high-priced mobile phones, such as smartphones, increased sharply in Korea, while the shipment of low-priced mobile phones, such as feature phones, decreased significantly. Thus, despite a decrease in the overall mobile phone exports, the real exports of mobile phones in terms of GDP, calculated by dividing the increased nominal export values by the export prices, increased, which significantly increased the gap between the growth rates of both indicators.

Third, according to the new SNA introduced in 2008, GDP reflects R&D expenditure and overseas production, which the IPI does not reflect. Furthermore, the BoK has introduced the chained weighted method in the compilation of GDP since 2009, changing the weight of different economic sectors every year to reflect changes in the economic structure. However, the IPI revises these weights only every five years, starting in 2010. Thus, even if the growth rates in the detailed sub-sectors of the economy are the same, differences in the growth rates of the two indicators may arise in the aggregations that add them up.

Fourth, their seasonal adjustment methods are different. GDP is seasonally adjusted upon a quarterly basis, whereas the IPI makes a monthly seasonal adjustment and then takes a three-month simple average to derive a quarterly series. This also contributes to the difference in the growth rates of the two indicators.

> It is practically impossible to remove the gap between the growth rates of GDP and IPI because their compilation goals are inherently different. Against this backdrop, the BoK has developed a monthly GDP series to supplement the IPI and to capture economic fluctuations quickly.[6]

In this regard, some monetary and interest rules, such as the Taylor rule, had been calculated by the BoK staff in the past. But they were no longer in use, particularly after the 2008 global financial crisis. Even though interest rates are not yet negative in Korea, they have nonetheless fallen significantly amid lower economic growth, and thus the Taylor rule could not provide the appropriate information as a guide for setting interest rates. Basically, as the economic environment becomes complicated and uncertain, the flexible judgement of the MPB members is more important than ever. Indeed, the identification of the prevailing economic status is completely subjective and discretionary. As Stephen Axilrod, who worked as a staff member of the US Federal Reserve System for more than thirty years, pointed out, 'rules can only serve as background music, whether it's a Friedman's monetary policy or a Taylor-style interest rate rule' (Axilrod, 2011).

Second, the MPB members try to forecast the future economic outlook. Because monetary policy affects prices and output with a time lag, a monetary policy decision should anticipate and respond to *future* economic conditions, rather than reflect *current* economic conditions. Furthermore, because monetary policy affects the economy through expectations, economic forecasting is crucially important, and working-level BoK staff provide the MPB members with annual GDP forecasts four times a year, in February, May, August, and November, which are regarded as some of the most important data for their decision-making. Based upon these forecasts, the MPB members check out whether actual GDP growth rates will rise or fall compared to potential growth rates, or whether inflation will move above or below the target inflation rate. The MPB members in Korea do not provide their own economic forecasts, and, therefore, have to reconcile the economic forecasts of the working-level BoK staff with

---

[6] In Korea, the GDP data are compiled by the statistical division of the BoK. This division publishes, albeit unofficially, monthly GDP data, which is extremely useful to forecast the quarterly GDP.

their own judgements. The economic forecasting may not be accurate if they ignore the economic forecasts of the BoK staff and only trust their own outlook, or, similarly, if they blindly accept the BoK forecasts without contributing their own judgement (see Box 5.2).

Economic forecasting by the BoK staff often relies on various economic models, such as the BoK macroeconomic model or the DSGE model. Such structural models are useful for explanation and policy simulation, but not for forecast accuracy. These models are merely tools for the mechanical understanding of the complex Korean economy. Thus, the judgement of the MPB members can play an important role in making the forecasts more accurate, though they currently do not contribute any input to the technical forecasts made by the BoK staff.

Economic outlooks also include an element of self-fulfilling expectations. In other words, if economic agents are optimistic about the economic outlook, the realised growth rate will be higher, and, inversely, if they are pessimistic, the growth rate will be lower. Therefore, the MPB members need to pay attention to possible changes in the expectations or psychology of economic agents. This is the reason why economic forecasts in monetary policy include not only economic indicators per se but also explanations and interpretations of the outlook.

5.3.2 Deliberation and Policy Rate Setting

The MPB members decide on the base rate after assessing both the current economic status and the future economic prospects. As they have already undertaken detailed discussions at the economic outlook-briefing meeting, the MPB members express their final opinions after only a relatively simple deliberation, and then they vote. At this stage, they will have to deliberate on the following points:

First, they consider whether the current economic status requires a change in the base rate in the light of the BoK's goals. If a temporary shock occurs that does not affect the economic outlook, they do not need to react with a change in monetary policy. For example, the outbreak of the MERS in Korea in 2015 caused a temporary decrease in national income, which was believed to have had little impact on the growth trend of the Korean economy. Notwithstanding this, the BoK reacted by cutting its base rate (see Box 5.3).

Box 5.2 Assessment of the Bank of Korea's Economic Forecasting Capability

How accurate are the economic forecasts made by the BoK staff? Figure B5.2 shows the GDP growth rate forecasts made by the BoK staff for the period 2007–2020.

Overall, the BoK's forecasts appear to be quite inaccurate with significant errors. Specifically, the BoK's economic forecasts reveal the following features:

First, the average forecast error represented by the forecast growth rate minus the actual growth rate is 0.8 percentage points, which means that the BoK forecasts tended to be over-optimistic. This was particularly the case during 2012–2016 when economic recovery was delayed. The reason for this positive error bias is that the BoK staff tended to make forecasts that were as uncontroversial as possible, based upon extrapolation. For example, they usually begin by forecasting the most optimistic two-years ahead growth rate and adjust it gradually downwards as they obtain more data over time. Figure B5.2 shows that the forecast errors have been consistently positive, except for the year 2017.[7]

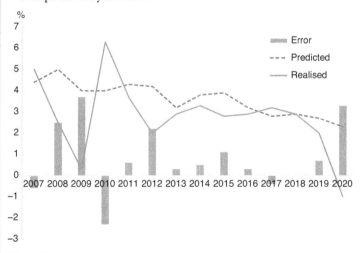

Figure B5.2 Actual and forecast growth rates compared
Note: Based upon one-year ahead growth rate forecasts.
Source: BoK.

---

[7] Due to the benchmark revision of the Korean National Account system, reflecting the R&D investment and digital-sharing economy, the real GDP growth rate of 2017 has risen unexpectedly by 0.1 per cent. See Quarterly Bulletin, BoK, 2019 (June).

Second, in times of economic crisis, such as the 2008 global financial crisis and the 2020 COVID-19 crisis, the BoK staff cannot correctly predict the severity of the prevailing economic downturn.

Forecasting makes the most use of the data available at the time of forecasting. Thus, after the initial long horizon forecasts are made, they are continuously revised over time, reflecting newly acquired data. Naturally, the forecast errors decline along with the shortening of the forecasting horizon, as Table B5.1 shows.

As the BoK staff rarely make major revisions to their previous forecasts, it is important to begin by relatively accurate long horizon forecasts. However, these forecasts show quite large forecasting errors. For example, even one-year ahead growth rate

Table B5.1 *Forecast errors by time horizon for selected years*

Time	Period t-1	Period t			
	October	January	April	July	October
2007	−0.6	−0.6	−0.6	−0.5	−0.3
2008	2.5	2.2	2	2.1	1.9
2009	3.7	1.7	−2.7	−1.9	−0.6
2010	−2.3	−1.7	−1.1	−0.4	−0.2
2011	0.6	0.8	0.8	0.6	0.4
2012	2.2	1.7	1.5	1	0.4
2013	0.3	−0.1	−0.3	−0.1	−0.1
2014	0.5	0.5	0.7	0.5	0.2
2015	1.1	0.6	0.3	0	−0.1
2016	0.3	0.1	−0.1	−0.2	−0.2
2017	−0.4	−0.7	−0.6	−0.4	−0.2
2018	0	0.1	0.1	0	−0.2
2019[1]	0.7	0.6	0.5	0.2	0
2020[1]	3.3	3.1	0.8	−0.3	−0.1

Note (1): The forecasting month for the annual GDP growth rate changed to February, May, August, and November since October 2019.
Source: BoK.

forecasts (made as of October, previous year) are often of little information value. The forecasts are meaningful only for short horizon of less than half a year. Because of the importance of the one-year ahead growth rate forecasts in monetary policymaking, it is necessary for the BoK to devise various ways to enhance its capacity for long horizon forecasting. In periods of high uncertainty, however, there is no guarantee that the small expert group of BoK staff is better than various outside groups at long horizon forecasting. Thus, the BoK should increase its efforts to reflect the various opinions held by the different outside groups, instead of adhering to its internal models and to the opinions of a few of its internal staff. This will be a first step towards increasing the accuracy of forecasting.

Second, when the movements in growth and prices have conflicting trade-off consequences, the MPB members decide which goal to prioritise. The BoK's adoption of a single goal can help to avoid such conflicts by prioritising price stability. In practice, however, the conflict between the inflation and unemployment goals may not be that meaningful. Even though the BoK officially only had the single mandate of price stability, the two goals have always been equally important. This is because the conflict between policy goals has not posed a major problem, particularly since the 2008 global financial crisis, as inflation remained near zero or below the target level, allowing the BoK to focus on employment or growth goals. Against this backdrop, the BoK announced, in the 'General Principles of Monetary Operations' published in 2016, that it would conduct its monetary policy to support real economic growth to the extent that this does not hinder attaining the inflation target over the medium term. However, setting priorities can become important with regard to financial stability issues, such as soaring household debt, which raises the possibility of a conflict between policy goals. This led the BoK to acknowledge the limits of maintaining financial stability solely by monetary policy, suggesting the need to complement monetary policy by macro-prudential policy (Bank of Korea, 2017: pp. 79–80).

Third, as a change in the base rate affects prices and the real economy through a variety of transmission channels and with a time lag, it is

Box 5.3 Temporary and Permanent Shocks: The Case of the MERS and COVID-19 Outbreaks

The most well-known example of a temporary shock that does not affect the trend of economic growth is bad weather. In this case, although there will be a drop in output, there is little need to respond with a change in monetary policy. The growth rate will rebound after the shock. Similarly, the outbreak of the MERS that occurred in Korea from May to July 2015 was an incidental and temporary shock that may have contributed to a drop in output, similar to the impact of the bad weather, but would affect neither the trend of economic activity nor the growth path. Thus, it would have been a hasty move to respond to it by way of an interest rate cut.

Nonetheless, the MPB decided to cut the base rate by 0.25 percentage points from 1.75 per cent to 1.50 per cent in June 2015. The GDP growth rate of the Korean economy was 0.4 per cent quarter-on-quarter in the second quarter, but it rose sharply to 1.2 per cent in the third quarter. This rise in the growth rate might reflect the effect of the interest rate cut, but, more importantly, came from the sharp rebound in consumption and investment after managing the MERS epidemic.

Given its high correlation with the global economy, the diffusion of the COVID-19 pandemic hit the Korean economy in early 2020. The COVID-19 outbreak was initially expected to be a temporary shock that would have little impact on the demand side. However, with the continuing spread of the disease, the temporary shock transformed into a permanent one affecting not just the demand side but also the supply side. The COVID-19 impact is certainly much more serious than the previous MERS epidemic, and has led to a change in the growth trend of the Korean economy. However, the initial reaction of the BoK was lukewarm, stating that 'we need more time and data to assess the COVID-19 impact on the economy'. Eventually, on two occasions, in March and May 2020, the MPB decided to cut the base rate by a total of 75 basis points from 1.25 per cent to 0.50 per cent. Indeed, the GDP growth rate fell by –1.3 per cent quarter-on-quarter in the first quarter, and by –3.2 per cent in the second quarter.

The decision-making regarding the outbreak of the two diseases can be analysed with the aid of the Figure B5.3. The top side of Figure B5.3 illustrates the negative impact of a temporary shock, which, although it means a loss in income, does not affect the growth trend of the Korean economy. It will not be necessary to rely on an interest cut. In contrast, the bottom side of Figure B5.3 shows the impact of a permanent shock that will continue to delay economic recovery and eventually lead to a decline in the growth trend. Clearly, this will justify a cut in interest rates.

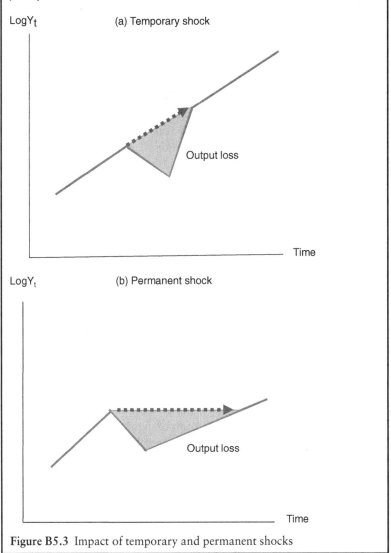

Figure B5.3 Impact of temporary and permanent shocks

not easy to grasp the effects of monetary policy in advance. Thus, it is always important for the MPB members to check and monitor the transmission channels when the base rate changes.

Fourth, once the MPB members decide to change the base rate, they also determine the scale of the adjustment. In general, unless the economy is in crisis, the MPB members prefer a gradual approach. This is because, in economic conditions full of uncertainty, they act more cautiously. From the beginning of the 1990s, the US Federal Open Market Committee has used a method of adjusting policy rates by a quarter percentage point, called 'Greenspan's baby step', named after Alan Greenspan, the chairman of the Board of Governors of FRS at the time. The MPB members in Korea have generally adopted this method. As shown in Figure 5.4, except for six cases out of the more than 40 rate adjustments made since the year 2000, there was no case for a sharp adjustment beyond a quarter percentage point. These exceptional sharp adjustments were made mainly during the period of the 2008 global financial crisis and the 2020 COVID-19 crisis.

Fifth, the MPB members consider policy measures other than interest rates. The BoK has several goals, including financial stability, and so it is difficult to meet all of them with only a single policy tool: the base rate adjustment. The MPB members prefer to use multiple tools because this can reduce the possibility of conflict between policy goals or objectives. For example, in addition to the base-rate adjustment, the BoK often relies on the lending facility largely geared towards SMEs called 'The Intermediated Lending Support Facility'. Thus, along with changes in the base rates, the BoK can simultaneously decide to fix the loan interest rate of this lending facility or increase the total amount of loans to relieve the financial difficulties of small- and medium-sized businesses. Moreover, if household debt rises amid an economic slump, the MPB members, while lowering the base rate, can decide to take further financial stabilisation measures that they deem necessary, either alone, or together with the government, to prevent a surge in household debt.

Sixth, the MPB members prepare a monetary policy direction statement, while considering its possible impact on the markets.

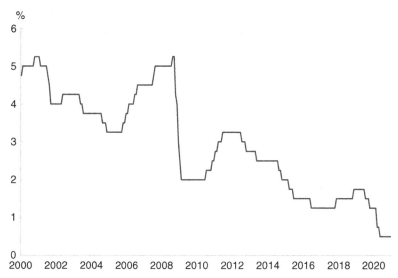

Figure 5.4 Adjustment of the Bank of Korea's benchmark interest rate since 1999
Source: ECOS, BoK.

5.3.3 The Announcement and Communication of Decisions

To secure credibility with regard to attaining its goal, the BoK relies on verbal communication as well as action, as J. Alfred Broaddus Jr. pointed out at the meeting of the Federal Open Market Committee in 1996:

I think a few well-chosen words stemming from the right source, backed up by deeds, can be a powerful credibility builder over time. (FOMC, 1996: p. 48)

Thus, immediately following its deliberations and decisions on the direction of monetary policy, the MPB announces its monetary policy direction by publishing its 'Statement on Monetary Policy Direction', while the governor holds a press conference to offer a detailed explanation on the policy decision and its background. Every decision on the adjustment of the base rate – including its freezing at its existing level – is subject to this procedure. Meanwhile, the MPB has made continuous efforts to enhance the effect of the announcement of its Statement on Monetary Policy Direction. As part of these efforts, the MPB has improved its statements by closely linking them with the economic forecasts released every quarter. The report on the economic outlook of Korea, along with the statements issued after the meetings in February, May, August, and November, all contain statistical projections of prices and economic growth that coincide with the scheduled release of economic forecasts, while the statements issued in other months describe the possible changes in or revisions to the previously projected developments in the economic forecasts. This change was made to increase the effectiveness of monetary policy by managing market expectations and conducting monetary policy in a forward-looking manner.

Furthermore, in a press conference after each meeting, the governor of the BoK announces the unanimity of the MPB members' decisions, and the number and names of the MPB members who voted against the decisions and their viewpoints. These procedures were all introduced to enhance further the signalling effects of monetary policy and the transparency of monetary policy decision-making. Moreover, the minutes detailing the deliberations by the MPB members are released on the BoK website on the first Tuesday two weeks after the date of the MPB meeting. The minutes are not a summary of the deliberations of the MPB members, but rather the equivalent of the transcripts of the meeting without specifying the members' names. Thus, the minutes accurately contain all the information related to the monetary policy decisions and the opinions of each member, which is an important source for the market to anticipate the future direction of monetary policy.

Traditionally, the BoK has been well known for its secrecy, and for avoiding public disclosure of information and policy decisions. This secrecy was, among other things, a means of protecting it from political interference in the absence of independence. Recently, however, communication has become the BoK's main policy tool, especially with the introduction of inflation targeting as an explicit way of conveying signals on future monetary policy directions. As a result, the BoK is strengthening its communications by disclosing their monetary policy goals, as well as increasingly detailed information, which include their economic forecasts and future monetary policy directions. In this regard, it is not just the inflation target but also the economic outlook provided by the BoK that is an important tool of communication. The BoK's economic outlook includes information on its assessment of the prevailing economic status and its future monetary policy direction, as well as simple forecast figures for growth and prices. However, apart from the economic outlook provided by the working-level BoK staff, the MPB members have not yet provided their own economic outlook. Nor do they provide their views on the future direction of monetary policy, such as the path of the future base rates. This should be reconsidered.

6 | *Inflation Targeting in Korea*

Inflation targeting was a very important operational tool in stabilising the inflation rate in many countries when the inflation rate was running high. Korea was no exception to the deployment of this tool. In the past, Korea suffered from relatively high inflation rates, and the introduction of inflation targeting contributed to stabilising inflation through the anchoring of the inflation expectations of private agents. The BoK initially set the target at 3 per cent and focused its operations on reducing inflation to below the target. Then it adopted a symmetric target of 2 per cent from 2016. This chapter conducts an assessment of the inflation targeting that Korea has experienced in the aftermath of the 1997 currency crisis.

6.1 Key Practical Issues for Targeting Inflation in Korea

The adoption of inflation targeting as a monetary policy framework required the BoK to decide on some practical questions: To wit, what price measure, target inflation rate, target horizon, and method of presentation to deploy?

6.1.1 Price Measure

What is the most appropriate inflation measure? In Korea, the issue centred on the choice between headline CPI, which includes food and energy prices, and core CPI, which excludes them. Initially, the BoK decided to use headline CPI, which is compiled by the Korea Statistical Office, mainly because of its familiarity to the Korean public. There was concern that the use of price indices other than the CPI might create public confusion in judging the inflation rate, given that the government had already been using the CPI in its communications with the Korean public. From the year 2000, however, the target price changed to core CPI. Given that Korea was a very open economy, the BoK decided to exclude those items whose prices were subject to very large short-lived fluctuations and unexpected external shocks from the target. Specifically, non-grain agricultural products, whose prices are greatly affected by weather conditions and harvests, and oil and related products, whose prices are likely to fluctuate reflecting international market conditions, were excluded. Core CPI is a more accurate indicator than headline CPI in the sense that it represents the basic underlying price trend, rather than short-term price swings, and reacts quickly to changes in the policy rate.

It does, however, suffer from the weakness of being divorced from the daily life of consumer households, in that it excludes the prices of agricultural products, and oil and related products that constitute major items in the cost of living. The effect of anchoring inflationary expectations to the target inflation rate is therefore likely to be weaker. Taking these points into consideration, the BoK shifted back to headline CPI as its target indicator from 2007. Since then, headline CPI has remained the target indicator for inflation targeting.

6.1.2 Target Inflation Rate

It is important for the BoK to determine a target inflation rate that is consistent with its goal of price stability. Currently, most central banks believe that an inflation rate of around 2 per cent will be the level that meets their goal of price stability. In the operation of an inflation targeting strategy, however, the target inflation rate does not necessarily have to be set at around 2 per cent. An inflation rate above or below 2 per cent can be set, reflecting the underlying economic fundamentals, policy priorities, and time horizon for achieving price stability. For example, for high-inflation countries experiencing difficulty in lowering general inflation expectations over short periods of time, lowering the inflation targets gradually, in stages over time, may be more desirable. The BoK has deployed such a strategy. Except for 1998, the first year of inflation targeting, when the exchange rate of the Korean *won* almost doubled in the wake of the currency crisis, the BoK set the target at around 3 per cent. The BoK set the target at 3±1 per cent in 1999, and then 2.5±1 per cent in terms of core inflation in the year 2000. It set the target again at 3±1 per cent annually from 2001 to 2003 and replaced it with a target range 2.5–3.5 per cent in terms of the three-year average CPI inflation from 2004 to 2006. For the period 2007–2009, the medium-term inflation target was set at 3±0.5 per cent and, for the period 2010–2012, it was set at 3±1 per cent. Then, for the period 2013–2015, the inflation target was set at 2.5–3.5 per cent with a narrower target range. Finally, for the first time since the adoption of inflation targeting, the BoK set the inflation target at 2 per cent from 2016 onwards.

6.1.3 Presentation of the Target

How should the inflation target be presented? For the successful implementation of inflation targeting, it is important for central banks to announce an explicit target inflation rate, one which affects the inflationary expectations of the general public. This is because the anchoring effect can work well only when everyone is well aware of the target. Thus, central banks need to decide on how to announce the target.

Currently, most central banks present a single target point, such as a 2 per cent target point, while some central banks present a target range, such as 2–3 per cent, or set upper and lower limits around a midpoint, such as 3±1 per cent. In this regard, it is important to note that the effectiveness of inflation targeting may depend on the presentation method of the target inflation rate. Presenting inflation targets as a single target point may be more useful in enhancing the anchoring effects than announcing a target range (Kahneman and Tversky, 1974).

The BoK has used the method of setting up a target range twice, first during the period 2004–2006, and then during the period 2013–2015. The main reason for this change was that, against the backdrop of increasing price stability, the BoK wanted to de-anchor the inflation expectations fixed at around 3 per cent and to move it towards 2 per cent. However, the method of presenting the target range changed again to that of a target point, with the objective of anchoring the inflation expectations around the newly set target. Thus, starting 2016, the BoK presented a single point 2 per cent inflation target. At the same time, it provides detailed explanations in cases in which the inflation rate diverges beyond the upper or lower 0.5 percentage point of the target inflation rate.

6.1.4 Target Horizon

What is the most appropriate time horizon for assessing inflation targeting? Up to 2003, the BoK fixed the target inflation rate annually and reviewed its inflation performance. However, the strategy was not very effective for two reasons:

First, since monetary policy affects inflation or the real economy with a time lag, it is desirable to stabilise inflation over a sufficiently long period. In the case of Korea, the effect of monetary policy is usually known to affect inflation with a time lag of six months to two years (Park et al., 2020). Therefore, it is necessary to make the attainment time horizon sufficiently long such that the transmission of monetary policy is fully under way.

Second, inflation conditions may be quite uncertain. Prices in small open economies like Korea are heavily influenced by many factors which the BoK alone cannot control, such as fluctuations of the exchange rates and the price of international raw materials. Taking these factors into consideration and setting different inflation targets each year will inevitably make it difficult to anchor inflation expectations. To maximise the anchoring effect, it would be desirable for the BoK to adhere to the inflation target from a long-term and consistent perspective, even if prices fluctuate in the short run due to uncertain factors.

Accordingly, the BoK switched to a medium-term system in 2004. While deciding to set the target every three years, it extended the target attainment period to three years, taking into account the time lag in the transmission channel of monetary policy. Simultaneously, the assessment of inflation performance was made in terms of the three-year average of the annual inflation rates during the target period. However, this average inflation targeting, similar to price level targeting, is 'history-dependent', making forward-looking monetary policy difficult, as past inflation performance affects current monetary policy. For example, if inflation rates are high in the first two years of the three-year period, the inflation rate in the third year should be sufficiently reduced to offset the past inflation overshoots, which implies adopting an excessively tight monetary policy in the third year regardless of future inflation trends. Consequently, starting in 2010, the BoK decided to assess the operation of its inflation targeting again upon a yearly basis, which has given the BoK more leeway to implement expansionary policies even if the actual inflation rates exceed the

Table 6.1 *Evolution of the inflation targeting system in Korea*

Year	Target	Indicator	Target-setting frequency	Assessment horizon
2001–2003	3±1%	Core CPI	Every year	Annual
2004–2006	2.5–3.5%	Core CPI	Every three years	Medium-term (average inflation targeting)
2007–2009	3±0.5%	CPI	Every three years	Medium-term (average inflation targeting)
2010–2012	3±1%	CPI	Every three years	Annual
2013–2015	2.5-3.5%	CPI	Every three years	Annual
2016–to date	2%	CPI	Every three years	Annual

three-year average target.[1] However, concern arose that this might weaken the accountability of the BoK. Against this backdrop, the BoK decided to increase the publication frequency of its Monetary Policy Report, a statutory requirement report submitted to the Korean National Assembly, from twice a year to four times a year from 2016, and to be more responsible for the breach of the target by providing more detailed explanations about inflation trends.

Table 6.1 summarises the evolution of the inflation targeting strategy in Korea. Since the introduction of inflation targeting in 2001, the BoK has experienced six separate phases of inflation targeting to date.

6.2 Assessing Inflation Targeting in Korea

6.2.1 Overall Performance

Despite the adoption of an inflation targeting strategy, which contributed, to a large extent, to containing the inflation rate, the CPI inflation rate in Korea continued to move above 3 per cent until the end of 2012, except for a short period before the outbreak of global financial crisis when it fell to around 2 per cent. But since then, the Korean economy started to see its inflation staying below 2 per cent. Although it recovered to around

[1] It is interesting to observe that, against the backdrop of extremely low inflation and lacklustre growth, price-level targeting and, in particular, average price-level targeting emerged as an alternative to inflation targeting in the United States and many advanced economies. See Svensson (2019).

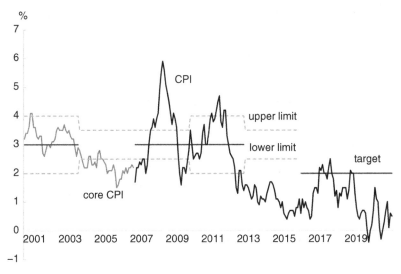

Figure 6.1 The CPI inflation rates and targets in Korea
Note: The inflation rate is expressed in terms of core CPI until the end of 2006 and thereafter in headline CPI. Inflation target was set at the range of 3 ±1 per cent between 2001 and 2003 and as a midpoint between 2007 and 2012. For other periods, only a range was set. Since 2016, only a target point without a range has been selected.
Source: BoK (2017) and ECOS, BoK.

2 per cent during the period 2017–2018, the CPI inflation rate fell again from the year 2019. Figure 6.1 shows the movement of this CPI inflation rate along with inflation targets in Korea.

Notwithstanding this, the inflationary expectations did not fall sufficiently. The inflation expectations of the general public, which remained around 4 per cent until 2012, dropped slightly but continued to remain near and slightly below 3 per cent. The long-term inflation expectations by the expert group remained higher than 2 per cent, although the actual inflation rate fell below 2 per cent. Against this backdrop, in December 2015, the BoK decided to lower its inflation target to 2 per cent, from the target range of 2.5–3.5 per cent put in place during the period 2013–2015. Despite this, the inflation rate continued to fall below the new target in the midst of the slow economic recovery, spreading concern that Korea, like Japan, would be entering into a deflation trap.

Given this, how could the actual performance of inflation targeting in Korea be assessed? In this regard, we rely on Demertzis et al. (2010)

and the IMF (2013) to assume that inflationary expectations are formed as follows:

$$\pi^e_{t+1} = \lambda\pi_t + (1 - \lambda)\pi^T$$

where π^e_{t+1} is the expected inflation rate for one period ahead, π^T the target rate, and π_t, the current observed inflation rate.

This equation means that the inflationary expectations of private agents π^e_{t+1} are affected by the announcement of the target π^T made by the central bank and by the actual performance of the observed inflation rate π_t, while the size of λ determines the effectiveness of the inflation targeting. That is to say, the smaller λ is, the stronger the effect of the targeting is. If the value of λ is near 0, for instance, the targeting is fully operative. In contrast, if λ is near 1, then the targeting is not operative at all, and the inflation expectations depend solely on the past inflation performance of private agents. Modifying the above equation, we obtain:

$$(\pi^e_{t+1} - \pi^T) = \lambda(\pi_t - \pi^T)$$

Thus, based upon the regression relationship of the inflation expectation error $(\pi^e_{t+1} - \pi^T)$ upon the actual inflation gap $(\pi_t - \pi^T)$, we can estimate the value of λ and test the performance of the targeting. However, the problem for the assessment of the targeting is that the inflationary expectations are not observable variables. Thus, we rely on the consumer survey conducted each month by the BoK to estimate the one-year ahead inflation expectations of consumers. Then, assuming that the inflation expectations adjust slowly over time, we run the following regression equation:

$$(\pi^e_{t+1} - \pi^T) = \alpha + \lambda(\pi_t - \pi^T) + \theta(\pi^e_t - \pi^T)$$

with α, λ, and θ all being constants.

Table 6.2 shows the short-run and long-run effects of anchoring in Korea for the whole inflation targeting period 2002–2019 and for the six sub-periods.

The targeting seems to have worked relatively well in Korea over the whole period. By announcing the target itself, the BoK has contributed to making the diverse inflationary expectations of private agents converge towards the target, and thus provided 'an anchor' to inflationary expectations. About 90 per cent of the inflation expectations turned out to be anchored by the target in the short run. However, in the long run, less than

Table 6.2 *Short-run and long-run effects of anchoring in Korea*

Phase	Date	Short-run anchoring effect $(1-\lambda)$	Long-run anchoring effect $(1-\lambda/(1-\theta))$	R2
1	2002.2–2003.12	0.86	0.61	0.65
2	2004.1–2006.12	0.91	0.79	0.65
3	2007.1–2009.12	0.90	0.18	0.96
4	2010.1–2012.12	0.91	0.12	0.95
5	2013.1–2015.12	0.88	0.41	0.91
6	2016.1–2019.12	0.87	0.72	0.71
Total	2002.2–2019.12	0.93	0.47	0.93

Note: The data on inflation expectations has newly been compiled since 2013.
Source: Author's estimation.

half of the inflation expectations were anchored by the target. The observed inflation had as much an impact as the target inflation, as inflation subsisted. For the different sub-periods, the short-run anchoring effects were much the same, but, in the long run, the anchoring effect worked little during the period 2010–2012 when large fluctuations of the observed inflation rates dominated the effects of the anchoring. After changing the target from 3 per cent to 2 per cent in 2016 amid the continuing low inflation trend, the long-term effect of anchoring improved.

6.2.2 Interpretation[2]

Currently, there seems to be a consensus that an inflation rate of 2 per cent is compatible with the price-stability mandate of many central banks,[3] with, perhaps the notable exception of the ECB,

---

[2] This section is based upon Moon (2020).

[3] In 1996, Janet Yellen, as a Federal Reserve governor, had an extensive exchange regarding the definition of price stability with the Federal Reserve Chairman at the time, Alan Greenspan. The latter defined it as 'the state in which expected changes in the general price level do not effectively alter business and household decisions', and said that zero inflation would guarantee it. In response to this remark, Yellen emphasised the need to 'grease the wheels of the labor market', allowing real wage adjustment through rising prices to cope with rigid nominal wages. It led her to propose 2 per cent inflation rate as compatible with the mandate of price stability. In 2012, the FOMC adopted, for the first time, an explicit longer-run inflation objective of 2 per cent, as measured by the Personal Consumption Expenditure (PCE) price index. See Federal Open Market Committee Transcripts (1996).

which set its target at slightly below 2 per cent. If the target is set at 2 per cent, then both overshooting and undershooting of the target should equally be cause for concern. Symmetry emerged as being important for the first time in 2012, when the FOMC in the United States referred to its inflation objective as a 'symmetric inflation goal', rather than just a simple 'inflation goal', in its 'Statement on Longer-Run Goals and Monetary Policy Strategy' (Federal Open Market Committee, 2012). This means that the central bank will endeavour to ensure that inflation is running neither persistently above nor below its target. Following the example of the FRS, the BoK also made public the 'General Principles of Monetary Policy Operation' in 2016, and emphasised the need to consider the risks of inflation remaining persistently above or below the target symmetrically. For some countries, however, the target can temporarily be set at higher levels than 2 per cent, let us say, 3 per cent, or at lower levels than the desirable level, which, let us say, is 1 per cent (3 per cent as the ceiling and 1 per cent as the floor[4]). For example, Korea initially set the target at 3 per cent because it suffered from quite a high inflation rate before the introduction of inflation targeting. It was clear that the implicit operational goal of this target was to stabilise the inflation rate below 3 per cent, not to maintain it at around 3 per cent. In contrast, if the target were temporarily set at 1 per cent, the implicit aspiration of the MPB members would be to raise the inflation rate above 1 per cent until it could be stabilised at around 2 per cent. Then, targeting cannot be symmetric. Figure 6.2 distinguishes three cases of inflation targeting operation depending on the level of the inflation target.

a) Inflation targeting under $\pi^T = 2$ per cent

Let us suppose, first, that the target is set at 2 per cent, which is the case for most central banks in advanced countries. In this case, the central bank should pay equal heed to the lower and upper limits of the target. Then, depending on the position of the actual inflation rate π_t and the inflation expectation π^e_{t+1}, three cases can be distinguished, as is shown in Table 6.3.

The first case is where π_t and π^e_{t+1} remain near the target 2 per cent. Clearly, the targeting is a big success here. The second case is where π_t

---

[4] J. Broaddus had already suggested that 3 per cent would be the ceiling. See, also, the Federal Open Market Committee Transcripts (1996).

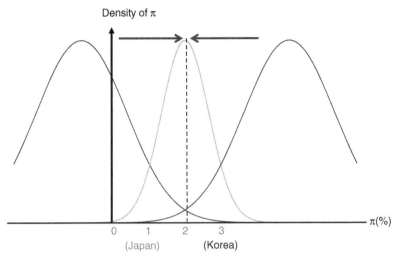

Figure 6.2 Probability density of inflation rate and the setting of the inflation target

Table 6.3 *Inflation targeting under $\pi^T = 2$ per cent*

	π^T	π_t	π^e_{t+1}	Performance Assessment
Case 1	2	2	2	Complete success
Case 2	2	3 or 1	2	Credibility is hurt but anchoring effect works well. No need to be concerned about inflation or deflation
Case 3	2	3 or 1	3 or 1	Complete failure. Through continuously missing the target, inflationary expectations are upwardly or downwardly adjusted. Concern about inflation or deflation.

rises above the upper limit, let us say 3 per cent, or below the lower limit, let us say 1 per cent, while π^e_{t+1} remains unchanged. Given that the target was set at 2 per cent and the actual inflation rate deviates from the target, it seems that the targeting operation appears to be a failure, but, as long as the inflation expectations are still anchored around 2 per cent, it may not necessarily be so, although large deviation of actual inflation rate from the target can do harm to the credibility of the monetary policy. The third case is where both π_t and π^e_{t+1} rise above the upper limit 3 per cent or fall below the lower limit 1 per cent. Then, the operation turns out to be a complete failure. There is no anchoring taking effect.

b) Inflation targeting under π^T = 3 per cent

Let us now consider the case in which the target is set at 3 per cent, instead of 2 per cent, as in Korea before 2016. Here, clearly, the objective of the targeting is to lower inflationary expectations below 3 per cent because the price stability defined by the Bank of Korea Act is not necessarily at 3 per cent. Thus, the targeting operation is not symmetric, as in the case of the inflation target of 2 per cent. Thus, two cases in which inflation rises above the upper limit, let us say, 4 per cent, and in which inflation falls below the lower limit, let us say, 2 per cent, are not perceived equally. If the inflation rate rises above 4 per cent and misses the target, there is no doubt that the targeting is a complete failure. But, even if inflation drops below 2 per cent, this cannot be considered to be a serious policy failure because the price-stability goal specified as the mandate of independent central banks is to maintain the inflation rate below 3 per cent (for instance, in the case of the ECB, price stability is interpreted as not achieving 2 per cent, but a little below 2 per cent). The reason why the BoK set the target at around 3 per cent for so long was not just because this 3 per cent target was considered to be desirable, but because it was thought that stabilising the inflation rate sufficiently below 3 per cent was unlikely to be attained quickly in the short run. Thus, when the BoK had a target of 3 per cent, preventing inflation from rising above 4 per cent was asymmetrically more important than stopping inflation from falling below 2 per cent. Against this backdrop, three cases of the targeting performance, as shown in Table 6.4, can be examined in more detail.

The first case is where π_t and π^e_{t+1} remain near the target 3 per cent. On the surface, it seems that the targeting operation is successful, but, in reality, it may not be necessarily so, in the sense that it failed to lower the inflationary expectations down to 2 per cent. There should be additional efforts to bring inflationary expectations down towards 2 per cent in the long run. The second case is where the inflation rate rises above 4 per cent or falls below 2 per cent, while inflationary expectations remain fixed around the target 3 per cent, probably

Table 6.4 *Inflation targeting under π^T = 3 per cent*

	π^T	π_t	π^e_{t+1}	Performance Assessment
Case 1	3	3	3	Not a complete success. The actual inflation is equal to the target inflation, but inflationary expectations are not anchored at 2 per cent, so that additional measures are needed to lower inflationary expectations.
		4	3	Because of the anchoring effect, inflationary expectations are not changed, but the credibility of the central bank is damaged due to its missing the target.
Case 2	3	2	3	Despite the drop of the actual inflation rate below 2 per cent, anchoring is working, and inflationary expectations are not downwardly adjusted. There is a long-term need to lower inflationary expectations further.
		4	4	Complete failure. Neither anchoring nor credibility is achieved. There is concern about inflation.
Case 3	3	2	2	Relative success. Through the drop of the actual inflation rate to below the 2 per cent target, inflationary expectations are downwardly adjusted. But, given the big divergence between the target and the expectations, anchoring does not work and the target needs to be reset.

thanks to the anchoring effect of the target. Here, the rise in inflation cannot be equally assessed as the drop in inflation. For instance, if the inflation rate rises above 4 per cent, it is bad. But, as long as the anchoring effect holds, the targeting operation is not that bad, with the exception of its putting the credibility of the monetary policy at risk. In contrast, if inflation rate drops below 2 per cent, it is good, but, as long as inflationary expectations fail to fall, additional efforts will be needed to lower inflationary expectations below 3 per cent. Against this backdrop, the BoK decided to adopt the band-targeting approach in 2012, in order to de-anchor inflationary expectations. Instead of a point target at 3 per cent, the BoK took the range or band between 2.5 and 3.5 per cent for the targeting operation. The third case is where the inflationary expectations fell along with the actual inflation rate, despite the setting of the target at 3 per cent. Here, again, the rise in inflation expectations should be distinguished from the fall in inflation expectations. If inflation expectations rise above 4 per cent, then the operation is a complete failure because the inflation expectations as well as actual inflation overshot the target. However, if inflationary expectations in addition to actual inflation fall to 2 per cent, this operation can be considered as being somewhat successful. Indeed, there were many criticisms of the BoK's inflation targeting operation, but they proved, for the most part, to be groundless due to misinterpreting the targeting operation as a symmetric operation, like those of other advanced countries. Although the targeting operation did not appear to be sufficiently satisfactory, the BoK nevertheless successively achieved its stabilisation.[5] The only problem is that the divergence between the target and the expected inflation rate might harm the credibility of the monetary policy and therefore suggests the need for the resetting of the target.

The ignorance of this asymmetric operation did indeed give rise to much inaccurate criticism, which considered the monetary policy of the BoK to be not sufficiently expansionary to increase the inflation rate to its target rate of around 3 per cent. But even if the inflation rate were very low, hovering below 2 per cent, it does not necessarily mean that the monetary policy was a failure. Rather, it could be a successful stepping stone towards the long-term goal of price stability, unless real output or employment fell below its potential or neutral level. As pointed out, the BoK decided to shift its inflation target from 3 per cent to 2 per cent in 2016, which was a landmark event, in the sense that, as the BoK rigorously interpreted its mandate for price stability, its inflation targeting operation also shifted from an asymmetric to a symmetric one.

c) Inflation targeting under $\pi^T = 1$ per cent

Another interesting asymmetric targeting operation is carried out when the target inflation rate is set at 1 per cent, as in the case of the BoJ, which had such a target before the launching of 'Quantitative and Qualitative Easing' in 2013. Clearly, the principal goal of the BoJ was

---

[5] However, there were no worries about deflation, as shown in the inflationary expectation, which remained between 2 and 3 per cent, even though the actual inflation rate fell below 1 per cent.

to escape from the deflationary spiral that Japan was in by raising the inflation rate above the target. Thus, the operational aim was to raise the inflation rate above 1 per cent, not to maintain it around 1 per cent. If the BoJ could raise the inflation rate near 2 per cent, it would be counted as a successful operation, but, if it had an inflation rate near 0 per cent, it is clear that the operation would be seen as a failure. The targeting assessments under $\pi^T = 1$ per cent and under $\pi^T = 3$ per cent will be very similar. But, concerning the effect of anchoring, there is an important difference between these two cases. In the former, the central bank attempts to raise inflationary expectations in a deflationary situation, while, in the latter, it tries to lower them in inflationary circumstances. It is taken for granted that lowering inflationary expectations in an inflationary situation has the same effect as increasing them in an economy trapped in deflation. But, as pointed out, the anchoring effect can be weaker in a situation in which the inflation rates – and consequently inflation uncertainties – are very low. Thus, when the actual inflation rate widely misses the target from below, the validity of the targeting in enhancing inflationary expectations can be called into question.

In this regard, O. Blanchard's proposal to set the inflation target intentionally higher than is actually appropriate may be erroneous (Blanchard et al., 2010). In effect, Erhmann (2014) shows that the effect of targeting is weaker in a low inflation environment. Apart from this empirical study, the recent experience of the BoJ also provides further strong evidence that a continuous expansionary policy fails to produce an increase in inflation. These results suggest that the arguments of Blanchard, and even the relevance of the targeting as an instrument to increase the inflation rate, can be flawed.

Is inflation targeting still a relevant operational framework for central banks? So far, it seems that the answer has been positive, highlighting the flexibility of targeting when faced with the flattening Phillips curve (Svensson, 2011). But low inflation or deflation raises a fundamental question about the usefulness of inflation targeting, because there is no guarantee that raising inflationary expectations under conditions of low inflation or deflation works. If this is the case, it is very likely that the anchoring mechanism itself will break down, and that central banks need to find an alternative operational framework to inflation targeting, no matter what that might be (see Box 6.1).

Box 6.1 Inflation Targeting and Price Targeting

With continuing low inflation after the recovery from the 2008 global financial crisis, there was increasing support for price-level targeting as an alternative to inflation targeting strategies. In Korea, as in many other economies such as the United States and the EU, inflation rates continued to undershoot the target inflation rates, which raised concerns about falling inflation expectations failing to boost the economy in the face of lacklustre economic growth. This led to the adoption of so-called make-up strategies, such as price-level targeting and average inflation targeting, to offset past inflation undershoots of the inflation target with future overshoots (Svensson, 2020). Against this backdrop, the US FRS, in its Statement on Longer-Run Goals and Monetary Policy Strategy made in August, 2020, hinted at the possible adoption of temporary price-level targeting, saying 'that, following periods when inflation has been running persistently below 2 percent, appropriate monetary policy will likely aim to achieve inflation moderately above 2 percent for some time'.

However, price-level targeting systems can be costly unless some preconditions are met. Economic volatility is likely to increase in the short term. If a price level deviates from its expected path, central banks should create sufficiently large surges in inflation or deflation to bring it back to its original path, and, in this process, the volatility of the economy may be excessively magnified.

The BoK conducted a strategy of average inflation targeting, by focusing on three-year average inflation rates over the medium term during the period 2004–2009. Because this system in which the average inflation rate over three years should be adjusted to the inflation target has a similar feature of path dependence, it can be said that the BoK had already incorporated some elements of price-targeting systems in its inflation targeting (BoK, 2018: p. 8). The result was that the closer the inflation target system was to the end of the target period, the more difficult it was for the BoK to operate a forward-looking monetary policy, given that monetary policy was dictated by past performance. For example, even though future inflation was expected to be low, high inflation in the past pushed the BoK to lower inflation rates further and to tighten monetary policy beyond the appropriate level.

Figure B6.1 shows the target price and actual price trends in both Korea and in selected major economies. The actual price began to undershoot the target price from the year 2014 in the United States and the euro area. In Japan, the actual price rebounded slightly since 2014 but the risk of deflation subsists as the actual price continued to undershoot the target-price level. In the case of Korea, however, the actual price tended to overshoot even the inflation target of 3 per cent until 2014, although a notable slowdown in CPI inflation rate was observed since then. The decision of the BoK to adjust the inflation target to 2 per cent is an essential first step towards attaining the long-term price stability goal. The introduction of a price-level targeting system is not yet a relevant topic.

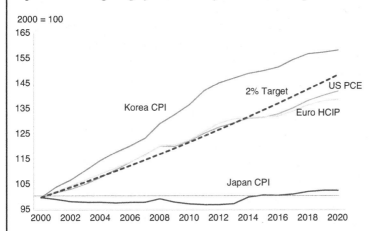

Figure B6.1 Target price and actual price trends in selected economies
Note: The price data used are the CPIs for Korea and Japan, the Personal Consumption Expenditures (PCE) index for the United States, and the Harmonised Index of Consumer Prices for the euro area.
Source: ECOS, BoK, and FRED, Federal Reserve Bank of St. Louis.

6.3 Low CPI Inflation and High-Rent Inflation

Although monetary policy has been sufficiently accommodative in Korea since 2012, the inflation rate measured by the CPI was running so low that the BoK was under strong pressure to lower its policy rate further in order to fight the risk of deflation. There were concerns as to whether the Korean economy, like the Japanese economy, was also entering into a deflation cycle. Is the inflation rate in Korea really as low as its CPI figure suggests? Officially, it seems so. However, this is just because the current CPI in Korea does not measure the impact of monetary policy on house-renting prices correctly.

Faced with low CPI inflation and low growth, the BoK has, in effect, undertaken a series of interest rate cuts, which continued from mid-2012 until the end of 2017. According to conventional wisdom, these cuts should have brought about a reduction in rental costs and CPI rent inflation by shifting the tenant demand from home-leasing to home-owning. In countries such as the United States and Japan, for instance, a fall in the interest rate allows tenants to buy homes, reducing the demand for rented accommodation and consequently a fall in rent prices. Contrary to this perceived wisdom, however, the Korean case suggests that the opposite is true. Lower interest rates in Korea do not generate this fall, but, instead, the rise in rent prices. Given the current unprecedented low interest rates, rent inflation seems to continue to figure prominently in the CPI inflation.

But why do low interest rates lead to rent inflation and why does it not lead to a rise in the published CPI inflation figure? First of all, the answers are associated with the special features of the Korean house-rental market, which are dominated by the leasehold deposit contracts called *chonsei*.[6] Second, it is because the CPI in Korea does not incorporate the homeowners' equivalent rent (OER).

6.3.1 *Hybrid* Chonsei *and Low-Rent Inflation*

Simple monthly rent contracts are extremely rare in Korea. Most of the rent contracts are *chonsei* contracts in which the tenant pays the landlord a large lump sum deposit upfront, which will be the equivalent of 50 to 70 per cent of the actual house value. The landlord pays the deposit back to the tenant at the end of the contract. The landlords, in lieu of the monthly rent paid by the tenant, rely on the interest income stream derived from the investment of the tenant's deposit. There are two types of *chonsei* contracts, to wit, pure and hybrid *chonsei* contracts. They are different to the extent that, while the tenant in pure

---

[6] For instance, see Ambrose and Kim (2003), KDI (2012), and Seong and Kang (2011) for the features of these contracts.

contracts pays only a deposit and pay no monthly rent, the tenant in hybrid contracts pays the deposits, but also pays a monthly rent.

Precisely for this reason, a cut in interest rates has a very strong positive impact on leasehold deposits, although not necessarily on house prices, which is the anticipated conventional monetary transmission channel. For instance, a cut in interest rates, by keeping the yield on deposits down, pushes landlords to charge tenants larger leasehold deposits so as to compensate for their decreasing interest income. As a result, the rent in pure *chonsei* contracts rises, which is captured by the change in the size of the leasehold deposits. However, the rent in hybrid *chonsei* contracts does not necessarily increase, because it is measured by monthly income stream, which is the sum of monthly rent paid and the monthly yield on the deposit invested upfront. A cut in interest rates lowers the yield on the leasehold deposits, which makes the rent in the hybrid *chonsei* contracts smaller, and leads to the underestimating of the increase in the rent for hybrid *chonsei* contracts.

Table 6.5 shows the effects of a cut in interest rates on the rents for the two types of *chonsei* contracts – one pure contract (with a KRW300 million deposit) and one hybrid contract (with KRW200 million as the deposit and KRW0.5 million as the monthly rent) – which have an identical monthly income stream worth KRW1.5 million when the yield on the leasehold deposit is 6 per cent. Suppose that the yield on the deposits declines from 6 per cent to 5 per cent due to a cut in the interest rate. Then, the leasehold deposit increases to KRW360 million for pure contracts because the landlords want to secure the same monthly income stream as when the yield on deposit was 6 per cent. Thus, although the monthly income does not change, the increase in rent is 20 per cent, as measured by the leasehold deposit. However, if the rent is measured in terms of monthly income as in the rent for hybrid contracts, the increase in rent will be zero. The incompatibility between the rents measured by deposit and by monthly income stream can only be solved if the yield on deposits is assumed to be unchanged at 6 per cent.

Let us now consider the hybrid *chonsei* contract. Faced with a cut in interest rates and in the yield on deposit, the landlords have two options. One option is to raise the amount of the deposit, leaving the monthly rent at the same level as before. That is, they can raise the deposit from KRW200 million to KRW240 million. Then, the monthly interest income to the landlords will be the same with KRW1.5 million

Table 6.5 *Impact of a cut in yield on deposit on pure and hybrid chonsei contracts (unit: million KRW)*

		6%	5%	Rent Increase
Pure *chonsei* (measured by deposits)	Original	D300	D360	20%
	Converted monthly income	D300 x 0.06/12 = M1.5	D360 x 0.05/12 = M1.5	0%
			(D360 x 0.06/12 = M1.8)	(20%)
Hybrid *chonsei* (measured by monthly income)	Original	D200 + M0.5	D240 + M0.5	NA
			D200 + M2/3	NA
	Converted monthly income	D200 x 0.06/12 + M0.5 = M1.5	D240×0.05/12+M0.5 = M1.5	0%
			(D240×0.06/12+M0.5 = M1.7)	(13.3%)
			D200×0.05/12+M2/3 = M1.5	0%
			(D200m×0.06/12+M2/3 = M5/3)	(11.1%)

Note: D and M denotes annual leasehold deposit and monthly payment, respectively. The figures in parenthesis are the rents calculated based on the assumption that the yield on deposit remained at 6 per cent.

(240×0.05/12+0.5 = 1.5). The other option is to increase the monthly rent, leaving the deposit constant. For instance, they will ask the tenants to pay KRW2/3 million as monthly rent instead of KRW0.5 million. In this case, the monthly income stream to the landlords will be the same KRW1.5 million (200×0.05/12+2/3 = 1.5). In both cases, the tenants are supposed to pay no extra rent as long as the rent for the hybrid contract is measured by converted monthly income stream. Therefore, the rent inflation will be recorded as 0 per cent. It is, however, clear that, in both cases, the tenants bear higher rent costs. For instance, when the tenants pay the landlords KRW240 million as a deposit with the same monthly rent, they should provide the landlord with KRW40 million more as a leasehold deposit compared to the previous contract. And when the tenants pay the landlords KRW2/3 million as monthly rent, while maintaining the same deposit, they pay KRW1/6 million more as monthly rent.

Figure 6.3 shows the divergent movements of pure and hybrid *chonsei* indices in Korea since 2012. As interest rates continued to drop until the end of 2017, the pure *chonsei* price rapidly increased, whereas the hybrid *chonsei* price increased only slightly. Only when interest rates started to increase in 2018 did their divergence cease.

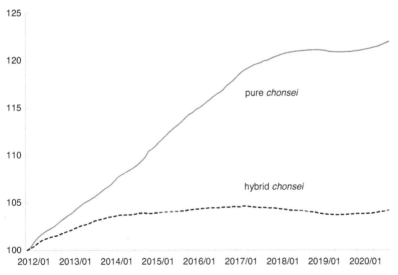

Figure 6.3 Movement of pure and hybrid *chonsei* prices
Source: Statistics Korea.

Given that the hybrid contracts account for more than 50 per cent of Korean rental contracts, the official CPI rent published by the Korea Statistics Office is therefore, to a large extent, underestimating the true rent inflation, widening the gap between the observed and the true CPI. It is therefore necessary to reflect the effect of the interest rate change on the rent for the hybrid *chonsei* contracts correctly and construct a true rent index. One method is to construct a rent index on the assumption that the yield on the deposits remains unchanged. If this method is used, the rent inflation represented by two hybrid *chonsei* contracts will be 13.3 per cent and 11.1 per cent, respectively, as shown in Table 6.5. In general, the more similar the hybrid contract is to the pure contract, the higher the increase in rent will be.

Figure 6.4 shows the movement of a new CPI inflation rate which can be obtained through the re-calculation of the rent of hybrid *chonsei* contracts by this method. According to this revised estimate (NEWCPI),

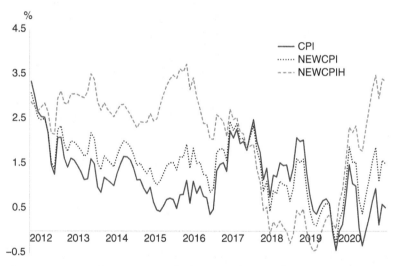

Figure 6.4 CPI inflation rates with the revised rent inflation (NEWCPI) and with the incorporation of OER (NEWCPIH)
Note: The rent was newly calculated based upon the assumption that the yield on deposit was assumed constant at the interest rate that prevailed in 2012. Also, it is assumed that 70 per cent of the monthly income stream from the hybrid *chonsei* contracts came from the leasehold deposit.
Source: Statistics Korea.

the CPI should have risen by around 2 per cent, instead of a little over 1 per cent during 2015. Thus, the official CPI would have biased inflation seriously downwards.

6.3.2 Owners' Equivalent Rent

Furthermore, unlike many other countries, such as the United States and Japan, Korea incorporates only tenant rent in its CPI, excluding owners' equivalent rent (OER). In fact, the Korea Statistics Office that compiles the CPI in Korea had been opposed to incorporating owners' equivalent rents on the grounds of lack of sufficient information, but one underlying reason behind this decision is a concern about excessively large speculative rises in house prices, which risk exaggerating the CPI movements. The Korea Statistics Office has thus decided to omit the owners' equivalent rent from the CPI and to incorporate solely tenant rents.

However, since 1995, the Korea Statistics Office has published a supplemental index (CPIH) that incorporates owners' equivalent rent, although this index has never been in official use. For the calculation of this index, the Korea Statistics Office draws on the tenant rents that are used to compile the CPI, and consider them as equal to owners' equivalent rents. This may also reflect the practical difficulties both in determining the most appropriate way of calculating the owners' equivalent rents and in obtaining the necessary data to do so. Thus, the only change is in the weight given to house rent. If the owners' equivalent rent is taken into consideration, the true inflation rate would be substantially much higher, owing to the increase in its weight, of up to 25 per cent of consumer expenditure.

For major economies that publish CPIH indices, housing costs account for 19–32 per cent of household consumption expenditure.[7]

---

[7] The CPIH has not yet been universally adopted as the most appropriate measure of the cost of living of households, but the consensus is that the OER should be incorporated into the CPI despite the differences in approaches to estimating the OER, ranging from the rent equivalent method to the user cost approach or the expenditure approach. Thus, many countries, such as the United States and Japan, are already reflecting the OER in the compilation of their CPIs. Other countries which have not yet done so have decided to incorporate it and are planning to do so (for instance, the United Kingdom and the EU). In the case of the United States, the share of housing expenditure is 32.10 per cent while the share of rent is 7.32 per cent. In Japan, the share of housing expenditure is

Compared to these countries, the share of housing costs in the Korean CPI is only 9.28 per cent of consumption expenditure, and thus suggests the under-representation of housing costs in Korea. If included in the CPI, the share of housing costs would increase to 27 per cent of household consumption expenditure.

It is clear that, as long as the OER is taken into consideration, the CPI inflation understates the true inflation by quite a huge margin. As seen in Figure 6.4, the gap peaked during the middle of 2015 with a magnitude of 1.5 percentage points, which explains about 50 per cent of the CPIH inflation. Thus, instead of 1.5 per cent, the true inflation rate (measured in NEWCPIH) would have risen to more than 3 per cent in 2015, meeting the inflation target set at around 3 per cent. Consequently, during the period 2013–2017, the inflation rate would not in reality be as low as to miss the target widely. As long as the cut in interest rates increased rents sufficiently, Korea's monetary transmission channel would have already been working well enough to increase both the inflation rate and real economic activity.

This suggests two important implications concerning monetary policy in Korea. First, once the official CPI inflation underestimates the real underlying inflation, the risk of choosing misguided monetary policies can be very high. In particular, relying on the official CPI can seriously bias monetary policy in the direction of excessively expansionary stances. For example, although real inflation seemed a lot higher than measured CPI inflation due to rent inflation in 2015, the BoK had to accept the request to fight deflation actively, lowering its interest rate in order to boost the Korean economy. Given that the current major transmission channel of monetary policy is largely through the real estate market, this risk might be greater. Monetary policy in Korea may be much more potent in influencing inflation than in many other advanced countries. Second, because the CPI is used as a benchmark for pricing in many services sectors, it can provide incorrect signals and amplify price fluctuations. In the case of Korea in particular, many service items such as public transportation tariffs and electricity bills are under the government control and their prices are determined based upon the CPI. This control, introduced during the

18.65 per cent while the share of rent proper is just 3.07 per cent. Similarly, in the United Kingdom where the CPIH is published separately from the CPI, the share of housing expenditure is 23.8 per cent while the share of rent is only 6 per cent.

period when inflation was high, is stricter if CPI inflation is high. If the official CPI inflation rate turns out to be lower than the real rate, these sectors could set their tariff rates higher than the level that would be justified by the real inflation and, in doing so, actually accelerate true inflation. It provides the monetary authorities with another justification for being less concerned with the seemingly low CPI inflation.

7 | *The Tools and Instruments of Monetary Policy*

The BoK has developed three monetary policy tools, to wit, the lending facility, the required reserve system, and open market operations, which have led to changes in its assets and liabilities. The BoK uses these tools to influence intermediate targets, such as the money stock and interest rates, and to achieve price stability as its final goal. It has also added to its existing toolbox a standby facility, which has gained in importance under the current interest rate-setting monetary policy framework. This chapter looks at the main components of the assets and liabilities of the BoK and examines its credit and monetary policy tools.

7.1 The Assets and Liabilities of the Bank of Korea

Just as commercial banks affect the economy through changes in their assets and liabilities, central banks do so through monetary and credit policies by changing the items in their assets and liabilities portfolios. However, the items on the balance sheets that can be changed depend on the degree of economic and social development of the country concerned. Consequently, preferred monetary and credit policy tools reflect national differences. This can be illustrated by the comparison of the balance sheets of the BoK and FRS of the United States. Table 7.1 shows their respective balance sheets before the 2008 global financial crisis.

The BoK's assets and liabilities before the 2008 global financial crisis show the following features:

First, on the liabilities side of the BoK, it is notable that cash in circulation accounted for only about 7 per cent of the BoK's total liabilities as of 2007. Thus, the cash ratio relative to reserve money was significantly lower in Korea compared to the United States where it accounted for about 90 per cent of the FRS's total

162

Table 7.1 *Balance sheets of the BoK and FRS as of the end of 2007*

Assets	BoK (Trillion KRW)	FRS (Billion Dollars)	Liabilities	BoK (Trillion KRW)	FRS (Billion Dollars)
Credits to banks	9.4 (3.1)	0.1 (0.0)	Cash in circulation	21.7 (7.2)	783.0 (89.7)
Credits to government	9.0 (3.0)	824.4 (94.4)	Reserves	84.4 (27.9)	18.7 (2.1)
Foreign reserves	252.4 (83.3)	33.6 (3.8)	Securities sold	161.2 (53.2)	29.6 (3.3)
Others	32.2 (10.6)	15.3 (1.8)	Government deposits and other debts	35.7 (11.8)	42.1 (4.8)
Total	303.0 (100.0)	873.4 (100.0)	Total	303.0 (100.0)	873.4 (100.0)

Note 1: Figures in parentheses denote the composition ratio compared to total assets or liabilities.
Note 2: Foreign reserves include gold and securities sold include MSBs and RPs.
Source: BoK and FRB.

liabilities. The BoK absorbed reserve money from circulation through the issuance of MSBs. The BoK is different from the FRS in that it can issue not only banknotes (cash) but also bonds (called MSBs) as its own debt. As of 2007, these bonds accounted for 53 per cent of the BoK's total liabilities. The BoK's main objective in its open market operations was to absorb the increase in reserve money, which ensued as a result of buying FX, by selling MSBs, and, thereby sterilising the inflow of foreign capital. The FRS was not equipped with equivalent monetary policy tools. This explains why Korea's cash ratio was significantly lower than that of the United States. In contrast, the open market operations of the FRS were, unlike those of the BoK, intended to supply reserve money, hence the purchase of US government bonds. In Korea, commercial banks also held quite a large amount of their reserves in the form of deposits at the BoK. For instance, commercial banks in Korea held about 30 per cent of the BoK's total liabilities in the form of reserves, compared to only 2 per cent in the United States. These reserves were held either due to legal reserve requirements or voluntarily to cope with interbank settlements or for emergencies.

Second, on the assets side, it is notable that the BoK had small government bond holdings of less than 3 per cent of its total assets. Compared to the FRS, which increased reserve money through the purchase of government bonds, the BoK tried to offset the increase in the reserve money caused by the purchase of foreign reserves. The government bond market in Korea remained relatively small until only recently. Thus, unlike in the United States, where the FRB purchased government bonds, the BoK had to sell its own MSBs through open market operations. Instead, the BoK provided a quite high proportion of its credit to commercial banks. Although commercial banks in Korea have greatly reduced their reliance on the BoK, the loans and discounts from the BoK were an important source of cheap money to them. They were often used to support the Korean government's industrial policy, as the loan rates were below market rates. Currently, they are limited to the so-called Aggregate Credit Ceiling Loans (renamed as 'Bank Intermediated Loans'). In contrast, commercial banks in the United States were reluctant to solicit loans or discounts from the FRS, fearing reputational loss as sound banks (the 'stigma effect'). Indeed, when US commercial banks took loans from the

FRS, they generally had to borrow at penalty rates that were higher than market rates. However, since Korea started to run current account surpluses from 1986, the BoK's asset expansion has principally been through FX purchases to replenish official FX reserves and to mitigate the appreciation of the Korean *won*. As of the end of 2007, Korea had 83 per cent of its total assets in foreign assets. In order to sterilise the excess liquidity created by the purchase of foreign assets, the BoK issued massive amounts of MSBs, which, in turn, contributed to the development of the Korean bond market. Thus, MSBs were the main type of securities used for open market operations, not government bonds.

The 2008 global financial crisis brought about significant changes in the size and composition of the assets and liabilities of many central banks. In particular, in the United States, the FRS launched a huge asset purchase programme in order to help overcome the crisis. As a result, Table 7.2 shows the FRS's assets, which stood at about US$870 billion at the end of 2007, increased approximately fivefold to US$4.45 trillion by the end of 2016. In comparison, the BoK undertook no significant asset expansion, with its assets growing only 1.6-fold from KRW303 trillion at the end of 2007 to KRW480 trillion at the end of 2016. There have also been significant changes in the composition of central bank assets. In the case of the FRS, loans extended to banks and other financial institutions increased sharply, reaching 40 per cent of total assets, which means a significant fall in the share of government bonds in the assets held by the FRS. In contrast, there have been no such changes in respect of the BoK. In addition, the issuing of reserve money increased rapidly in the United States in line with the aggressive asset purchase programme. This increase, however, came about in the form of bank deposits at the FRS, rather than cash in circulation. Thus, the proportion of reserves held in the form of deposits at the FRS increased sharply from 2 to 40 per cent of total liabilities, and, consequently, the ratio of cash in circulation dropped from 90 per cent to 33 per cent of total liabilities. As a result, the assets and liabilities structure of the BoK is currently more like that of the FRS than was the case prior to the 2008 global financial crisis.

In a sense, it can be said that the BoK already had a quantitative easing programme through the purchase of foreign assets, while simultaneously conducting a sterilisation operation through the sale of

Table 7.2 *Balance sheets of the BoK and FRB as of the end of 2016*

Assets	BoK (Trillion KRW)	FRS (Billion Dollars)	Liabilities	BoK (Trillion KRW)	FRS (Billion Dollars)
Credits to banks	17.3 (3.6)	1811.6 (40.7)	Cash in circulation	86.8 (18.1)	1462.9 (32.8)
Credits to government	15.7 (3.3)	2567.4 (57.7)	Reserves	117.3 (24.4)	1759.7 (39.5)
Foreign reserves	441.9 (92.0)	41.2 (0.9)	Securities sold	200.0 (41.6)	725.2 (16.3)
Others	5.4 (1.1)	33.1 (7.4)	Government Deposits and other debts	76.4 (15.9)	405.5 (11.4)
Total	480.3 (100.0)	4453.3 (100.0)	Total	480.3 (100.0)	4453.3 (100.0)

Note: Figures in parentheses denote the composition ratio compared to total assets or liabilities.
Source: BoK and FRB.

MSBs. As such, sterilisation operations decline along with the reduction of FX market interventions. However, outright sales of MSBs are also declining. Moreover, against the backdrop of population aging and burgeoning social spending in the aftermath of 2020 COVID-19 pandemic, fiscal deficits in Korea are likely to increase rapidly. These changes will further increase the resemblance between the balance sheet structures of the BoK and the FRS in the future.[1]

7.2 Credit Policy Tools

As outlined earlier, the government has had only limited borrowings from the BoK, with the notable exception of the early years of economic development when the tax base was weak and capital markets were undeveloped. The purchase of FX could lead to an increase in reserve money, as long as the Korean economy recorded current account surpluses, but this increase was sterilised by the BoK. Thus, the extension of credit to commercial banks has been the principal source of reserve money in Korea.

7.2.1 The History of the Lending to Banks

Central banks discount bills from commercial banks, or advance loans to banks, just as banks do with companies and households. Closely associated with the role of central banks as the bankers of the banks, central banks' credit policies stem from re-discounting the bills discounted by commercial banks. In the past, therefore, re-discounting by central banks was a major money-supply channel. The BoE, one of the world's oldest central banks, supplied money mainly through the re-discounting of bills until the early twentieth century, and the US FRS held re-discounting to be the most important source of money during the early years of its establishment. This was due to the spread of the 'real bills doctrine', which stated that central bank money supply could never be inflationary when issued against commercial bills arising from real transactions in goods and services (Bindseil, 2014).

Similarly, the re-discounting of bills was the most important credit policy tool since the establishment of the BoK. Supporting rapid

---

[1] If FRS normalises its monetary policy by absorbing excess liquidity created by the quantitative easing, this resemblance will also be accelerated.

economic growth, the BoK extensively used it as a means of monetary policy financing to support the government's industrial policy and development programme, rather than just as a liquidity adjustment tool. For instance, when commercial banks provided financial support for a strategic industry or company, the BoK refinanced part of the funds at rates lower than market interest rates. This made it difficult for the BoK to control the supply of credit to the economy and focus on price stability, because interest rates that stayed at lower levels for long periods created excessive credit demand.

To reduce the volume of preferential policy loans and strengthen the control of the money supply, the BoK revamped its credit policy and introduced the ACCL system in March 1994. While dismantling most preferential policy loans or transforming them into fiscal budget programmes, the BoK incorporated diverse loans into this system, such as the re-discounts of commercial bills, trade financing, and the special loans for the production of basic materials and parts. Then, setting a ceiling on its overall refinancing provided to banks, it abolished automatic re-discounts. Thus, the BoK was able to take the lead in determining the amount of credit supplied in the form of ACCLs and in limiting eligibility for refinancing.

This represented a big step forward in the BoK's evolution from an institution providing preferential policy loans (called 'growth money'), to an institution implementing monetary policy. Notwithstanding this, the new system did not represent a complete departure from the old system, because the allocation of re-discounts and loans was linked to the preferential loans of commercial banks to SMEs, and the lending rates were lower than the prevailing market interest rates. Thus, until the 1997 currency crisis, the orientation of the BoK's credit policy was gradually to lower the credit ceiling supplied by the ACCL and to adjust the lending rates to market interest rates. However, the subsequent deterioration of the domestic economy and financial market conditions turned the achievement of this goal into a long-term objective. The ACCL had to be used extensively as an instrument to overcome the large-scale liquidity shortages and credit crunches that resulted from financial and economic crises. In the meantime, the Korean economy's slowdown continued and, particularly in the aftermath of 2008 global financial crisis, its economic performance was lacklustre. There was thus a pressing need to stimulate the Korean economy.

The BoK decided to change the ACCL again. This time, the goal of the ACCL was no longer to reduce the credit supply but to expand it in order to help stimulate the economy. Against this backdrop, in April 2013, the BoK made comprehensive changes in its covered target sectors, credit ceilings, and loan interest rates. In December of the same year, even the name ACCL was changed to the 'Bank Intermediated Lending Support Facility (BILSF)'.

7.2.2 Operation

Currently, the BoK's lending to banks is implemented under the label of the BILSF with the objective of supporting bank lending to SMEs. While changes in interest rates by monetary policy affect the whole economy, the BILSF has the advantage of supplementing monetary policy by allocating funds to strategically selected sectors. To this end, the BoK provides funds to the banks in proportion to the volume of their loans extended to SMEs, setting their funding costs at a lower interest rate than the base rate. The MPB determines the ceiling and interest rates of this lending facility when necessary, taking into consideration many factors, such as the general economic outlook, financial market conditions, and the funding conditions of the SMEs in question.

Along with the introduction of the BILSF, the BoK has continued to elevate its ceiling. In particular, in order to mitigate the impact of the COVID-19 on the Korean economy, it increased its ceiling by 16 trillion KRW to 43 trillion KRW in 2020 (see Figure 7.1). The interest rate on loans has also been cut to 0.25 per cent in 2020. The expansion of this facility was due to the fact that the BoK aggressively utilised it as a supplementary package to its interest rate cut, to support and stimulate the Korean economy further.

The composition of the BILSF has been adjusted as well, reflecting the changes in the credit policy priorities of the BoK. Table 7.3 shows that the BILSF currently comprises six programmes categorised by their objectives and by the status of the recipients.

This reorganisation has important implications, although changes in policymaking are not very visible yet.

First, the BoK has officially accepted the view that money and credit can be endogenous under the interest rate-oriented monetary

Table 7.3 *Ceiling and interest rates of the BILSF programmes, end of 2020 (Trillion KRW, %)*

Programme	Date of Introduction	Ceiling (Trillion KRW)	Objectives
Support for trade financing	1994.3	2.5	Support for export financing
Support for regional SMEs	1994.3	5.9	Support regional SMEs
New growth and job creation	2013.6	13.0	Support for high-tech start-ups
Stabilisation of SME lending	2017.9	5.5	Mitigate the volatility in lending to SMEs
Support for SMEs affected by COVID-19	2020.2	13.0	Support companies affected by COVID-19
Support for self-employed individuals	2020.9	3.0	Support individuals affected by COVID-19
Total		43.0[1]	

Note: Includes retained ceiling 0.1 trillion KRW.
Source: BoK.

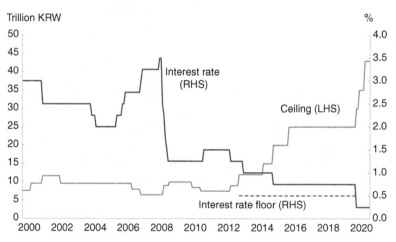

Figure 7.1 Ceiling and interest rates of the BILSF
Source: BoK.

policy framework. Given that monetary targeting had been in place for much longer in Korea than elsewhere, it took longer for the BoK staff to free themselves from the influence of this long-held monetarist doctrine. To the extent that any level of credit supply is compatible with a given interest rate level, the BoK, therefore, can begin credit easing even before the interest rate reaches zero bound.

Second, the new facility is no longer a credit-rationing tool, as its aim has changed to reinforcing its counter-cyclical function and, through it, to enhancing the effectiveness of monetary policy. It was necessary for Korea to boost the economy actively, as the post-2008 recovery was anaemic, and low economic growth continued. Against this backdrop, the BILSF may be a very effective counter-cyclical tool. Many similar programmes had already been implemented in other major advanced economies, including the United Kingdom's funding for lending, which the BoK closely benchmarked in its reorganisation of the ACCL system. Furthermore, funding costs at interest rates lower than market rates are not a matter of preferential credit provision made by central banks, but rather an incentive for all commercial banks willing to increase their loans to the economy and to strengthen the effectiveness of monetary policy to stimulate the economy.

7.3 Monetary Policy Tools

The BoK has at its disposal two main monetary policy tools: the required reserve system, and open market operations.

7.3.1 The Reserve Requirement

The reserve requirement policy obliges commercial banks to hold a certain proportion of their assets in the form of reserves in their central bank accounts. The reserve requirement policy was enacted by the BoK at the time of its establishment in 1950. Initially, its use was limited because direct credit rationing was the most commonly used policy tool. Then, as the Korean economy began to run current account surpluses, and with the consequent monetary expansion from the late 1980s, it became a major instrument to absorb excess liquidity.[2] However, against the backdrop of ongoing financial liberalisation from the early 1990s, the role of the reserve requirement as a means of liquidity adjustment has greatly declined. The main reasons for this are as follows:

> First, there was a growing demand for market-based monetary policies amid financial liberalisation. Because the required reserve policy was a regulation that restricted the autonomous operation of financial institutions, open market operations have emerged as the main monetary policy instrument. Second, as the BoK came to shift its operational framework of monetary policy from money targeting to interest rate targeting, the importance of steering the call rate to the base rate increased. The change in the required reserve ratio, which indiscriminately affects all banks, is not appropriate for such fine-tuning operations. Third, the issue of regulation fairness was raised. The reserve requirement system mainly applied to banks and other deposit-taking institutions, but not to other non-banking financial institutions, such as money market funds. Against the backdrop of financial innovation that blurred the division between banks and non-bank financial firms, the required reserve system put the banks at an unfair competitive disadvantage, which resulted in the substantial lowering of the required reserve ratio to alleviate the burden on the banks. Fourth, independently of whether it was required or not, banks voluntarily held reserves for the purposes of payments and settlements, which removed the need to enforce it by legislation or regulation.

For these reasons, the required reserve system lost its usefulness as a habitually deployed monetary policy tool in Korea. However, the BoK still maintains the system, albeit at a very low required reserve ratio. The current operation of the required reserve system in Korea is as follows:

> First, the MPB decides the minimum required reserve ratio to be held by each bank within a range of 50 per cent of its liabilities subject to reserve requirements. However, in periods of pronounced monetary expansion, the MPB can impose a marginal reserve requirement

---

[2] Like Korea, the reserve requirement was a useful instrument for a country such as China, which once tried to prevent the excessive expansion of credit supply in the wake of the abrupt expansion of foreign reserves due to current account surpluses.

ratio of up to 100 per cent. Second, each bank must hold its reserves in its current deposit with the BoK or in its own cash vault. A bank is allowed to hold up to 35 per cent of its required reserves as vault cash, the amount of which is calculated based upon the amount held during the reserve calculation period. In cases where a bank fails to maintain sufficient balances to meet its reserve requirements during the reserve maintenance period, it pays a penalty of 2 per cent of the average balance of the deficiency. If its actual reserves fall short for three periods in a row, it can be prohibited from making new loans, investments, or paying dividends to shareholders until it has maintained the required reserves continually for more than a month. Third, required reserve ratios cannot differentiate between banks and vary according to the type and size of the pertinent liabilities. Currently, the BoK has established different required reserve ratios only upon the basis of the types of liabilities, not upon their sizes, at the range between 0 per cent and 0.7 per cent. Fourth, in respect of the method of maintaining reserves, each bank calculates its required reserves, and maintains the calculated reserves on a monthly basis. The reserve calculation period is from the first to the last day of each month, and the reserve maintenance period is from the Thursday of the second week of the following month to the Wednesday of the second week of the subsequent month. Fifth, in principle, no interest payments are made on reserve deposits with the BoK. However, if necessary, the MPB may decide to pay interest on reserve deposits. During the 2008 global financial crisis, for instance, the MPB decided to make a one-off interest payment of KRW500 billion into the reserves of banks, so as to improve their BIS capital adequacy ratios as a means of enhancing their credit supply capacity.

7.3.2 Open Market Operations[3]

a) Historical Overview

Open market operations are the policy instruments through which central banks purchase or sell securities, including government and public bonds with their financial institution counterparts in open

---

[3] This part is based upon the BoK (2017).

markets, such as money or bond markets, and change the funding conditions of their counterparts, through adjusting bank reserves or short-term interest rates.

Open market operations in Korea were first launched with the issuance of MSBs in 1961. These bonds were sold to banks to absorb their temporary excess liquidity. Although these operations were called open market operations, they were actually compulsory bilateral transactions with banks as the direct counterparts. Non-bank financial institutions were included as eligible counterparts for the open market operations from 1977. It is important to note that government bonds (KTBs) were suitable for open market operations as well, but operations involving the buying and selling of government bonds were rarely undertaken because of the shortage of outstanding government bonds. As a result, open market operations in Korea were largely in respect of MSBs.

From 1986, open market selling of MSBs on a large scale was conducted to absorb excess liquidity arising from the increase in FX holdings following the first current account surplus in the Korean economy. However, these operations were still compulsory transactions as interest rates remained regulated.

Since the early 1990s, open market operations based upon the prevailing market interest rates have been conducted. In 1993, a competitive tender method was introduced for transactions in government and public bonds under RPs. From 1997, bonds that failed to attract successful bids at auctions, in respect of the sales of RPs or the issuance of MSBs, were no longer allocated by direct sale to financial institutions. This effectively resulted in open market operations based upon fully competitive bidding. With the introduction of electronic bidding through BoK-Wire, the BoK's Real Time Gross Settlement System established in 1997, open market operations based upon market mechanisms were firmly established.

Since the 2000s, efforts have been made to relieve the burden of roll over and the accumulation of MSBs, and make open market operations more market-friendly and efficient. For example, a regular timetable was instituted for the auction of MSBs based upon maturity; the minimum bid price and minimum successful bid price were adjusted upwards, reflecting common transaction practice in the bond market; and subscription to MSBs, fungible issue, and early redemption of MSBs were introduced. Meanwhile, the method of conducting RP transactions with financial institutions was changed from the borrowing and lending of funds using securities as collateral to the buying and selling of securities. With the reform of the monetary policy operational framework in March 2008, RP transactions were undertaken upon a regular basis and fixed interest rate tenders were introduced. In the 2010s, the BoK further enhanced the transparency and effectiveness of its open market operations. In October 2010, alongside the existing compulsory deposit requirement, a market-friendly system of competitive bidding was adopted for deposits with the BoK's MSA. In December 2011, securities lending and borrowing and intra-day RP systems were introduced, which strengthened the role of open market operations in financial stability. Since June 2014, MBSs issued by the Korea Housing-Finance Corporation were included in the types of securities eligible for open market operations as a means to improve the structure of household debt by stimulating the mortgage securitisation market. In April 2015, the margin requirement ratio applied to RP purchases was differentiated, based upon the type of eligible security and the remaining maturity, in order to reflect better the market price risk of the eligible securities. In 2020, to cope with the COVID-19 crisis, the BoK strengthened the open market operations further with the introduction of unlimited Repo transactions, as well as the expansion of the eligible collateral and institutions for the OMOs. The BoK also performed outright purchases of Treasury bonds.

b) Operation

The primary aim of the BoK's open market operations is to steer the call rate to the base rate set by the MPB, by buying and selling its own MSBs. The call rate is significantly affected by the amount of bank reserves, because banks attempt to deal with the shortages or surpluses of reserves through the call market, where short-term funds are traded (typically overnight loans). Thus, in order to achieve the goal of open market operations, the shortages or excesses of bank reserves must be identified and appropriately resolved.

The demand for reserves is equivalent to the required reserves that a bank has to hold for a certain period. The required amount is calculated every month based upon a bank's liabilities, subject to the reserve requirements, and the bank must hold it from the Thursday of the second week of the following month to the Wednesday of the second week of the subsequent month. The supply of reserves takes place through various channels. For instance, when taxes are paid, funds are transferred to the government account from the accounts at the BoK opened by commercial banks, and, consequently, bank reserves are commensurately reduced. Conversely, if the government makes a payment to a private contractor for a construction project, the paid funds are transferred from the government account to the private contractor's bank account, and, consequently, bank reserves increase. When the BoK pays Korean *won* for the purchase of US dollars from commercial banks, or when the BoK extends loans to banks, the reserves also increase.

If the supply of reserves far exceeds demand, banks will try to place their non-profit excess reserves (actual reserves minus required reserves) on the call market, leading to downward pressure on call rates. Conversely, if actual reserves fall short of the required reserves, banks will borrow more money from the call market, leading to upward pressure on call rates.

The BoK estimates the supply of reserves by reflecting the various factors which affect the reserves, comparing it with the demand for reserves in order to calculate the amount of reserve surplus or deficit. If a deficit is forecast, the BoK will inject liquidity, and if a surplus is forecast, it will absorb liquidity. In this way, it conducts open market operations so that call rates do not deviate significantly from the base rate. To achieve this objective, the Financial Markets Department (see Box 7.1), in charge of the BoK's open market operations, relies on two types of market adjustment: structural and fine-tuning adjustments.

First, as Figure 7.2 shows, the Financial Markets Department conducts structural adjustments, which aim to absorb the excess

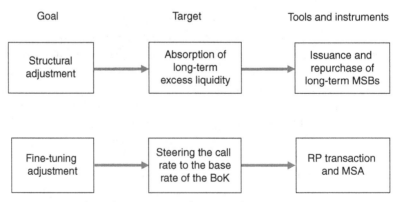

Figure 7.2 Mode and instruments of open market operations

Box 7.1 Government–BoK Compact on Open Market Operations

The Financial Markets Department, which is the second most important department next to the Research Department within the BoK, manages the commercial banks' reserves and conducts open market operations by issuing MSB to sterilise the supply of money related to FX market interventions. Meanwhile, the Office of Treasury and Debt Securities inside the Payment and Settlement Systems Department is a small team in charge of the issuance and redemption of Korean government bonds (KTBs). Their operations are largely undertaken in the primary market, but they can intervene in the secondary market if necessary. However, their operations are carried out after instructions from, or consultations with, the MOEF.

At present, the two departments (or offices) are strictly separated inside the BoK. While the operation of the Financial Markets Department is regarded as an integral part of the BoK's competence, the operation of the Office of Treasury and Debt Securities pertains to the government, and, therefore, operations involving government bonds are not reported to the MPB. Furthermore, against the backdrop of the main function of OMOs to date being to absorb excess liquidity from the market, the BoK has been reluctant to purchase KTBs. As a result, the BoK's holdings of KTBs have remained negligible. As of June 2020, the BoK has only KRW17 trillion KTB holdings, which accounts for 2.7 per cent of the total outstanding KRW630 trillion KTBs. For these reasons, the function of the Office of Treasury and Debt Securities has been under-represented in the BoK's operation of monetary policy. There is, however, a need to rethink the role of the Office of Treasury and Debt Securities and to strengthen its policy collaboration with the Financial Markets Department.

First, faced with the current deteriorating economic outlook and the spread of the COVID-19 pandemic, there is an increasing demand to stimulate the economy through more expansionary monetary policies unless the follow-on inflation rate increases excessively. The issuing of MSBs is basically an operation to absorb the excess liquidity created by FX market interventions. As the Korean government cannot continue its interventions in the FX market, there will be little chance of increasing the issue of MSBs.

Furthermore, the use of MSBs is likely to shrink because their issue would collide with the objective of stimulating the economy through continuing cuts in the interest rate, thereby increasing market liquidity. Given that the issue of MSBs is an operation to absorb liquidity, stabilise FX rates, and prevent the appreciation of the Korean *won* against the US dollar, there is no longer any justification for their use. The continued use of MSBs could result in the twisting of the yield curve in Korea. Despite a cut in the base rate, short-term yields were not able to fall sufficiently because of the outright sales of MSBs, an outcome which affects long-term yields and ends up harming the normal transmission channels of monetary policy.

At the same time, there are increasing concerns about budget deficits. Starting in 2019, the Korean government began to experience serious budget deficits due to social security-related expenditure. This trend is likely to be stronger in the future amid the spread of COVID-19. The burgeoning budget deficits will require financing by the issuing of deficit-financing government bonds, raising concerns over the potential increase in bond yields, as increased bond issuance may result in a steep decline in bond prices. It is expected that the BoK will have to play a 'proactive role' in cushioning the possible shocks in the financial markets.

Second, the open market operations of the BoK, under the current corridor system, will not necessarily be required except for fine-tuning operations that consist in matching the call rate with the base rate. The current monetary policy framework, which changes short-term interest rates in order to achieve the monetary policy goals, such as price stability, is based upon the stable transmission channel that links short-term interest rates to long-term interest rates. However, there is no guarantee that this relationship always works smoothly, and, as this channel is frequently damaged, there is an ongoing need to repair it.

However, the BoK is not operating on the long end of the yield curve because its open market operations are conducted through MSBs with relatively short-term maturities of less than two years. There is an implicit agreement between the BoK and the MOEF that the former specialises in its MSB operations only in money markets and short-term financial markets, while the latter conducts its KTB operations in the long-term capital market, and that they do not interfere with each other on the issuance and redemption of MSBs and KTBs. However, what will be important for the normal transmission of monetary policy will be the impact of the long-term interest rates on the economy. Currently, the Korean government issues KTBs with three-, five-, ten-, twenty-, thirty-, and fifty-year maturities, while the maturities of MSBs are less than two years. Thus, for the smooth functioning of monetary policy, it is necessary to strengthen the collaboration between the Financial Markets Department and the Office of Treasury and Debt Securities. To stem the money financing of government deficits, interventions by the Office of Treasury and Debts Securities should only be conducted in the secondary market, and not in the primary market.

Notwithstanding this, there is still a high risk that this collaboration will put monetary policy independence in jeopardy, if the interests of the debt management by the MOEF prevail. There seems to be quite strong resistance from the BoK with regard to the extension of open market operations for fear of losing monetary independence, and it may be necessary for the BoK and the government to reach agreement about the division of tasks and competences between them, as was concluded between the US Treasury and Federal Reserve Board under the Treasury-Fed Accord. What is likely to happen in Korea is that, irrespective of whether the two institutions reach such agreement, there will be strong political pressure to force such collaboration in order to lower the cost of financing government debt under conditions of low inflation and low growth.

liquidity supply arising from the sterilisation of large FX inflows, which is a long-term trend. To this end, it issues MSBs, which have relatively long maturities, and, once issued, these MSBs are not, in principle, redeemable prior to maturity. A ceiling on the issuance of MSBs is set quarterly by the MPB. There are various MSB types with maturities ranging from fourteen days to two years. However, only 91-day, 182-day, one-year, and two-year MSBs are issued regularly to absorb the excess structural liquidity. For two-year MSBs, the Financial Markets Department also conducts RP transactions before maturity if there is a need to ease maturity concentration and boost liquidity. For this structural adjustment, the outright sale of the government bonds could be considered, but, in practice, it is rarely used because of the very meagre amount of government bonds held by the BoK.

Second, after absorbing the long-term liquidity, the Financial Markets Department conducts short-term fine-tuning operations, which consist largely of steering the call rate towards the base rate. To this end, the principal adjustment is conducted through the RP transactions, without outright sales or purchases of MSBs, which have little use. The RP transactions are the most important tools for the fine-tuning adjustments, and, for these transactions, government bonds are usually utilised. The longest RP maturity is ninety-one days, but the majority of RP transactions involve seven-day RPs, whose interest rate is the base rate of the BoK. Meanwhile, if the BoK lacks sufficient government bonds for the RPs that it needs to sell, it may borrow them from financial institutions.

For short-term fine-tuning adjustments, the BoK also uses the MSA, a term-based deposit facility, which it started to operate in competitive auctions from 2010. In normal times, the BoK accepts deposits from financial institutions in a process of market-friendly competitive bidding. However, it can also oblige financial institutions to make deposits with the MSA in exceptional circumstances, including rapid credit expansion. The maturity period of deposits with the account is less than ninety-one days, but the BoK generally receives deposits in the MSA with maturities of less than one month. Early withdrawal of MSA deposits is restricted, and the sums deposited are not regarded as part of the reserves.

Figure 7.3 shows that, as of the end of 2019, the outstanding MSBs balance was KRW165.4 trillion, while the outstanding RP sales and deposit balance of the MSA stood at KRW11.5 trillion and KRW6.7 trillion, respectively.

The BoK conducts most of its open market operations through public offerings, and, if necessary, it also makes bilateral transactions with individual financial institutions. The public offerings are divided into subscriptions and competitive auctions. Subscriptions refer to the fixed interest rate allocation of securities to bidders according to their bidding amount, while competitive auctions mean the allocation of securities according to bid rates. The subscription method is used for

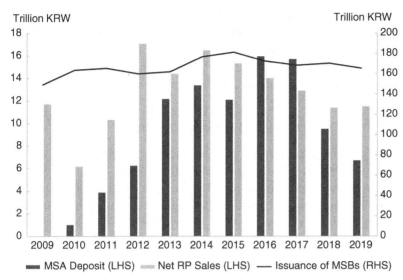

Figure 7.3 Structural and fine-tuning adjustments by open market operations
Source: BoK.

regular subscriptions to MSBs and the sale of seven-day RPs, while the competitive auction method is used for other types of operations.

In competitive auctions, there are two methods for determining interest rates for transactions: the single rate (Dutch auction method) and multiple rate methods (conventional method). The former applies the highest rate from among those offered by successful bidders, while the latter applies the rate that each bidder offers. The BoK uses the single-rate method to absorb liquidity and the multiple-rate method to supply liquidity. For instance, if the BoK issues MSBs or sells RPs through competitive auction to absorb liquidity, any financial institution that offers the lowest rate (or the highest price) will be at the top of the allocation order. Then, this highest successful bid rate is applied to all subsequent bidders. In contrast, if the BoK seeks to supply liquidity by re-purchasing MSBs before maturity or by buying RPs in a competitive auction, the financial institution that offers the highest rate (or the lowest price) will be at the top of the allocation order. The bid rates that each subsequent successful bidder offers then become the successful bid rates. Meanwhile, if the bid rate of more than two successful bidders is the same, the amount allocated will be in proportion to the amount bid for.

Besides public offerings, the BoK can re-purchase MSBs prior to maturity or sell or lend securities to specific financial institutions through bilateral transactions. However, the use of bilateral transactions is limited to some exceptional cases, such as liquidity support to a financial institution suffering a temporary shortage of funds.

7.4 Stand-by Lending and Deposit Facilities

After initially introducing an inflation targeting system, the BoK subsequently shifted to a call-rate targeting framework. However, as call rates remained rigidly fixed around the target level regardless of liquidity supply and demand conditions, its liquidity allocation and information signalling functions weakened greatly. Furthermore, the rigidity of call rates led to an over-concentration of short-term borrowers in the overnight call market and the distortion of RP markets and other short-term financial markets, harming the seamless working of the monetary policy transmission channel running from the adjustment of policy rates to the real economy, through the adjustment of long-term interest rates. Thus, the BoK realigned its monetary policy operational framework in March 2008, changing the policy rate from the overnight call rate to the base rate, which is the seven-day RP rate between the BoK and its counterpart financial institutions (see Table 7.4). Specifically, it is the fixed offer rate for the sales of securities, while it is the minimum bid rate for the purchases of securities. In addition, the BoK has introduced two standing facilities under the label of 'Liquidity Adjustment Loans and Deposits'. The Liquidity Adjustment Loans facility allows financial institutions to borrow from the BoK in order to comply with their overnight liquidity requirements, while the Liquidity Adjustment Deposits facility allows banks to deposit their surplus funds freely with the BoK. These facilities contain the volatility of money-market interest rates within the upper and lower bounds set by their loan and deposit rates, similar to the standing facilities of the BoE and the ECB, which are benchmarked by the BoK.

The operational methods of the Liquidity Adjustment Loans and Deposits were further improved in 2009 and 2011. In February 2009, it became possible for the maturities of Liquidity Adjustment Loans to be extended by up to one month so as to allow them to be used flexibly as a tool for stabilising the financial market, and the restrictions on interest rate adjustments were eased so that they could be changed

Table 7.4 *Major realignments of the monetary policy operation framework in March 2008*

	Before	After the realignment
Policy rate	Overnight call rate	Base rate
Operating target	Overnight call rate	Overnight call rate
RP transactions	Transaction: any time on demand Main instrument: any one-day to fourteen-day RPs Interest rate: variable tender	Transaction: regular tender (every Thursday) Main instrument: Seven-day RPs Interest rate: fixed offer rate for RPs (minimum bid rate for reverse RPs)
Lending and deposit facilities	Loans for temporary shortage of funds – Maturity: One day – Interest rate: call rate+2% Liquidity adjustment loans – Maturity: less than a month – Interest rate: call rate –25bp	Introduction of two standing facilities: liquidity adjustment loans and deposits facilities. – Interest rate: Base rate+/–100bp Abolition of loans for temporary shortage of funds. Liquidity adjustment loans revamped

Source: BoK.

along with the BoK's base rate. In 2011, as the reserve maintenance period of financial institutions changed from a half-monthly to a monthly basis, the BoK adjusted the interest rates of Liquidity Adjustment Loans and Deposits on the last business day of the reserve maintenance period to the same level as on other business days, in order to discourage financial institutions from delaying their reserve adjustments until the last business day of the reserve maintenance period. This measure was designed to mitigate violent fluctuations in the overnight call rate arising from significantly increased amounts of fund excesses or shortages requiring adjustment around the last business day of the maintenance period, although it was also expected to allow financial institutions to increase their flexibility and autonomy in terms of their fund management.

The financial institutions eligible to make use of these standing facilities are those institutions that are required to hold reserves. The use of Liquidity Adjustment Loans may be restricted so that they do not become a tool for the support of financial institutions in trouble. Liquidity Adjustment Loans and Deposits carry overnight maturities. But if the MPB decides it necessary for the smooth working of the financial markets, the tenor for Liquidity Adjustment Loans may be extended by up to one month. The interest rate for Liquidity Adjustment Loans is 1 percentage point higher than the base rate of the BoK, and should the base rate be below 1 per cent, the rate is twice the base rate. Meanwhile, the rate for Liquidity Adjustment Deposits is 1 percentage point lower than the base rate, and should the base rate be below 1 per cent, the lower limit is 0 per cent.

The volume of Liquidity Adjustment Loans suggests that banks do not routinely access this facility even when faced with temporary fund shortages, and it is used intermittently, when bank-funding conditions go temporarily awry. This is probably because, when banks experience temporary fund shortages, it is more advantageous for them to borrow money from the call market at lower interest rates than to use the Liquidity Adjustment Loans, which impose a rate that is one percentage point higher than the base rate, and also because those banks that use the facility run the risk of acquiring the stigma effect mentioned earlier for being unable to raise funds in the financial market.

In the case of Liquidity Adjustment Deposits, it has been observed that banks preferred depositing surplus funds in the facility because of the intensification of credit risks in the wake of the 2008 global financial crisis. The crisis led to an increased volume of Liquidity Adjustment Deposits, which exceeded KRW300 trillion during March 2009 (based upon the accumulated daily balances for each month) before decreasing again when the crisis abated.

8 | Monetary Policy without Money

Monetary policy is no longer the decisions to determine money, but just to decide on the short-term interest rates. Notwithstanding this, old principles consider these decisions as being equivalent, based upon the negative correlation between the bank reserve and the interest rate in the money market. Moreover, the BoK staff had a firm belief that the open market operation in the money market was the most desirable policy tool. In practice, however, the interest rate is neither determined by the interplay of demand and supply in the money market, nor is the open market operation an indispensable instrument, given the increasing role of the standby facility. This chapter examines the determination of the short-term interest rate under the 'corridor' system.

8.1 Equivalence between Reserve Targeting and Interest Rate Targeting

Managing the reserve positions of banks through open market operations has been the most common operating framework of monetary policies for many central banks around the world. The BoK, under the monetary targeting strategy, used this standard framework, adjusting the reserves of commercial bank as an operating target or instrument, while using open market operations as a tool. After adopting the inflation targeting strategy, the BoK began to use interest rates as an operating target. However, it continued to use open market operations as a major tool for adjusting the interest rates.

This regime shift can be assessed in terms of three criteria for choosing the operating target: observability, controllability, and predictability (Mishkin, 2011: pp. 411–412):

> First, the use of the short-term interest rates as an operating target yields better observability than that of the reserves. Unlike the short-term interest rates, which can be observed in real time and

186

monitored immediately, there is a time lag in reporting monetary aggregates, including bank reserves. However, with the computerisation of data collection and the reporting system integrated under the BoK's economic statistical system, the BoK could quickly collect the information on the reserves and the monetary aggregates. Thus, observability was not a main reason for the regime shift.

Second, the short-term interest rates are easier to control than the reserves. The reserves of the banks are not completely controllable because of constant shifts in the demand for cash. The BoK, however, monitored the reserve positions of individual banks upon a daily basis and managed to control them. Controllability was not an issue, either

Third, and most important, the short-term interest rate targeting is more predictable than the reserves targeting, as far as the impact of monetary policy is concerned. Predictability refers to the linkage between the operating instrument and the goals of the BoK, and high predictability means high efficiency in terms of monetary policy. In the case of the targeting of the reserves, the efficiency is assured through the transmission channel of the monetary policy that goes from the changes in reserves through the changes in money stock (M1 or M2), to the changes in real economic activity. This operation framework, however, had two predictability problems for the BoK and many other central banks. First, controlling the reserves did not necessarily lead to controlling the supply of monetary aggregates. Second, controlling the supply of money would not affect the real economy in the expected way. The first problem is associated with the instability of the money multiplier (see Box 8.1), while the second is linked to the instability of the velocity of money or the demand for money, as already examined in Chapter 2.

Against this backdrop, the BoK shifted to targeting short-term interest rates, managing the reserves by open market operations. Along with the introduction of standing facilities in 2008, however, open market operations have no longer been inevitable in order to determine short-term money-market interest rates. Figure 8.1 shows this change in the operating framework of the monetary policy in the BoK.

Box 8.1 Money Multiplier in Korea

A change in a bank's reserves leads to a change in the monetary base, which, in turn, affects the money in the economy through the monetary creation process known as the money multiplier. Mathematically, this relation is captured by the following equation:

$$M = m \times MB$$

Here, M denotes the money stock in the economy, MB the monetary base and m the money multiplier. If C and D denote, respectively, cash in circulation and deposits in banks, then $M = C + D$. If R denotes bank reserves, also $MB = C + R$. Let us assume that the desired holdings of currency C grows proportionally with the money M, such that $C = cM$. Let us also assume that banks hold a proportion of their deposits in the form of the required reserves, such that $R = \theta D$. Then, the money multiplier is expressed as follows.

$$m = \frac{1}{\theta(1 - c) + c} > 1$$

Thus, m is explained by its two components, c and θ, and the lower the reserve ratio θ or the cash ratio c is, the higher the multiplier m is. In the case of Korea, the movement of money multiplier since the 2008 global financial crisis is mostly explained by the changes in the cash ratio. Figure B8.1 shows the trend of the money multiplier and its components in Korea.

In Korea, the money multiplier tended to fall after incurring a sharp rise during the 1997 currency crisis. This movement was first determined by the variation of the reserve ratio. After the 1997 currency crisis, the cash ratio decreased but the reserve ratio increased sharply. Recovering from the financial restructuring, Korean banks replenished their reserves quickly, which led to a drop in the multiplier. Since the 2008 global financial crisis, however, the cash ratio started to increase, in tandem with the tendential decrease in interest rates. In particular, as the issue of large-denomination banknotes was made from 2008, the holdings of cash by the Korean public increased sharply. The share of KRW50,000 bill increased from 26 per cent in 2009 through 70 per cent in 2014 to 84 per cent in 2020. This led to the decline in the money multiplier. However, the reserve ratio did not vary much. In contrast, the rise in the reserve ratio was a main factor that led to the sharp drop in the money multiplier in countries such as the United States and Japan that adopted quantitative easing policies.

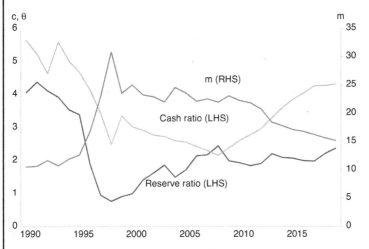

Figure B8.1 Money multiplier in Korea
Source: ECOS, BoK

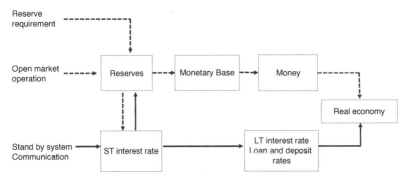

Figure 8.1 Operating instruments and tools for monetary policy
Note: The dotted line is the transmission channel under the monetary targeting framework while the solid line is the channel under the current interest rate targeting framework.

Nevertheless, it is still customary to explain that, when the central bank wants to change interest rates, it changes the bank reserves through open market operations, as under the monetary targeting regime. According to this traditional view, a change in bank reserves determines the short-term interest rate in the money market. If such a view is correct, then it will make no difference which variables central banks use as an operating instrument, be it the short-term interest rates or the bank reserves. Using the interest rates as an operating instrument is equivalent to using the reserves as an instrument. Until recently, the BoK took this view as well. For instance, the BoK stressed the equivalence between the two operating instruments in its monetary policy book in 2013:

> The central bank cannot achieve its reserve-money target and short-term interest target at the same time through open market operations, which leads to its achieving only one of the two targets. At present, central banks in major advanced economies, including the Bank of Korea, are adjusting the provision of the reserve so that the call rate moves closer to the policy rate, using open market operations as the most important monetary policy tool. (Bank of Korea, 2013: p. 102)

It is therefore necessary to examine this equivalence question in detail. Let us consider, first, the demand for overnight reserves by banks in the call market. In Korea, the demand for reserves comes largely from the required reserves set by the MPB. In addition, banks hold additional reserves at the BoK as a precaution against a shortage of the required reserve and as settlement balances. Then, banks' demand for the reserves in the call market is inversely related to the call rate. Let D be the demand for reserves and r_c the call rate. Then, D can be represented by the downward sloping function of r_c as follows:

$$D = D(r_c) \text{ with } \partial D / \partial r_c < 0 \tag{1}$$

If the BoK increases its supply of reserves from R^1 to R^2 in the call market through open market operations, the call rate r_c must fall from $r^1{}_c$ to $r^2{}_c$ along the demand curve for reserves D, and, inversely, if it reduces the supply of reserves R, the call rate r_c will rise along the demand curve. This negative response of the call rate to a change in the supply of reserves is referred to as the 'liquidity effect'. Therefore, at least in theory, there is a one-to-one correspondence between the movements of interest

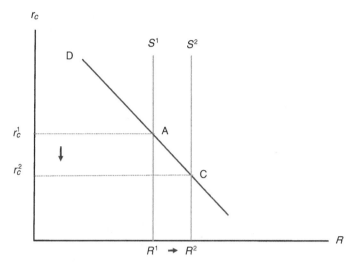

Figure 8.2 The relationship between the reserves and call rate along the demand curve for reserves

rate and reserves, which will make interest rate targeting equivalent to reserve targeting. This relationship is summarised in Figure 8.2.

In practice, however, there is no such correspondence. Let us suppose that an increase in the bank demand for reserves occurs. This will shift the demand curve for the reserves to the right. Under the framework of reserve targeting, the interest rate should be allowed to fluctuate widely whenever there is such a change in the demand for reserves. Under the framework of interest rate targeting, however, the provision of reserves is adjusted through the open market operations in order to offset the fluctuations in the demand for reserves. Reserve supply is endogenously determined in response to changes in demand, which will lead to a smoothening of the interest rate fluctuations.

This adjustment process is shown in Figure 8.3. Let us suppose now that the reserve demand shifts to the right from D to D'. The call rate should soar from $r^1{}_c$ to r_c' under the reserve targeting regime, because the reserves should be kept at R^1. Under the interest rate targeting scheme, however, the supply of the reserves will increase to R' in order to maintain the call rate constant. Thus, it is possible to maintain different levels of the reserves at the same given interest rate.

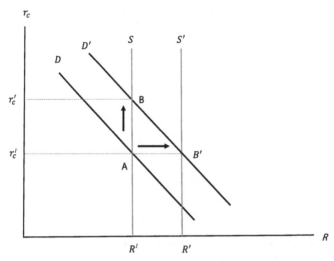

Figure 8.3 The relationship between the reserves and call rate when the demand for reserves shifts upwards

Thus, as Borio and Disyatat (2009) pointed out under the title of the 'decoupling principle', the traditional view that the change of interest rate corresponds one-to-one to the change of reserves is no longer valid. 'Under the same reserve supply, different interest rates may coexist and, inversely, different reserve levels may exist at the same interest rate'. Indeed, according to Friedman and Kuttner (2011), short-term money-market interest rates in the United States and the euro area fluctuated independently of the changes in the amount of reserves. Thus, interest rate movement was independent of reserve movement, and the liquidity effect could not be confirmed. The quantitative easing through which many central banks in the advanced economies supplied as many reserves as they wanted at zero interest rates after the 2008 global financial crisis was an extreme example of this decoupling.

8.2 Decoupling under Interest Rate Targeting

Currently, the BoK is adopting an interest rate targeting regime, like many other central banks, such as the FRS and ECB, do. Thus, whenever there is a shift in the demand for reserves, the BoK accommodates it by adjusting its supply of reserves. Thus, the interest rate movement is decoupled from the changes in reserves.

It is important to note that the BoK's policy rate, that is, the base rate, is separated from the call rate, which it considers to be an operational target to steer towards the policy rate. In the United States, federal fund rates were used as policy rates and also as operating target rates prior to 2008 global financial crisis, but both do not need to be the same.[1] In Korea, too, the policy rate was the overnight call rate, the operation target for open market operations. In March 2008, however, the BoK changed its policy rate from call rate to base rate, which is the reference rate applied for the transactions between the BoK and its counterpart financial institutions, thereby separating the policy rate from the call rate. Specifically, the base rate is the seven-day RP rate between the BoK and its counterpart financial institutions. Thus, a change in the base rate leads to a shift in the demand curve for reserves, not a movement along the demand curve for reserves.

To examine this relation in more detail, let us consider bank demand for reserves in the call market, D. Let r_p and r_c be the policy rate and the call rate, respectively. Then, D can be represented by the negative function of r_c and the positive function of r_p as follows:

$$D = D(r_c : r_p) \text{ with } \frac{\partial D}{\partial r_c} < 0 \text{ and } \frac{\partial D}{\partial r_p} > 0 \tag{2}$$

The demand for the bank reserves is negatively related to the call rate as before. It is, however, to be noted that bank demand for the reserves is also affected by the policy rate, namely, the interest rate in the seven-day RP market. Both the call market and RP market are closely substitutable for each other. If banks can borrow at lower interest rates from the BoK or other money markets than from the call market, the demand for the reserves in the call market will go down for any call rate. Inversely, if banks have to borrow at higher interest rates in the alternative RP market, the demand for the reserves in the call market will go up for any call rate. Thus, the demand for the reserves in the call market is positively related to the policy rate, which is under the complete

---

[1] For example, the ECB sets the seven-day RP rate as the policy rate for MRO and directs the EONIA rate to the policy rate level. Before the global financial crisis, the BoE also used the one-week RP rate as its policy rate and used an open market operation to make the overnight interest rate, the index of the short-term financial market, equal to policy rate.

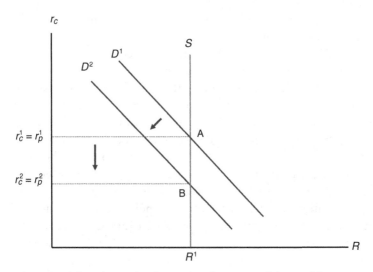

Figure 8.4 The relationship between policy rate and demand for reserves in the call market

control of the BoK. Let us suppose that the BoK cuts its policy rate, say, from r_p^1 to r_p^2. Then, the demand for reserves in the call market drops, which will be represented by a parallel shift to the new demand curve D^2 from D^1 (see Figure 8.4).[2] This will immediately lower the call rate at r_c^2. Thus, a drop in the policy rate will induce a downwards shift of the demand for reserves leading to a drop in the call rate without any change in the supply of the reserves. Let us suppose that r_c^2 happens to deviate from r_p^2. Then, all market participants anticipate that the BoK will intervene in the call market through the open market operations, such that they match each other. In other words, they know that, if the call rate r_c^2 exceeds r_p^2, then the BoK will supply reserves in the call market by open market purchase, and, if r_c^2 falls below r_p^2, then the BoK will absorb reserves from the call market by open market sales. Thus, the changes in the policy rate lead to changes of the same size in the call rate. Figure 8.4 shows that, when the policy rate is cut, the demand for

---

[2] In the United States, the federal funds rate is both a policy rate and a target-operation rate. Thus, in order for a change in policy rate to shift the demand for reserves to a new demand curve, it is assumed that the demand for reserves is affected by the expected future policy rate as well as policy rate. Then, a change in policy rate can shift the demand for reserves through the corresponding change in the expected future policy rate. See Friedman and Kuttner (2011).

reserves will shift from D^1 to D^2 and the call rate will fall from r_c^2 to r_p^2. Thus, different levels of call rates can coexist at any given reserve supply.

The concrete operation of interest rate targeting by the BoK can be summarised as follows:

> First, the MPB sets its policy rate, or base rate, at a desired level, taking the economic conditions into account. Then, it announces its decision, and this information is instantaneously communicated to the market. The change in policy rate is a signal to adjust market expectations. As soon as the announcement has been made, the call rate immediately adjusts to match the policy rate and the monetary policy takes effect, even without any intervention to adjust the liquidity in the call market by the open market operations. The BoK can set the base rate at any level that it wants. This is because, among other things, market participants believe that the BoK can provide (or absorb) as much liquidity as it wishes through its power to print money, and consequently they will not stand against the BoK's decision. For example, if the BoK announces that the base rate is 2 per cent, they will neither trade at a rate that is less than 2 per cent, nor at one that is more than 2 per cent. Market participants think that they can borrow from, or lend to, the BoK at 2 per cent at any time. As a result, monetary policy is often called the 'open mouth policy', by which the signal effect through the announcement replaces the liquidity effect through the open market operations.
>
> Second, through the Financial Markets Department, the BoK intervenes in the interbank market to prevent the short-term call rate from deviating from the announced policy rate, by supplying and absorbing liquidity through the open market operations in the call market. This is because the call rate, the overnight interbank-market interest rate, serves as the starting point of the monetary policy transmission channel. Thus, the BoK wishes to ensure that the call rate does not deviate significantly from the policy rate. It means that that the term-risk of the seven-day collateral-based RP rate can be offset by the credit risk of the unsecured call transaction. However, this fine-tuning operation of the BoK is implemented just to reduce unnecessary fluctuations in the call rate and to smooth its movement. Thus, the call rate is adjusted endogenously, rather than exogenously (Thornton, 2004). Figure 8.5 shows how the BoK's open market operation is used to keep the call rate in line with the policy rate, and not to determine the call rate (fine-tuning).

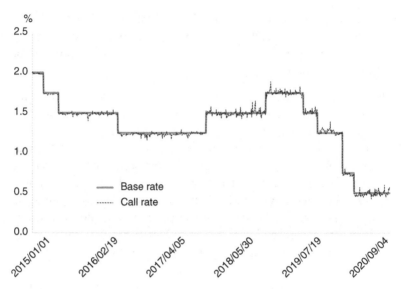

Figure 8.5 Base rate and call rate
Source: ECOS, BoK.

Figure 8.6 shows that, under this interest rate targeting, the relationship between the reserves and policy rate is independent. The policy rate is determined just by signalling, and requires no operation or action to change the supply of the reserves in the short-term financial market. Signalling works as a device for changing market expectations.

Notwithstanding this, the principle of this decoupling does not seem to have been clearly understood. Even some members of the MPB, for example, seemed to have suffered from this confusion, especially when the BoK decided to shift from the monetary targeting regime to the interest rate targeting one. The confusion came from the observation that interest rate cuts did not necessarily lead to an increase in the supply of reserves and money stocks. The problem that troubled them is well illustrated by the following comment.

Despite a cut in the interest rate, the growth rate of money has not increased and in this respect the effectiveness of the monetary policy seems to be severely constrained. (Bank of Korea, 2004)[3]

---

[3] This sentence has been translated into English from the 2004 Minutes of the BoK written in Korean.

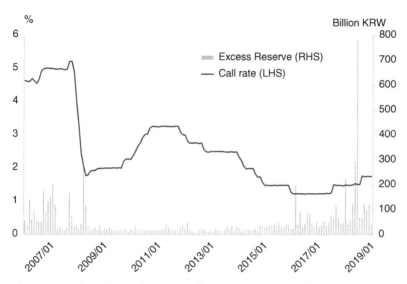

Figure 8.6 The relation between call rate movement and reserves changes
Source: ECOS, BoK.

Currently, the BoK does not determine the short-term interest rates by adjusting the reserves held by banks. Instead, it determines them by announcement, regardless of their liquidity positions. In other words, it is conducting *monetary policy without money*. Under these circumstances, the open market operations are no longer critically important for interest rate setting.

8.3 The Operation of the Corridor System

As already examined, once the MPB decides on the policy rate, it immediately announces it. Then, following this decision, the Financial Markets Department of the BoK makes sure that the short-term call rate does not deviate from the policy rate in order to maintain the confidence of the market participants in its monetary policy and to ensure the effectiveness of its monetary policy. To smoothen the volatility of the call rate, the Financial Markets Department normally relies on two instruments: open market operations and the standby facility system. In the past, the open market operations had been actively used to achieve the reserve targets. Under the interest rate targeting system, however, the daily open market operations are carried out passively in order to reduce call rate fluctuations (fine-tuning transactions), leaving thereby the open market operations and standby facilities some-what indifferent to their impact. With two standing facilities, Liquidity Adjustment Loans and Deposits, the BoK is currently operating a corridor system which establishes a ceiling and a floor in order to limit the fluctuation of short-term call rates.

To derive the equilibrium call rate under the corridor system, let us consider a model developed by Woodford (2001). Then, a representa-tive bank j maximises expected profit by lending its surplus reserves in the interbank market. But, because the bank is subject to the liquidity shock, ε_j, which has the probability distribution of mean 0 and stand-ard deviation σ_j, it should receive a standby loan from the central bank and pay interests if its reserves are in shortage. Conversely, if the net reserve turns out too ample, the bank will place it to the central bank as standby deposit and thus earns interests. Then, the bank j's desired reserves, R_j, are determined from the first order condition for the maximisation of expected profit. Let i denote the call rate, and i_l and i_d the standby lending and deposit rates. Then, the marginal return from interbank loan, i, must equal the marginal expected cost of using the standing facilities, which can be derived as $i_l F_j(-R_j) + i_d(1 - F_j(-R_j))$ with F_j being the cumulative probability function of liquidity shock ε_j.[4] In equilibrium, the aggregate demand for reserves equals the supply from the central bank such that $\sum R_j = R$, where R is the aggregate bank reserves at the central bank. The equilibrium call rate is thus given by:

$$i = i_d + (i_l - i_d)F(-R/\sum \sigma_j) \tag{3}$$

---

[4] Let ε_j be the liquidity shock that arrives at the end of the day. If $\varepsilon_j + R_j < 0$, then the net reserve of the bank becomes negative at the end of the day, and the bank should pay the cost i_l for its stand-by loan from the central bank. Conversely, if $\varepsilon_j + R_j > 0$ such that the net reserve turns out positive after the arrival of liquidity shock, the bank earns i_d from its stand-by deposits to the central bank. Because $F_j(-R_j)$ denotes the probability that $\varepsilon_j + R_j < 0$, the marginal expected cost of using the standing facilities is $i_l F_j(-R_j) + i_d(1 - F_j(-R_j))$. See Woodford (2001) and Sveriges Riksbank (2014) for the detailed derivation.

where F is a cumulative probability distribution function with a mean of zero and a variance of one.

Thus, in this corridor system, the BoK can theoretically determine the call rate, which is an operating target, either by controlling the reserves of the entire banking system through its open market operations or by altering the upper and lower bounds of the interest rate corridor. Clearly, if the width of the corridor is so small that the upper and lower bounds are not much different, the interest rate is almost set by the lower bound.

Generally speaking, the standby facilities can have the same function as the open market operations. For instance, by ensuring a slight shortage of the reserves in the interbank market, the BoK can conduct the open market RP purchase of the bonds based upon the fixed-rate tenders, which will be equivalent to the standby loans in its effect. In practice, however, the adjustment of the interest rate corridor was hardly ever used in Korea. This may be due to the fact that, while the fine-tuning open market operations could be conducted routinely by the BoK staff, the change of the corridor should be determined by the MPB members during their regular interest rate-setting meetings. Thus, frequent adjustments of the corridor are neither possible nor efficient. Furthermore, the width of the corridor is very large. This has made the BoK conduct its fine-tuning open market operations so strictly that the call rates varied too little to the point of nullifying the rationale of actually setting up the corridor. It may be necessary for the BoK to refrain from intervening too meticulously in the call market while reducing the width of the corridor.

Let us consider the fine-tuning operation of the BoK. In this case, the goal of the BoK is to keep the net reserve positions of interbank markets at zero through an RP operation such that $F(0)=1/2$. Then, the fundamental equation is simplified as follows:

$$i = \frac{1}{2}(i_l + i_d) \tag{3'}$$

Thus, the target rate is in the middle of the upper and lower bounds of the corridor, which is referred to as a symmetrical corridor scheme. Figure 8.7 illustrates this system.

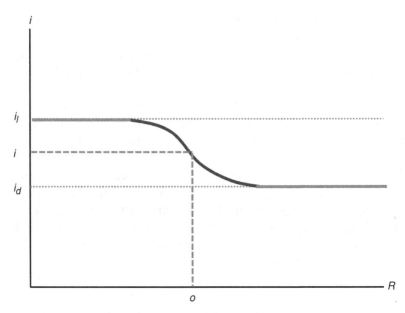

Figure 8.7 Interest rate under a symmetric corridor system

If the BoK intends to absorb bank reserves in the interbank market, the target call rate will start to rise, and, as sufficiently large reserves are absorbed, the banks will rely on the standby Liquidity Adjustment Loans from the BoK. Then, the call rate will be equal to the standby loan interest rate under the corridor system. That is, $i = i_l$ because $F(-R/\sum\sigma_i) = 1$, when R has a large negative value, say, R'. Figure 8.8 illustrates this case. During the high-growth period of the Korean economy, the BoK was under such a system. For example, the Korean economy was suffering from a chronic shortage of funds, and credit rationing prevailed. In order to cope with the Korean banks' persistent shortages of the reserves and to support their liquidity adjustments, the BoK operated the re-discount facility which had a feature of automatic loans. Under this system, the commercial banks could obtain the loans from the BoK, at any time when they needed them, by offering their commercial bills for re-discount. The re-discounting facility resulted in commercial banks becoming dependent to a high degree on the BoK

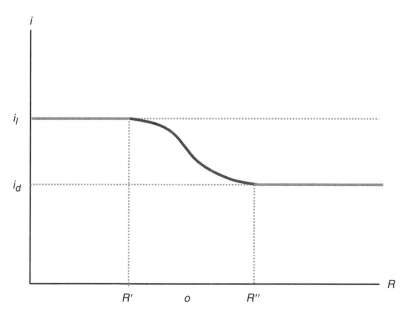

Figure 8.8 Interest rate under the ceiling and floor systems

loans.[5] The BoK often relied on the 'Window Guidance' to discourage the banks to use it. Currently, as already mentioned, such a facility is rarely used because of the so-called stigma effect. Under normal circumstances, the banks are reluctant to borrow from the BoK, for fear of damaging their reputation.

Conversely, if the BoK supplies sufficiently large reserves in the interbank call market, as shown in Figure 8.8, the target call rate can be determined at the lower bound of the corridor. In other words, $i = i_d$ because $F(-R/\sum \sigma_i) = 0$, when R has a large positive value, say, R''. This system is called the floor system. Korea has yet to enter into such a system, but this system became common in many central banks of the advanced economies, such as the US FRS, after the global financial crisis of 2008.

The advantage of the corridor system is that central banks could provide the market with as much liquidity as it desires *independently* of

---

[5] According to Bindsell (2004), the German Reich Bank in the early twentieth century was also under such a system.

the interest rate level, thereby securing additional policy instruments than that of the interest rate (Goodfriend, 2002). Thus, if a crisis like the 2008 global financial crisis causes liquidity shortages in the financial markets, central banks can use both interest rates and liquidity-supply instruments simultaneously in order to stabilise the market. However, as already pointed out, the use of the standing facilities is very rare because of the obsession, on the part of the BoK staff, to adhere to strict open market operations, which rendered the corridor mechanism obsolete by setting the width of the corridor too wide.

8.4 Guiding Yield Curve

Once the BoK's policy rate has been set, it affects the short-term interest rates, which, in turn, influence the long-term interest rates, as well as bank deposit and loan interest rates. Thus, although monetary policy is usually understood as setting the policy rate, in practice, it is a process through which short-term interest rates, bank loans and deposit rates, and long-term interest rates all move in the desired direction in order to ultimately affect both prices and the real economy. Therefore, the essential step for the BoK to take is to monitor all the different financial markets and thereby ensure that the transmission of monetary policy comes into play as anticipated. The monitoring process carried out by the BoK is as follows:

> First, the BoK makes sure that a change in the policy rate leads to a change in interest rates in the call market and in the other short-term financial markets. The short-term financial market in Korea is a market for financial instruments with a maturity of less than one year, which consists of the call market, the re-purchase agreement market, the CD market, the commercial paper (CP) market, the short-term MSB market, and so on. A distortion in the short-term interest rates, therefore, can lead to a breakdown in the transmission channel of the monetary policy. For instance, CD rates in Korea were often too rigid, obstructing the smooth transmission from call rates to the financial markets (see Box 8.2).
> Second, bank loan and deposit interest rates have traditionally been the sole most important transmission channel of monetary policy in Korea because of the underdevelopment of its capital markets. The question is whether the deposit and loan rates appropriately

Box 8.2 KORIBOR and COFIX as Reference Interest Rates

The BoK does not have any effective authority to monitor the movement of bank deposit and loan rates. This is, above all, because the Office of Bank Supervision was separated from the BoK after the reorganisation of the financial supervisory system in Korea in 1998. As the newly created FSC along with the FSS monopolised the regulation and supervision of banks, the BoK lost all its power to oversee the rate-setting processes of the commercial banks.

Against this backdrop, the FSC took the initiative in the reform of the market reference interest rate, based upon which the commercial banks fix their deposit and loan interest rates. The CD rate in Korea has long been used as a reference rate for commercial banks' deposits and loans, in particular, for variable rate mortgage loans. Collecting the data on the yields of the CDs issued by commercial banks with a credit rating of AAA from ten securities companies, the Korea Financial Investment Association calculates the CD rate as a simple average of the eight yields, after excluding the highest and lowest yields submitted. However, the CD rates are too rigid to reflect the banks' funding costs properly, due to the small size of primary and secondary markets. Given the uncertainty in the issuing amount, the movement of the CD rate often differed from short-term interest rates. Figure B8.2 shows that there has been constant controversy over the rigidity of CD rate.

In July 2004, the FSC introduced the KORIBOR, benchmarking the United Kingdom's LIBOR (London Inter-Bank Offered Rate). The KORIBOR is the offered rate for uncollateralised interbank Korean *won* borrowing. KORIBOR is calculated and announced by the following procedures:

First, the twelve Korean banks quote their offered rates for each maturity every business day to the KORIBOR calculator ('Yeonhap Informax'). The calculator determines the KORIBOR by arithmetic averaging of the middle six of the twelve interest rates. However, as a result of the LIBOR crisis in July 2012, efforts to improve the credibility and utilisation of the KORIBOR were made. As a part of these efforts, the KORIBOR's basic principle of quoting the rates, and the internal control system for the reference banks, were further strengthened. As a result, from July 2014, the KORIBOR has not been calculated for some maturities with low usability. Thus, the announced rates were reduced from ten to six.

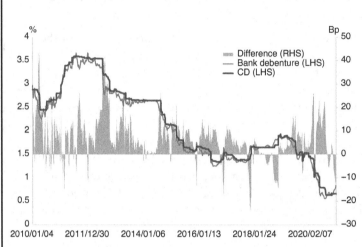

Figure B8.2 Movement of the CD rate
Source: ECOS, BoK.

In addition, the FSC introduced the COFIX calculated as the average interest rate of bank funding products in 2010 as a new loan reference interest rate. Since then, banks have been actively launching loan products with their rate linked to the COFIX (COFIX-linked loans) and making it easier to switch from existing loans to COFIX-linked loans. As a result, they have been rapidly replacing CD rate-linked loans. Based upon the financing information provided by eight banks, the COFIX is calculated by the Korea Federation of Banks, and it is announced on the fifteenth day of every month. As of the end of 2016, COFIX-linked loans accounted for 31.3 per cent of the total floating rate loans, while CD rate-linked loans accounted for 14.3 per cent. In the case of mortgage loans, in particular, COFIX-linked loans accounted for 66.5 per cent. The COFIX is the average cost of funds, with an average maturity of nine to ten months, and is announced only once a month. Thus, banks still tend to prefer CD rates to COFIX as a reference base for floating rate loans with one to two years of maturity. In July 2012, as a short-term reference rate, a short-term COFIX was introduced for use in corporate loans with short maturities and household credit loans. The short-term COFIX is the average interest rate of short-term (three-month) funding products and has been announced once a week upon the basis of weekly acquired new funds.

It is important to note that, in order to monitor short-term interest rates and deposit and loan interest rates effectively, the BoK has strengthened its collaboration with the FSC and the FSS. Currently, the BoK can request the FSS to conduct a joint bank examination if the MPB deems it necessary for the implementation of monetary and credit policies, but, clearly, this will not be sufficient for the BoK to ensure the smooth functioning of monetary policy.

reflect the short-term market interest rates or not. For instance, although there was no change in base rate, loan interest rate increased by almost 25 bp amid the dampened economic activity in 2020. The Korean government (FSC) pushed it through just to reduce the demand for real estate. In general, the commercial banks in Korea set their own loan rates, adding their profit margins to their internal base rates, based upon the market reference interest rates. But, in determining the profit margins, the Korean banks are able to wield considerable discretion and arbitrariness, which often results in their undermining the smooth transmission of the BoK's monetary policy. It is therefore important for the BoK to monitor the movements of deposit and loan interest rates closely.

Third, along with the development of the capital market, the Korean economy is rapidly shifting from a bank-centred economy to a financial-market-oriented economy. Accordingly, long-term interest rates have emerged as the principal transmission channel of monetary policy. However, there is no way of ensuring a smooth transition from short-term interest rates to long-term interest rates. In general, long-term interest rates are affected by various factors, such as the outlook for economic growth and prices, turbulence in international financial markets, and variations in the supply and demand conditions for government bonds, in addition to monetary policy factors. For this reason, it remained a long-standing taboo for the BoK to attempt to manage long-term interest rates. For the BoK staff, long-term interest rates were not controllable and therefore could not be an operating target of monetary policy, although their movement was more important in stabilising real output and inflation than the short-term interest rates. In particular, the BoK staff who conduct the open market operations in the Financial Markets Department were extremely reluctant to engage in the operations of managing or guiding the long-term interest rates, citing the uncertainties in being able to *control* the long-term interest rates as a main hurdle or obstacle. It is probable that they are too concerned about their possible failure to guide the long-term interest rates in a desired direction if this becomes their new operating target.

But, if the BoK abandons trying to influence the long-term market interest rates on the grounds of the difficulty to control them, it would be tantamount to carrying out a monetary policy with no concern about the actual goal of the monetary policy. BoK staff who are tasked with the mechanical operation of steering the market interest rates towards the policy rate tend to forget about the goals, while the MPB members are basically responsible for the goals, rather than the operations. In this regard, it is necessary to distinguish between *controlling* long-term market interest rates and *guiding* long-term market interest rates. Even if the BoK cannot *control* the long-term interest rates as much as the short-term interest rates, it can still *guide* them through the open market operations and communication tools. In particular, the BoK needs to strengthen its communication tools, such as the forward guidance. Furthermore, since financial stability has become a new mandate from 2013, the BoK is responsible for stabilising volatile movement of long-term interest rates, especially when the financial market is turbulent. Therefore, there is no reason why the uncertainties in the *guidance* of long-term market interest rates should present too big a hurdle so as to prevent the BoK from pre-emptively and proactively influencing the long-term interest rates.

It goes without saying that the BoK should consider extending its operating target to the long-term interest rates if it wants to enhance the effectiveness of monetary policy in order to attain price, output, and financial stability. In this regard, monetary policy can be said to be an action that *guides* the interest rates on all the maturities of the yield curve.

Let R_t, be the long-term interest rate, with maturity n at period t. Then, R_t is expressed as the average of the current short-term interest rate r_t and future short-term interests r_{t+j} and term and risk premiums as in the following formula:

$$R_t = \frac{\left(r_t + E(r_{t+1}) + \ldots + E(r_{t+n-1})\right)}{n} + term_t + risk_t \qquad (4)$$

where $E(r_{t+j})$ is the expected short-term interest rate at period j while $term_t$ and $risk_t$ are, respectively, term and risk premiums.

As shown in equation (4), long-term interest rates are affected not only by the current and expected future short-term interest rates, but also by the term and risk premiums. Thus, to guide long-term interest rates and to adjust the slope of the yield curve, it is important that the BoK affects the expected future interest rates through its communication tools, such as forward guidance, or attempts to change the term and risk premiums by open market operations and other non-conventional actions, such as asset purchases or 'Operation Twist' used by the US FRS.

Figure 8.9 illustrates the movement of yield curve in normal times when monetary transmission works smoothly such that a fall in short-term

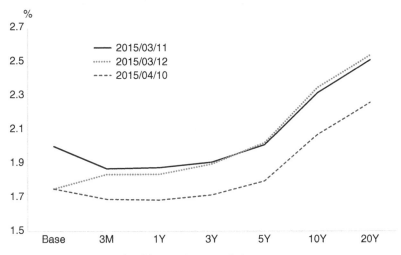

Figure 8.9 Reaction of yield curve in normal times

Note: The three-month interest rate is the yield on the MSBs, while long-term interest rates are based upon government bonds with maturities of more than one year.

Source: ECOS, BoK.

interest rates induces a corresponding drop in long-term interest rates. For example, by cutting its policy rate on 11 March 2015, the MPB was able to guide a downward shift in long-term interest rates with a short time lag. Thus, the BoK's policy action was appropriate in ensuring a smooth working of the monetary transmission channel.

However, long-term interest rates do not always respond as anticipated. For instance, the MPB decided to raise the policy rate on 30 November 2017. However, by postponing the chances to raise the interest rate for too long, the MPB's delay failed to guide long-term interest rates. Its decision, when it was finally announced, had no forward-looking effect. As the MPB was not leading the market participants' expectations, but was, instead, lagging behind them, its decision had no repercussions at all beyond the call market. Figure 8.10 shows that long-term interest rates barely moved, despite the hike in the policy rate.

As Figure 8.11 shows, the case in which long-term interest rates move in the opposite direction to short-term interest rates offers a much more serious case, one which puts the monetary authorities in great difficulty. This phenomenon is well known as the so-called Greenspan's conundrum. When the US FRS raised its policy rate

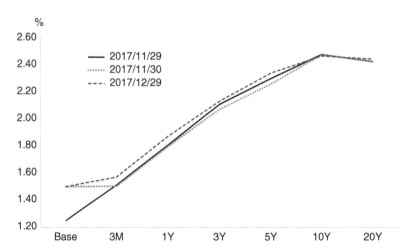

Figure 8.10 Reaction of yield curve with disconnected long- and short-term rates
Source: ECOS, BoK.

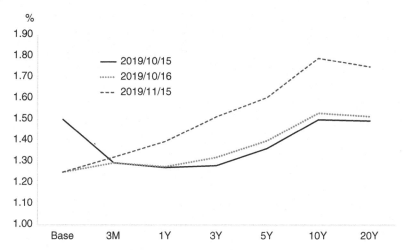

Figure 8.11 Reaction of yield curve under the 'Greenspan conundrum'
Source: ECOS, BoK.

from 1.0 per cent to 3.50 per cent between June 2004 and August 2005, the ten-year government bond yield in the United States fell from 4.7 per cent to 3.9 per cent, which Alan Greenspan, the Fed chairman at the time, found puzzling. This conundrum can frequently be observed in Korea as well. For instance, a policy rate cut in May 2015 failed to decrease, but actually increased the long-term interest rates, in complete contrast to the MPB's intentions. Most recently, this occurred again on 15 October 2019 when the MPB decided to cut the base rate by 25 bp, from 1.5 per cent to 1.25 per cent in order to boost the economy. Following a short delay, the long-term interest rate went up, completely nullifying the intentions of the MPB, which was to stimulate the economy.

It is clear that long-term interest rates are more difficult to control compared to short-term interest rates. Notwithstanding this, long-term interest rate targeting policy is carried out by the BoJ. In September 2016, the BoJ shifted from a QQE to the so-called QQE with Yield Curve Control, through which the BoJ controls both short-term and long-term interest rates. That is to say, the BoJ decided to purchase JGBs to maintain ten-year JGB yields at 0 per cent, while setting short-term interest rates at –0.1 per cent for the banks depositing their reserves at the BoJ.

At the time of writing, it is too premature for the BoK to consider introducing QQE with Yield Curve Control. But, given that, more and more frequently, long-term interest rates have a different movement from short-term interest rates, it will be important for the BoK to develop some appropriate tools, particularly communication tools, which should be based upon the communication capacity of the MPB members, with regard to the future paths of macroeconomic variables. Successful communication is, indeed, a very effective tool to change the slope of the yield curve without necessitating any direct actions.[6]

---

[6] This is particularly illustrated by the speech of Mario Draghi, former ECB president. On 26 July 2012, in the midst of the euro crisis, Draghi delivered the momentous speech in which he avowed: 'Within our mandate, the ECB is ready to do whatever it takes to preserve the euro. And believe me, it will be enough' (Draghi, 2012). A week later, the ECB announced a programme to buy the bonds of its distressed countries, known as Outright Monetary Transactions (OMTs). Traders reacted immediately. Although the ECB never actually used this programme, the mere promise was sufficient to calm investors and bring down the long-term bond yields across the euro zone.

9 | Foreign Exchange Market Intervention and Monetary Policy

There are three key questions with regard to the exchange rate policy in Korea: (1) the determination of the appropriate level of the exchange rate; (2) the reduction of exchange rate volatility; and (3) the connection between the interest rate and the exchange rate. Until very recently, the Korean exchange authorities put a primary emphasis on keeping the exchange rate of the Korean *won* at an appropriate level. Along with the liberalisation of capital flows, the priority shifted over time towards reducing excessive fluctuations of the exchange rates. Furthermore, as interest rate changes increasingly have a stronger impact on capital movement, monetary policy has also become inseparable from exchange rate policy. This chapter examines the direct and indirect FX rate policies of the Korean government and the BoK.

9.1 Overview of Foreign Exchange Market Intervention in Korea

9.1.1 The Goals of the FX Market Interventions

Foreign exchange market intervention is a policy designed to achieve exchange rate stability. Currently, FX policy in Korea is conducted jointly by the MOEF and the BoK (collectively called the FX authorities). When the BoK was first established in 1950, it was responsible for all FX policies, including the formulation and execution of the policies, as well as FX regulations. However, with the enactment of the Foreign Exchange Control Act in December 1961 and the subsequent revision of Bank of Korea Act in May 1962, these responsibilities were largely transferred to the government. Since then, the BoK has no formal authority or responsibility for FX rate policy. According to Article 83 of the Bank of Korea Act, 'the Bank of Korea shall exercise an advisory function over the government's policies on exchange rates, the foreign currency loans and deposits of banking institutions, and the setting of FX overbought and oversold position limits on them'. Thus, the MPB, even though it is the highest decision-making body of the BoK, has little competence over FX policies or market interventions.

Notwithstanding this, the MOEF conducts FX policy in close consultation with the BoK. The BoK takes charge of the daily management of FX policy and implements market interventions because it owns the payment and settlement system of Korean *won*, along with the banks, and has a well-trained staff to conduct such interventions. Furthermore, two institutions separately manage the official FX reserves with the BoK, through its own account and with the MOEF through the Foreign Exchange Stabilisation Fund. Thus, it can be said that the BoK exercises FX policy jointly with the MOEF, although the latter holds the final responsibility for these policies.

Foreign exchange market intervention (FX intervention) usually takes the form of purchasing or selling foreign currencies against the Korean *won* to influence the exchange rate of the Korean *won* against the US dollar. However, the FX authorities frequently express their positions or views verbally on the exchange rate movements to change the exchange rate expectations of the market participants. The most recent verbal intervention was to cope with the market volatility after the outbreak of the COVID-19 pandemic, as indicated in the Korean government's statement that it would take 'pre-emptive and decisive' actions if the volatility in the FX market became too 'excessive'.

Reasons for FX intervention include both the targeting of the exchange rate level and the reduction of exchange rate volatility. Prior to the 1997 currency crisis, the Korean government targeted an appropriate level for the exchange rate and intervened in the FX market to steer the nominal exchange rate of the Korean *won* to the target rate. However, the determination of the optimum target exchange rate remained for a long time the most critical and difficult question for the Korean FX authorities. Conceptually, an equilibrium exchange rate that simultaneously attains both internal and external equilibria can be considered to be the optimum target exchange rate. In practice, however, this concept is of no practical use because the estimation of the equilibrium exchange rate is extremely arbitrary, and diverse estimates are made, depending on the model and methodology deployed. Thus, one of the most commonly used methods is to use the real effective exchange rate, the weighted average of the bilateral exchange rates of the Korean *won* against its partners' currencies adjusted by relative prices. The real effective exchange rate is favoured by policymakers in many countries, including the BoK, because its concept is clear and is easy to calculate.[1]

However, as Korea moved to the free floating exchange rate system after the 1997 currency crisis, exchange rate targeting intervention was interrupted in favour of intervention to replenish foreign reserves from an empty vault. Subsequently, as the Korean authorities came to accumulate sufficient foreign reserves, the goal of FX intervention changed again. Currently, the goal is to limit excessive exchange rate fluctuations by undertaking smoothing operations, as the exchange rate varies with wide margins (see Box 9.1). The Korean *won* is subject to a high degree of volatility, especially because of the elevated openness of Korean capital markets. International financial market turbulence always has major repercussions on exchange rates through capital movements.

Another objective of FX intervention is to alleviate the funding demand for FX by commercial banks experiencing US dollar shortages, especially during crises. As FX funding shortage will put depreciatory pressure on the Korean *won* and increase exchange rate volatility, the Korean authorities often provide US dollar liquidity to banks to ease imbalances in the FX fund (loan) market (Ryoo et al., 2013).

The Korean authorities thus carry out their FX intervention operations both in the FX market and in the foreign currency fund market. While the FX market is a market in which FX trading occurs through the transfer of ownership between currencies, the foreign currency fund market is a market in which foreign currency funds are lent and borrowed. Thus, while an intervention in the FX market is reflected in a change in Korea's official foreign reserves, which will directly affect the exchange rate of the Korean *won*, the interventions through the foreign currency fund market lead to a change in the supply of, and demand for, foreign currency loans, which indirectly affect the exchange rate through the interest rate related to foreign currency loan transactions. It is noteworthy that these interventions were particularly important during the 1997 and 2008 financial crises. The Korean authorities were then the lenders of last resort in foreign currency when Korean banks experienced serious FX-funding difficulties.

---

[1] It is noteworthy that, in some countries, such as Singapore and Taiwan, the nominal effective exchange rate is targeted (see Chow and Wong, 2020).

Box 9.1 Optimal Exchange Rate that Minimises Exchange Rate Volatility

The intervention of the Korean FX authorities in the FX market has been criticised as manipulating exchange rates in favour of Korean industry. Reflecting upon the fact that Korea has annual trade surpluses of around US$20 billion with the United States, the US Treasury Department, in particular through its semi-annual 'Report to Congress on Macroeconomic and Exchange Policies of Major Trading Partners of the US', attempts to assess whether the Korean government intervenes unfairly to stem the appreciation of the Korean *won* against the US dollar, and to maintain its trade surpluses with the United States. In the event that Korea was found to be a currency manipulator, the United States could designate Korea as such and thereby impose trade sanctions. However, such claims are no longer true because the current goals of the Korean FX market interventions are to reduce the volatility of exchange rates.

Currently, Korea has important trade relationships with many trading *bloc*s in the world, including Japan, China, and the euro area, as well as the United States. Thus, stabilising the bilateral exchange rates with all its trading partners is important. But, the *won*–dollar exchange rate affects the *won*–yen, *won*–*yuan* and *won*–euro exchange rates through cross rates. For instance, the *won*–*yen* exchange rate is calculated by multiplying the *won*–dollar rate by the dollar–*yen* rate. So, the *won*-dollar rate affects Korea's trade relationship with all partners. Furthermore, whenever there are fluctuations in the bilateral exchange rates between Korea's trading partners, such as the *yen*–dollar rate or the euro–dollar rate, then the Korean FX authorities have to offset them by adjusting the *won*–dollar exchange rate. When the JPY depreciated by 40 per cent against the US dollar during 2013 due to the quantitative and qualitative easing by the BoJ, for instance, the *won*–*yen* exchange rate would have appreciated by the same proportion, unless it was offset by the FX market interventions of the Korean FX authorities. Because Korea has chronic trade deficits with Japan, this would only serve to aggravate them. In fact, the

Korean *won* appreciated sharply from about 1,400 *won* per 100 yen in 2012 to about 900 *won* in 2015. Thus, the Korean authorities tried to offset the effect of the depreciation of the *yen*–dollar by the deprecation of the *won*–dollar in order to mitigate the *won*–*yen* exchange rate volatility.

Against this backdrop, we can consider an optimal exchange rate that minimises exchange rate volatility V defined as follows:

$$Min\ V = \sum_{j}^{4} w_j (s_j^{krw} - \bar{s}_j^{krw})^2$$

where w_j is the trade weight for country j, which can be the United States, Japan, China, and the EU, and s_j^{krw} represents the bilateral exchange rates of the KRW against country j's currencies, such as the USD, the JPY, the CNY, and the EUR.

It is noteworthy that the *won*–*yen*, the *won*–*yuan* and the *won*–euro exchange rates are determined by the cross-rates between the *won*–dollar rate, on the one hand, and the dollar–*yen*, the dollar–*yuan* and the dollar–euro exchange rates, on the other hand. That is, $s_{jpy}^{krw} = s_{usd}^{krw} \times s_{jpy}^{usd}$, $s_{cny}^{krw} = s_{usd}^{krw} \times s_{cny}^{usd}$ and $s_{eur}^{krw} = s_{usd}^{krw} \times s_{eur}^{usd}$. Finally, $\bar{s}_j^{krw}$ represents the base year exchange rates of the Korean *won* against the currencies of its trading partners.

From this optimisation, we can calculate the exchange rate that will minimise volatility if it is targeted by the Korean FX authorities. Figure B9.1 shows the actual and optimal target exchange rates of the Korean *won* against the US dollar.

It is notable that, since the latter half of 2013, the optimal *won*–dollar rates hover far above the actual *won*–dollar rates, which means that the exchange rate of the *won* should depreciate substantially against the US dollar in order to minimise its exchange rate volatility. This gap occurred because of the sharp depreciation of the JPY. Clearly, the interventions to prevent the appreciation of the Korean *won* were not acts of manipulating the exchange rate, but a response to reduce the exchange rate volatility caused by the exchange rate instability between Korea's two major trading partners, the United States and Japan.

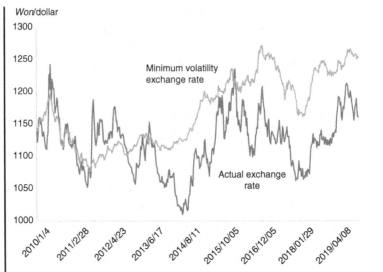

Figure B9.1 Actual and optimal target *won*–dollar exchange rates
Note: The year 2010 is taken as the base year. The exchange rates for 2010 were 1,156 *won*/dollar, 1,532 *won*/euro, 1,320 *won*/yen, and 171 *won*/ *yuan*.
Source: ECOS, BoK.

9.1.2 Direct FX Market Intervention

The BoK intervenes in the FX market through agents selected from among the major banks. To this end, it imposes a confidentiality requirement on these agent banks to maintain secrecy concerning their interventions. As for the criteria used to select the agent banks, priority is given to the banks with no default risk that play an active role as market makers, providing the BoK with instant market information (Ryoo et al., 2013).

Information relating to interventions has remained confidential until very recently. Thus, the exact extent of FX interventions was not known. However, concerned about the possible designation of Korea as an exchange rate manipulator by the US Treasury Department, the government decided to publish the FX intervention data from the second half of 2018 onwards. Figure 9.1 shows that, except for

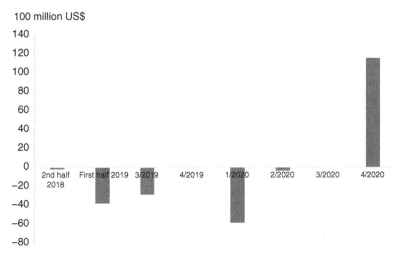

Figure 9.1 FX net balances of the Korean authorities (US$100 million)
Source: BoK homepage.

the fourth quarter, 2020, the FX interventions were not made to absorb the excess supply of US dollar liquidity, thereby intentionally stemming the appreciation of the Korean *won*, but rather to provide US dollar liquidity to Korean banks in order to prevent the Korean *won* from depreciating too much.

The Korean authorities also carried out interventions based upon forward contracts. During the 1997 currency crisis, the authorities conducted its first forward intervention to defend the value of the Korean *won*. Forward intervention was the preferred intervention tool because selling the US dollar and buying the Korean *won* through forward contracts allowed the authorities to intervene without depleting the official foreign reserves until the due date and thus camouflaged the size of the freely available foreign reserves. However, the BoK was not the first central bank that intervened in the forward market.[2]

---

[2] According to Bordo (2009), for example, the BoE had actively used forward market interventions to defend the value of the British pound during the sterling crisis in 1964–1967. This allowed the BoE to deploy twice as much as the amount of its official foreign reserves. However, as the interventions failed, this resulted in huge losses at the BoE. Like the BoE, the Korean authorities also incurred huge losses through these interventions (see Chapter 10).

Since 1999, the market has grown for NDF transactions in which the settlement of the difference between the contracted forward rate and the prevailing spot exchange rate takes place at maturity. The notional amount is never exchanged, hence the name 'non-deliverable'. These NDF transactions are settled in US dollars, and trade over-the-counter in offshore markets. Currently, the NDF market for the Korean *won* is the world's largest and most liquid market with a daily turnover of US$60 billion (Schmittmann et al., 2020). The Korean authorities, especially led by the MOEF, have frequently intervened in this offshore forward market. One reason why the Korean government preferred to intervene through offshore NDF transactions was that, as in the case of forward market interventions, these operations had a large leverage effect, allowing the FX authorities to conduct them with much smaller settlement risks than ordinary forward operations.

But how do the NDF transactions between Korean banks and non-residents affect the exchange rate of the Korean *won*? Suppose that a non-resident purchases US dollars in the *won*-dollar NDF market. Then, the Korean bank, which will be selling the US dollars as the counterparty, is exposed to currency risk due to its short position. To hedge against this risk, the bank will square its FX position by purchasing US dollars in the spot market. This will increase the demand for US dollars in the spot market and exert depreciation pressure on the Korean *won* against the US dollar. Conversely, if the difference between the contracted and the spot rate is settled on the due date, the FX position of the Korean bank will be unwound, and the bank will end up with the sale of its US dollars in the spot market to clear its long position. Thus, contrary to the NDF purchase contracts, the supply of US dollars will increase in the spot market and exert downwards pressure on the *won*–dollar exchange rate, which will nullify its initial effect. The effect of these interventions on the exchange rate is, at best, temporary until the maturity date.

Figure 9.2 shows that the variation of the *won*–dollar exchange rate was significantly related to the size of the NDF net purchases of US dollars by non-residents.

Given the sensitivity of Korean exports to the exchange rate of the Korean *won*, the Korean government continued to intervene in the NDF market in order to stem the too rapid appreciation of the

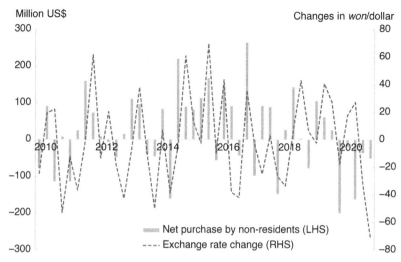

Figure 9.2 The net purchases of NDF contracts by non-residents and the variation of the *won*–dollar exchange rate
Source: BoK.

Korean *won* until the outbreak of the global financial crisis in 2008. These interventions ended up with significant losses for the Korean government (Moon and Rhee, 2006).

9.1.3 Indirect Intervention through FX Swaps

FX interventions in Korea are also carried out through the foreign currency fund market. The largest foreign currency fund market in Korea is the FX swap market. An FX swap agreement is a contract in which one party borrows one currency from, and simultaneously lends another to, a second party. Each party uses the repayment obligation of its counterparty as collateral and the amount of repayment is fixed at the forward rate as of the start of the contract. Thus, FX swaps can be viewed as FX risk-free collateralised borrowing and lending, and are mostly transacted on terms shorter than one year. Figure 9.3 shows the daily average turnover of the various FX transactions in the interbank Korean market, according to which, the FX swap turnover was the largest transaction, accounting for 50 per cent of the interbank FX turnover in 2020.

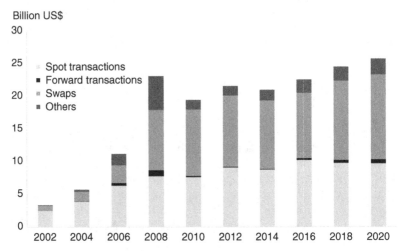

Figure 9.3 Daily average turnover of foreign exchange transactions by type in the interbank market
Source: BoK.

FX swaps have been employed to raise foreign currencies, both for financial institutions and their customers, including exporters and importers, as well as institutional investors who wish to hedge their FX positions. To look at the basic mechanism of FX swap transactions, consider the following CIP condition:

$$r_t - r_t^* = \frac{(F_t - E_t)}{E_t} \tag{1}$$

where r_t and r_t^* denote domestic and foreign interest rates while F_t and E_t are the forward and spot market exchange rates, respectively.

According to the CIP, the swap rate, which is denoted by $\frac{(F_t - E_t)}{E_t}$, should – at least theoretically – be equal to the interest rate differential between two countries $(r_t - r_t^*)$. In practice, however, the swap rate often deviates from the interest rate differential. For instance, if commercial banks have difficulties in funding US dollars or have a large demand for US dollars, the swap rate is likely to fall below the interest rate differential. The spot rate will go up, while the forward rate will go down, because they will have to buy US dollars in the spot market and sell them in the forward market. Conversely, when banks have plenty of foreign currency liquidity, they will sell on the spot market and buy on the forward market, which will result in the swap rate exceeding the

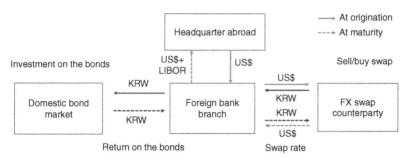

Figure 9.4 Example of an arbitrage transaction by a foreign bank branch using an FX swap

interest rate differential. A large deviation between the interest rate differential and swap rate can thus create an opportunity for arbitrage gain. In the case of Korea, foreign bank branches have played a central role in this arbitrage. Figure 9.4 shows the role that they have been playing in the swap market.

Let us consider, first, the case in which the swap rate falls below the interest rate differential. Let us suppose that the spot market exchange rate is 1,200 *won*/dollar and the three-month forward exchange rate is 1,205 *won*/dollar. Let us further suppose that the three-month MSB interest rate is 3 per cent per year, and the three-month LIBOR for borrowing US dollars is 1 per cent per year. Then, the swap rate is calculated as 1.67 per cent – (((1205–1200)/1200) × 4 × 100) – per year, which will be below the interest rate differential of 2 per cent per year (see Bank of Korea, 2016b). Thus, the foreign bank branches can earn arbitrage profits through carry trades. The detailed process is as follows:

> First, let us suppose that the foreign bank branches each borrow 1 US dollar at an interest rate of 1 per cent from their headquarter banks abroad. They then obtain Korean *won* through a sell/buy FX swap transaction (selling US dollars at the spot rate and re-purchasing the sum forward). For borrowing the Korean *won*, they pay the swap rate of 1.67 per cent as cost.
>
> Second, the foreign bank branches invest the Korean *won* thus obtained in MSBs, which will yield a profit of 2 per cent due to the interest differential between Korea and United States (3 per cent less 1 per cent). They then repay the borrowed

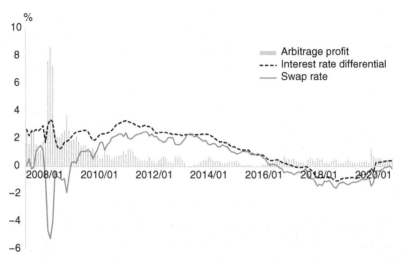

Figure 9.5 Swap rate and interest rate differential after the global financial crisis
Source: BoK.

Korean *won* with the acquired dollars when the forward transaction is due. As a result, the foreign bank branches will earn a return of 0.33 per cent, deducting the swap rate of 1.67 per cent from the interest rate differential of 2 per cent. Conversely, let us suppose that the swap rate is higher than the interest rate differential. Then, the foreign bank branches reimburse their borrowed US dollar, carrying out an FX buy/sell swap (buying US dollars at the spot rate and selling it forward).

Figure 9.5 shows the gap between the interest rate differential and the swap rate since 2008. As Korean banks were under the squeeze of the US dollar, the swap rate fell sharply. Korea's FX swap markets have persistently shown an excessive positive gap between the interest rate differential and the swap rate since the 2008 global financial crisis, thereby creating the potential opportunity for arbitrage profit.

The FX market in Korea is directly linked to the FX swap market. As indicated, when the swap rate fell sufficiently low due to the high demand for foreign currency caused by foreign capital outflows during the 2008 global financial crisis, banks found it very difficult to borrow foreign currency. Instead, they bought it in the spot market, which accelerated the depreciation of the Korean *won*, destabilising the FX market. As a result, the BoK had to intervene in the FX swap market, by directly providing foreign currency liquidity to banks. The BoK was a dual lender of last resort, as it provided foreign currency liquidity as well as domestic currency liquidity. For example, during the global financial crisis, the BoK helped to stabilise the FX swap market by lending a total of US$26 billion to the banks. Through competitive auction, it provided US$10 billion out of its official FX reserves and US$16.3 billion out of the US dollar currency swap with the US FRS.

In the aftermath of the global financial crisis, however, the BoK continued to provide the swap market with US dollars. These operations could have been the object of the complaints of exchange rate manipulation by the US Treasury Department, because the BoK bought US dollars in the spot exchange market and, at the same time, lent them in the FX swap market. The Korean authorities probably wanted to hide the increase in the amount of official foreign reserves, which might be interpreted as indirect proof of FX market intervention aimed at stemming the appreciation of the Korean *won*. Figure 9.6 shows the total amount of Korean foreign currency reserves, which was larger than the reported official foreign reserves because of the unreported foreign currency loans in the swap market.

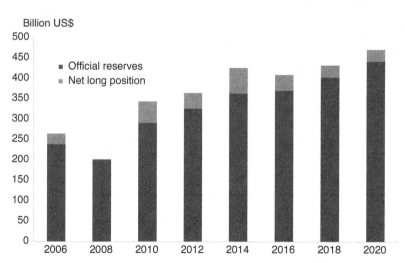

Figure 9.6 Total foreign reserves held by Korea (billion US$)
Source: BoK, IMF.

9.2 Intervention by the Bank of Korea and the Foreign Exchange Stabilisation Fund

Although the MOEF and the BoK constitute the FX authorities together, their FX interventions need to be examined separately because they respectively manage their own FX accounts.

9.2.1 Intervention by the BoK

If the BoK intervenes in the FX market, it affects the Korean economy through a change in the asset portfolio and money stock. In turn, a change in the asset portfolio affects the exchange rate of the Korean *won*, while a variation in the supply of money influences inflation or interest rates.

In general, the BoK's FX interventions are divided into non-sterilisation interventions that do not offset the change in the money supply resulting from the purchase or sales of FX, and sterilisation interventions that offset the change in the money supply through open market operations. Thus, non-sterilisation intervention is theoretically a combined operation of FX rate policy and monetary policy, while sterilisation intervention is a pure FX policy. For this reason, the BoK almost automatically carries out sterilisation operations, attempting to separate its monetary policy, which is independently decided by the MPB, from the exchange rate policy, which is set up by the MOEF. For example, when the BoK purchases US dollars, by selling Korean *won*, it simultaneously tries to absorb the subsequent increase in the money supply by open market operations, either through the outright sales of its own MSBs or through RP transactions, thereby preventing exchange rate policy from affecting monetary policy.

Figure 9.7(a) shows the trend of the MSBs, which are issued as a result of the BoK's FX purchases. The BoK began to issue MSBs on a large scale to replenish the official foreign reserves, which were depleted in the wake of the 1997 currency crisis. As the Korean economy continued to record current account surpluses, then the BoK increased the purchases of US dollars to stem the appreciation of the Korean *won* and, at the same time, sold the MSBs to sterilise the excess liquidities in the economy. However, from the mid-2000s onwards, when the interest rate in Korea remained higher than that of the United States, the costs associated with the sterilisation of the excess liquidity by open market operations became exorbitant. In particular, the economic costs of selling *won*-denominated MSBs at higher interest rates than those of the US dollar-denominated assets held, caused great controversy. This led to the establishment of the Reserve Management Group in 2011, which specialised in the investment management of the foreign reserves as a quasi-independent organisation within the BoK. Figure 9.7(b) shows that the BoK made a net loss in the mid-2000s. But, as the interest rates in Korea moved closer to US interest rates in the aftermath of the global financial crisis, the losses turned into profits.

Meanwhile, there has been controversy over the effectiveness of the sterilisation interventions in influencing the exchange rate. In the case of non-sterilisation interventions, the fall in domestic interest rates, which can arise from the increase in the quantity of money accompanied by the purchase of FX, may induce investors to prefer to hold foreign assets rather than domestic assets denominated in Korean *won*. The consequent portfolio adjustment effect can lead to a depreciation of the Korean *won*. In the case of sterilisation interventions, in contrast, there is no such change in the quantity of money. Thus, as long as the domestic interest rate remains unchanged, the interventions of the BoK should only have a limited impact; this will be particularly so, if the FX market is sufficiently large with ample liquidity. However, given the fact that the FX market in Korea is not yet big enough, and that the Korean *won* is not an internationally traded currency, the impact of the FX interventions is nonetheless significant. Furthermore, although the portfolio adjustment effect will be small, the signalling effect may be important in affecting the exchange rate. The BoK's interventions, even though they were sterilisation interventions, contain important information and signals about future exchange rate movements, and thus can change the expectations of market participants and affect the exchange rate of the Korean *won* to that extent.

9.2.2 Intervention by the Ministry of Economy and Finance through the Foreign Exchange Equalisation Fund (FEEF)

The MOEF can carry out FX intervention, relying on its own resources, which are mobilised through the FEEF. The fund was first established in 1967 to stabilise the FX market and then authorised in 1987 to issue its own bonds, called Foreign Exchange Equalisation Bonds, in

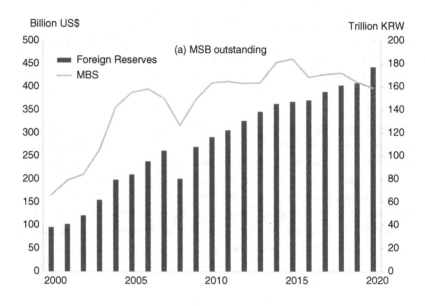

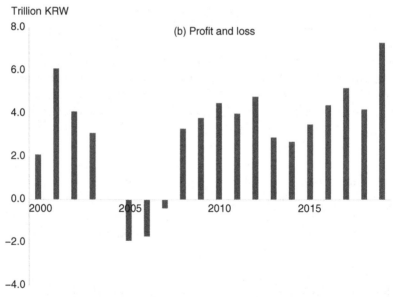

Figure 9.7 Monetary stabilisation bonds outstanding and the BoK's profit and loss
Source: ECOS, BoK.

a similar manner to the BoK issuing its own MSBs. Currently, the FEEF is allowed to issue its own bonds only in foreign currencies, as the issue of bonds denominated in Korean *won* has been replaced by the Public Capital Management Fund, which issues Treasury Bonds for the sake of the Korean government.

Unlike the operation of buying or selling the foreign reserves held by the BoK, the MOEF has exclusive decision-making authority over the operation of the FEEF, although the BoK is charged with helping in the operation of the fund. If the FEEF acquires foreign currency funds either through the issue of Foreign Exchange Equalisation Bonds or by purchasing them in the FX market with money borrowed from the Public Capital Management Fund, these foreign currency funds are deposited with the Korea Investment Corporation and the BoK as part of Korea's official FX reserves. Thus, if there are FX market interventions through the FEEF, they are automatically sterilisation interventions.

Figure 9.8(a) shows the assets and liabilities of the FEEF. The FEEF's debts jumped fourteen-fold from about KRW15 trillion in early 2000 to about KRW248 trillion in 2019. In contrast, during the same period, its assets increased from about KRW14.5 trillion to KRW228 trillion. The difference in assets and liabilities is attributable to the FEEF's cumulative net loss of about KRW30 trillion. Figure 9.8(b) shows the net profit and loss of the FEEF.

The government's FX interventions through the FEEF were again highly controversial because of the huge cost of the interventions. Much of its net loss was incurred as the result of the reverse margin between the cost of funding that derived from issuing the bonds denominated in Korean *won* and the returns on the US dollar-denominated foreign assets, as was the case for the MSBs. But the FEET's operations were managed much more inefficiently. For example, the FEEF's reverse margin was extremely large, exceeding 5 per cent in the early 2000s. In 2004 alone, the interest loss from reverse margins stood at KRW6 trillion, reflecting the massive FX interventions carried out by the Korean government. In particular, the FEEF recorded a loss of about KRW4.5 trillion due to the forward intervention in the NDF market. The reverse margin widened again after the outbreak of the 2008 global financial crisis, with the interest losses reaching KRW3.6 trillion to 6.5 trillion per year. Meanwhile, thanks to the sudden depreciation of the Korean *won* in 2008, the FEEF recorded a big

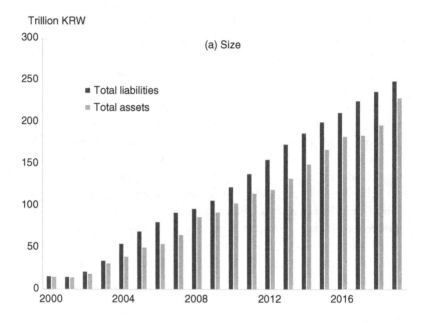

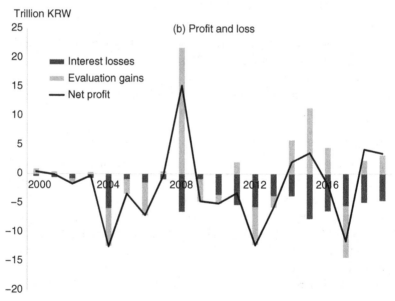

Figure 9.8 The size and profit and loss of the Foreign Exchange Stabilisation Fund
Source: MOEF and the National Assembly.

asset re-evaluation gain of KRW21.7 trillion, which contributed to offsetting the previous yearly re-evaluation losses of KRW2.5 trillion to 6.6 trillion. Since 2010, re-evaluation gains and losses have alternated.

9.3 Exchange Rate Adjustment through Monetary Policy

Attempts to intervene in the FX market and affect the level of exchange rates are very likely to cause trade frictions, making exchange rate policy difficult, except in exceptional circumstances. But central banks can indirectly affect exchange rates through monetary policy, in particular, through adjustments in interest rates, which lead to a change in exchange rates by inducing short-term capital movements. Along with increasing capital movements and financial linkages across borders, this issue is increasingly important. Currently, most advanced economies maintain free-floating exchange rate systems, which imply that there should not be any explicit FX intervention targeting exchange rates. Monetary policy is thus the sole instrument available to exert an influence on the exchange rate. Furthermore, as interest rates dropped to zero in the wake of the global financial crisis, the usual transmission channels of monetary policy through interest rates weakened. Thus, one important transmission channel of the quantitative easing policies adopted by major central banks was the depreciation of their currencies, which could be regarded as a 'beggar-thy-neighbour policy', or what is often labelled as 'currency wars'. For example, the BoJ, through its quantitative and qualitative easing programmes, was successful in depreciating the Japanese currency (see Fukuda, 2017), which was to have important repercussion on the Korean economy.

However, unlike these advanced economies, the Korean authorities have been relying on direct FX market intervention to affect exchange rates. To date, there has been a strict separation in Korea between responsibility for FX rate policy and monetary policy. While the monetary policy is the sole competence of the MPB, the exchange rate policy is under the control of the MOEF. This means that monetary policy was rarely used to stabilise exchange rates, particularly after the independence of the BoK in 1998. As long as the exchange rate stabilisation was monopolised by the MOEF, the MPB had little input. Thus, although interest rate movement tends to exercise greater influence on exchange rates through inducing short-term capital movements, there is no explicit targeting of exchange rates by the MPB. Even the sharing of information regarding the desired exchange rate policy was rare between the two institutions.[3]

More importantly, the problem with deploying monetary policy as an exchange rate policy is that the BoK cannot control both domestic and foreign interest rates. As a result, the relationship between domestic interest rates and exchange rates does not always move in the expected direction, which prevents the MPB from relying on the transmission mechanism through exchange rates. Table 9.1 shows that the relationship between interest rates and the *won*–dollar exchange rate in Korea was not stable. In the case of the twelve interest rate cuts carried out since 2010, the exchange rate of the Korean *won* rose (depreciated) in only six cases on the day of the rate-cutting decision, in five cases on the next day, and in seven cases one month later. In the case of two interest hikes, the exchange rate of the Korean *won* rose on the decision day but declined the next day and also one month later. Furthermore, it seems that the exchange rate of the Korean *won* one month later was more affected by the US Federal Reserve's monetary policy than by home decisions.

Thus, attempts to control the exchange rate through interest rates are not effective in normal times. In small and open economies such as Korea, the attempts can trigger short-term capital movements and increase the instability of the FX market, which will do more bad than good. Instead, what the MPB attempts to do is to strengthen the coordination of its monetary policy stance to global monetary policy and US monetary policy in particular. As implied by the so-called impossible trinity or trilemma theorem, the BoK cannot simultaneously achieve both exchange rate stability and monetary policy autonomy, as long as capital movement is free. Thus, it should choose either monetary policy autonomy, letting exchange rates float, or choose exchange rate stability, sacrificing the independence of its monetary policy. However, the officials in the MOEF have been extremely distrustful of floating exchange rate systems, based on their belief that the 1997 currency crisis was caused by the excessive appreciation of the Korean *won*. Given their

---

[3] Although the MPB is the highest decision-making body of the BoK, the BoK staff consider the responsibility in respect of exchange rate policy to reside in the MOEF and do not provide any information to the MPB. Thus, by bypassing the MPB, the BoK staff conduct exchange rate policy with the MOEF, which is a curious way to address this issue, and one which should be reconsidered.

Table 9.1 *Changes in the* won–*dollar exchange rate after interest rate changes since 2010 (unit: KRW)*

Date	Domestic policy stance	Interest change	T	T+1	T+30	US monetary policy stance
2012/07/12	easing	3.25→3.0	10.6	–1.2	–20.4	QE
2012/10/11	easing	3.0→2.75	–0.3	–3.1	–25.7	QE
2013/05/09	easing	2.75→2.5	4.5	15.1	36.3	QE
2014/08/14	easing	2.5-→2.25	–7.7	–	16.8	QE tapering
2014/10/15	easing	2.25→2.0	–1.4	–1.6	37.4	QE tapering
2015/03/12	easing	2.0→1.75	–0.1	2.1	–27.8	QE tapering
2015/06/11	easing	1.75→1.5	0.6	5.9	20.9	QE tapering
2016/06/09	easing	1.5→1.25	–0.6	9.5	5.8	tight
2017/11/30	tight	1.25→1.5	11.4	–1.8	–17.7	tight
2018/11/30	tight	1.5→1.75	2	–1.5	–5.5	tight
2019/07/18	easing	1.75→1.5	–2.5	–4.3	32	tight
2019/10/16	easing	1.5-→1.25	2.6	–0.8	–21.2	easing
2020/03/17	easing	1.25→0.75	17.5	2.2	–25.6	easing
2020/05/28	easing	0.75→0.5	5.2	–1.1	41	easing

Note: T indicates the change of the *won*–dollar exchange rate on the day when the base rate was changed. T+1 and T+30 indicate changes the next day and one month later, respectively. The signs (+) or (–) represent the depreciation or appreciation of the Korean *won* against the US dollar.
Source: BoK.

'fear of floating', it is very unlikely that they will abandon FX market intervention, leaving the movement of the exchange rate completely to the market. This means that the BoK finds it difficult to exercise full autonomy in its monetary policymaking, even though it may wish to do so. If the US Fed raises or cuts interest rates, for instance, the BoK is obliged to do likewise, in order to narrow the interest rate gap between the two countries. Otherwise, ensuring massive capital outflows or inflows could generate quite wide fluctuations in the exchange rates.

Even when the exchange rate is left to float freely, the BoK may not be able to conduct an autonomous monetary policy. As H. Rey pointed out (Rey, 2015), the transmission of monetary policy through capital flows, in particular credit flows, which cannot be hindered by exchange rate flexibility, can transform the 'trilemma' into the 'dilemma' between autonomous monetary policy and free capital movement. For example, if the US Fed cuts interest rates, there will be increasing capital inflows to Korea with global risk-on market sentiment, which will amplify the credit market boom in Korea. Conversely, if the US Fed raises interest rates, global risk-off market sentiment will trigger capital outflows from Korea and have an adverse effect on the domestic credit market in Korea. Thus, the Korean economy cannot remain insulated from the US Fed's monetary policy regardless of the exchange rate regime, which it deploys. For this reason, the monetary policy stance of the BoK *cannot* be too different from the policy of the US Federal Reserve Board. The monetary policy stance of the US Federal Reserve Board is always one of the most important pieces of information when the members of the MPB decide upon Korean monetary policy.

PART IV

How Is Financial Stability Pursued in Korea?

10 | *Financial Crisis and the Role of Government*

Financial markets are subject to constant shocks, which can lead to crises when markets fail. Theoretically, the government can prevent such market failures. In practice, however, crises are often caused or amplified by government failure. This was particularly the case for the 1997 currency crisis in Korea. Not only did the Korean government's inappropriate intervention trigger the crisis, but its inappropriate policy responses further transformed the initial mistakes into an economic disaster. This stands in sharp contrast to the government's responses to the 2008 global economic crisis and the 2020 COVID-19 pandemic. This chapter overviews the roles played by the Korean government during these three crises.

10.1 A Brief Overview of the Currency and Financial Crises in Korea

Korea was hit by three crises in 1997, 2008, and 2020. The underlying origins of these crises may be multifaceted, but, broadly speaking, they were all related to short-term capital outflows, in particular, the refusal on the part of foreign banks to roll over short-term debts owed by Korean banks.

Figure 10.1 shows the trend of foreign capital flows in Korea. Since the early 1990s, favourable international market conditions have contributed to the surge in private capital inflows in Korea. Low interest rates in Japan and the United States encouraged international investors and lenders to expand their activities in Korea and in East Asian markets. The capital inflows reached US$100 billion during the period from January 1995 to July 1997.

This increase was, above all, due to the borrowings from private lenders, including commercial banks and non-bank creditors. With hindsight, the Korean crisis highlighted the structural and institutional challenges posed by financial liberalisation. Korea was ill-prepared for

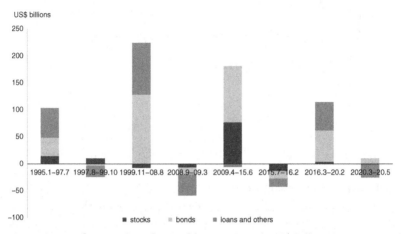

Figure 10.1 Inflows and outflows of foreign capital (US$ billions)
Source: ECOS, BoK.

fast integration into the global financial market. Korean financial institutions borrowed short-term funds from foreign banks and used them recklessly in long-term domestic loans and risky international investments. During the 1997 crisis, however, the inflow suddenly reversed, leading to a net capital outflow of US$24 billion. In particular, the sharpest capital outflow came from the drop in loans to Korean banks. Moreover, the inappropriate intervention by the Korean government to defend the overvalued exchange rate parity of Korean currency against the backdrop of the capital outflow turned out to be disastrous.

In 2008, Korea was again hit by a financial crisis. This time, the epicentre of the crisis was the United States, but Korea was not immune to this crisis. After capital inflows attained a peak in 2007, they reversed dramatically in late 2008. From September 2008 until March 2009, capital outflows amounted to US$58 billion (more than 5 per cent of Korean GDP). Capital outflows surged again in tandem with US monetary policy normalisation in 2015. However, this had little impact on the Korean economy. In 2020, against the backdrop of the spread of the COVID-19 pandemic, the Federal Reserve Board undertook many extraordinary measures that went beyond those in 2008 in speed and size. This triggered capital outflow amounting to US$15 billion from Korea.

Figure 10.2 Korean *won* exchange rate against the US dollar
Source: ECOS, BoK.

Figure 10.2 shows the movement of the exchange rate of the Korean *won* against the US dollar, which mirrors the movement of foreign capital flows.

During the 1997 Asian financial crisis, the exchange rate of the Korean *won* increased to 1,700 *won*/dollar. Korean foreign reserves were completely depleted as foreign investors withdrew their capital and refused to roll over their existing loans to Korean banks. As Korean banks and companies went bankrupt, a simple currency crisis turned into a serious economic crisis. As Figure 10.3 shows, the GDP growth rate fell for three consecutive quarters. In particular, the GDP growth rate in the first quarter of 1998 was –6.8 per cent quarter-on-quarter, the largest drop since the 1979 oil shock. During the 2008 global financial crisis, the exchange rate of the Korean *won* soared to 1,400 *won*/dollar, the highest rate since the 1997 currency crisis. Korea had had more than US$250 billion worth of FX reserves, but this large stock of reserves, albeit nine times as large as the FX reserves in 1997, did little to help stabilise the FX market. The sharp depreciation in the value of the Korean *won* was caused by the decline in global demand, which led to a drop in Korean exports. The GDP growth rate dropped to –3.3 per cent quarter-on-quarter in the fourth quarter of 2008, but rebounded quickly from the

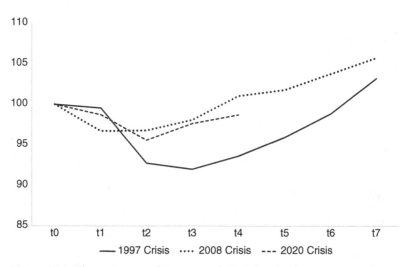

Figure 10.3 The trajectory of Korean real GDP for the three economic crises
Note: The base periods are the third quarter 1997, third quarter 2008, and fourth quarter 2019.
Source: ECOS, BoK.

first quarter of 2009. In 2020, the exchange rate of the Korean currency rose to 1,230 *won*/dollar, the highest level since the 2008 global financial crisis, amid increasing risk aversion that followed the domestic and global spread of the COVID-19 pandemic. Economic growth shrank again, due to the decline in domestic demand and exports. The real GDP growth rate dropped to –1.3 per cent quarter-on-quarter in the first quarter of 2020, and to –3.3 per cent in the second quarter. From the third quarter, the Korean economy started to rebound. Figure 10.3 compares the movement of the real GDP during these three crises.

Reflecting the drop in GDP, the unemployment rate also increased. Figure 10.4 illustrates the unemployment rate trend in Korea during the three crises. During the 1997 Asian financial crisis, the unemployment rate soared from a mere 2 per cent in 1996 to nearly 9 per cent in 1998. More than 1 million people lost their jobs, which left the number of employed people down by 6 percentage points. There were large-scale lay-offs, which had been illegal in Korea for a long time. Until the outbreak of the 1997 currency crisis, there had been few lay-offs, and job security was well protected. Strong job security in exchange for weak workers' rights had been an integral part of the implicit social contract under the

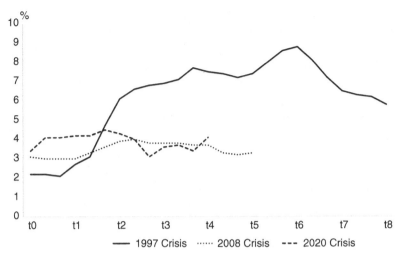

Figure 10.4 The trend of unemployment rates during the three crises in Korea
Source: ECOS, BoK.

authoritarian regimes in Korea. It is important to recall that these massive lay-offs were only permitted because of the labour market reform undertaken by the Korean government. To compensate for the labour market changes, the Korean government started to strengthen the social safety net, by extending the coverage of the unemployment insurance system, introduced in Korea in 1995. Unemployment dropped to more normal levels only when the Korean economy regained its normal growth path after the year 2000. Compared to the 1997 currency crisis, the unemployment rate during the 2008 global financial crisis and the recent COVID-19 pandemic remained rather stable. The unemployment rate temporarily increased above 4 per cent, but averaged below 4 per cent throughout the whole period of the crisis. The serious social and economic hardships experienced in the 1997 currency crisis were not repeated.

10.2 The 1997 Currency Crisis and Government Failure

10.2.1 *Mismanagement of Exchange Rate Policy*

a) Misalignment of the Exchange Rate
In an open economy such as that of Korea, where exports account for almost half of the GDP, exchange rate flexibility is a key factor in

maintaining economic growth and stabilising the economy. Notwithstanding this, the Korean *won* remained overvalued for too long from the early 1990s. As Figure 10.2 illustrates, the exchange rate of the Korean *won* remained rigidly in the range 700–800 *won*/dollar until 1997. To make matters worse, the JPY depreciated by more than 30 per cent in 1995, which further eroded the export competitiveness of the Korean economy. As a result, Korea's current account deficit increased to a record high of US$23 billion in 1996. But why did the exchange rate of the Korean *won* remain so rigid, preventing the Korean *won* from depreciating in the face of the accumulating current account deficits? The following reasons were highlighted during the hearings of the National Assembly on the causes of the 1997 currency crisis, which was held in 1999.

There was a need to accommodate the depreciation pressure on the Korean *won* into an appropriate exchange rate alignment in the face of the increasing shortage of foreign currency liquidity. However, given the concerns about price stability and the increase in foreign debt costs from depreciation, along with the President's election campaign pledge to raise the annual *per capita* income of Korea to US$20,000 by the end of 1997, the Korean government stuck to the fixed exchange rate of the Korean *won*. (National Assembly, 1999)

Although it is difficult to assess which factors were the most crucial in stemming exchange rate flexibility, it is clear that the government intended to stabilise the exchange rate of the Korean *won* even at a highly overvalued rate. Historically, the main reason for interventions by the Korean FX authorities had been to correct the current account deficits: if the Korean *won* had tended to appreciate, they would have actively intervened in the FX market, whereas, if it had moved in the opposite direction, they would have refrained from doing so. Interventions were limited to the passive purchase of US dollars in order to replenish their foreign reserves (Rhee and Song, 1996). By the time of the 1997 crisis, however, this pattern had changed. Interventions were largely to stem the depreciation of the Korean *won*, rather than its appreciation. Thus, the Korean *won* was overvalued despite the continuing current account deficits. If the movement of the exchange rate was left to market forces, rather than in the hands of the government, Korea might have avoided the subsequent sudden collapse of its currency, thereby mitigating its disastrous effect on the real economy.

b) Continuous Market Intervention

Against this backdrop, the FX market interventions during the 1997 crisis turned out to be fatal mistakes (Moon and Rhee, 2006). Figure 10.5 shows the relationship between the *won*–dollar exchange rate and the amount of FX market interventions carried out by the FX authorities[1] during the two periods, January to March 1997, and September to November 1997. As is clear, the Korean *won* depreciated only slightly during the first period. To defend the *won*, the government spent foreign reserves totalling US$9.5 billion, which amounted to one-third of the total official foreign reserves in Korea. Given that the depreciation of the Korean *won* stopped, this intervention can be seen to have been a success. It is noteworthy that, in addition to spot market intervention, the Korean government used forward market intervention for the first time. From April 1997, the FX rate of the Korean *won* remained stable at around 890 *won*/dollars until the middle of August.

From September, however, the Korea *won* again started to depreciate rapidly. In October, in particular, it became apparent that the Korean government could not maintain its previous levels of official reserves, amid increasing worries about the spreading of the currency crisis, which had initially broken out in Southeast Asia, to neighbouring Asian countries. For instance, Taiwan devalued its currency on 17 October 1997, and the stock market in Hong Kong crashed on 20 October 1997. On the same day, the fall in the value of the Korean *won* accelerated, forcing the government to sell ever greater amounts of US dollars. The government ended up selling half a billion to a billion dollars per day (2–3 per cent of the total foreign reserves). Despite these interventions, the steep fall of the Korean *won* continued. All the efforts to defend the Korean *won*, including the forward market interventions, failed, and the Korean *won* collapsed. Over a period of less than three months, the government sold a total of US$15.4 billion, which completely depleted its foreign reserves. These interventions were doomed to failure because the demand for dollars was also coming from domestic financial institutions, such as the merchant banking corporations, which were in illiquid states to repay dollar-denominated debts to

---

[1] As pointed out, the government was mainly responsible for the exchange rate policy. Therefore, unless otherwise stated, we will refer to government interventions instead of interventions by the FX authorities.

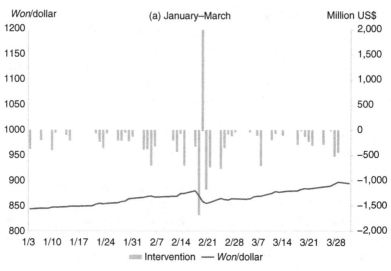

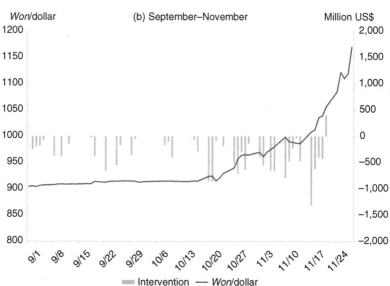

Figure 10.5 FX interventions and the *won*–dollar exchange rate: January–
March and September–November 1997
Note: '–' denotes the selling of US dollars in place, and '+' the purchase of US
dollars.
Source: Moon and Rhee (2006).

foreign creditors after being denied rollovers on their debts. On 21 November 1997, the government decided to ask for an emergency loan from the IMF. But this loan request came far too late. The government abandoned its interventions only after depleting all its foreign reserves unsuccessfully in its attempts to defend the Korean *won*.

Figure 10.6 shows the extent of the arbitrage profit opportunities measured by the difference between the forward premium and the interest rate differential between Korea and the United States during these two periods in 1997. Arbitrage profit opportunities soared, reaching nearly 20 per cent by early November. It was already clear that any further intervention by the government could not be sustained. Nevertheless, the government continued its interventions, bringing Korea to the verge of bankruptcy.

Why did the Korean government officials continue to pursue such relentless interventions to the extent of depleting all the country's FX reserves? The FX market interventions conducted by the government officials were opaque. No checks and balances mechanisms were in place inside the government, which allowed the government officials to camouflage their FX operations. On 21 November 1997, when the Korean government decided to go to the IMF for emergency funding, the published free foreign reserves held were around US$7.2 billion. But when the forward market interventions and other secret forms of support to banks were taken into consideration, it turned out that the Korean government had only between US$400 and US$500 million in foreign reserves. If the Korean government had decided to float the Korean *won* earlier, and had given up its interventions, at least it might have saved some of its foreign reserves – albeit substantially reduced – and might have had sufficient time to negotiate with the IMF from a more advantageous position.

c) Lack of Transparency
Perhaps the Korean government officials were so confident about their ability that they thought they could control the FX market in their favour. In order to hide the true size of their market operations, they relied on two schemes.

As Table 10.1 shows, the first scheme was the provision of secret FX support through the overseas branches of Korean banks. The FX authorities provided their foreign reserves to Korean banks in US dollar-liquidity difficulties, but this support was concealed. For

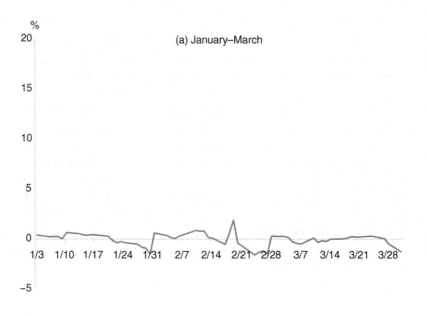

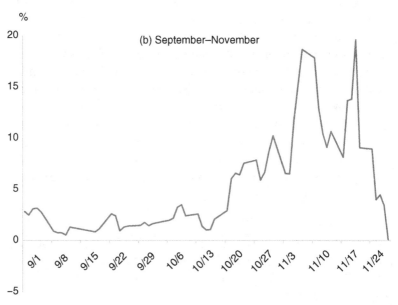

Figure 10.6 Forward premium less interest rate differential: January–March
and September–November 1997
Note: Arbitrage profit is measured by the forward premium (measured by the log
difference between the three-month NDF bid rate and the spot exchange rate) and
the interest rate differential between three-year Korean and US government bonds.
Source: Moon and Rhee (2006).

Table 10.1 *The trend of free foreign reserves 1997 (US$ billions)*

	Jan	Feb	Mar	Apr	May	Jun	Jul	Aug	Sep	Oct	Nov	Dec
Foreign Reserves	31.0	29.8	29.1	29.8	31.9	33.3	33.7	31.1	30.4	30.5	24.4	20.4
Non-liquid Foreign Reserves	3.8	9.3	11.8	11.3	9.5	7.9	8.6	10.1	11.0	14.1	23.3	17.4
(Overseas Branch Deposits)	3.8	7.0	8.0	8.0	8.0	8.0	8.0	8.0	8.0	8.0	16.9	11.4
(Forward Balances to Be Settled)		2.3	3.8	3.3	1.5	-0.2	0.6	2.1	3.0	5.9	6.2	5.8
Free Foreign Reserves	27.2	20.5	17.3	18.5	22.4	25.5	25.1	21.0	19.4	16.4	1.1	3.0

Source: Moon and Rhee (2000).

instance, the Korean government moved the foreign reserves that it held in the form of short-term safe deposits with the US banks to the overseas branches of the Korean banks, which, in turn, lent these US dollar deposits to their mother banks in Korea. In appearance, there was no statistical change in respect of the official foreign reserves held by the government. In practice, however, free foreign reserves (the official foreign reserves less the FX authorities' deposits at the overseas branches of domestic banks and less the unsettled forward market interventions) decreased in the sense that these deposits could not be freely used to repay foreign creditors. In February 1997, the overseas branch deposits increased to USS$7 billion, and, in November 1997, they more than doubled to reach US$16.9 billion, which amounted to more than half of the official Korean foreign reserves. In fact, as Korean banks could not roll over their short-term debts to foreign creditors, they were obliged to rely on this support from the official foreign reserves.

The second scheme was interventions in the forward exchange market. If the government concluded a forward contract to sell US dollars, it would not change the amount of the official foreign reserves held until the settlement date, but its effect would be almost the same as the selling of the US dollars on the spot market. As Figure 10.7 illustrates, the government intervened in the forward market for the first time in February–March 1997, selling a total of US$3.8 billion, compared to US$5.7 billion in the spot market. During the months of September to November 1997, the government also sold a total of US$5.3 billion in the forward market, compared to US$10 billion in the spot market. With the collapse of the Korean *won*, these forward market interventions cost the government a substantial amount of money. On 4 December 1997, when the Korean government reached an agreement with the IMF for the emergency bailout loans, these forward interventions had cost the country between US$2 and US$3 billion.

The two schemes used by the Korean FX authorities proved quite successful in the February to March period. In March, when the first wave of capital withdrawals by foreign investors took place, the changes in free reserves were kept secret from investors, both domestic and foreign. However, this success was not repeated in the September to November period. Despite continued withdrawals of foreign capital and FX market interventions, the reported official foreign reserves changed little. More and more foreign investors began to doubt the

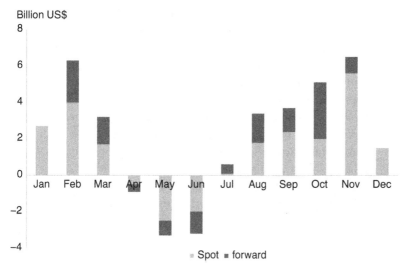

Figure 10.7 Spot and forward exchange market interventions 1997
Note: Negative values imply buying US dollars.
Source: BoK.

credibility of the government reports on its official foreign reserves. This precipitated speculative attacks on the Korean *won*, resulting in the free foreign reserves falling to a record low level. Although the government reported that its official foreign reserves had declined only slightly to US$24 billion by the end of November 1997, its free foreign reserves had fallen below US$1.1 billion, a situation that was close to the total bankruptcy of the Korean economy.

10.2.2 Supervisory Negligence

The second government failure originated from excessive regulation which was not always accompanied by corresponding supervision.

The Korean government was overly ambitious in trying to control cross-border capital flows meticulously. First, against the backdrop of large capital inflows in the early 1990s, the government took measures to induce capital outflows and restrict inflows in order to avoid the appreciation of the Korean *won*. Korean banks were encouraged to increase their overseas investments while promoting their internationalisation through the competitive establishment of overseas offices, branches, or subsidiaries. Second, the government incentivised Korean banks to undertake short-term foreign borrowing by making the notification of long-term foreign borrowing mandatory, while abolishing the regulations on short-term foreign borrowing. These policies led Korean financial institutions to fall into a double mismatch of maturities and currencies, borrowing short-term foreign-currency-denominated capital and investing it in long-term domestic assets (Moon and Rhee, 2000).

Unaccompanied by government supervision, the double mismatch was an important factor that triggered a run on the Korean banks. Until 1997, the MOEF had financial supervisory authority over all non-banking financial institutions except commercial banks, but it had neither sufficient technical expertise nor the staff necessary to undertake effective supervision. Consequently, the Ministry delegated parts of its supervisory power to the Office of Bank Supervision of the BoK, the Securities Supervisory Committee, and other related institutions. The problem with this fragmented delegation was that, while the MOEF was drafting the regulations and rules that it wanted implemented, it failed to ensure that the necessary supervision was executed properly. In particular, the supervisory negligence in respect of the merchant banking corporations, which were part of the non-bank financial institutions, had severe consequences.

Merchant banking corporations were originally established to help promote inflows of foreign capital. Until the early 1990s, there were only six merchant banking corporations in Korea, which were joint ventures between domestic and foreign financial companies. Subsequently, the number of merchant banking corporations increased sharply. This growth was again due to the differing regulations applicable between banks and non-banking institutions, in particular, the less onerous regulations in favour of merchant banking corporations. Except for deposit-taking, which was the traditional activity of commercial banks, the merchant banking corporations were permitted to undertake all other financial activities including overseas borrowing and lending. Compared to the banks, which were subject to strict interest rate and loan regulations, they were also given much more leeway in their management. There was, for instance, no regulation on the holding of required reserves. Furthermore, they benefited from the early and preferential de-regulation of interest rates, while commercial banks still suffered from delayed liberalisation. Against this backdrop, the Korean government allowed investment finance companies, which specialised in short-term financial activities, to convert themselves into merchant banking corporations en masse. The number of merchant banking corporations jumped to thirty in 1996. However, faced with increasing competition between themselves, the merchant banking corporations saw their profits decline and sought to strengthen their international business undertakings.

The merchant banking corporations borrowed short-term foreign funds extensively, including low interest rate borrowings from Japanese banks, while they lent long term to big domestic companies or invested in low-grade foreign fixed assets. Given the high interest spread between Korea and the United States or Japan, there was a good reason for them to devote themselves to the dollar or *yen* carry trade. However, few bank managers were accustomed to international banking, risk management assessment practically did not exist, and almost all Korean banks, not to mention the merchant banking corporations, were seriously exposed to liquidity and currency risks. Table 10.2 shows that the liquidity ratios in foreign currency for these merchant banking corporations were only 3–6 per cent in the run-up to the 1997 currency crisis.

Naturally, the absence of risk management came to increase the vigilance of foreign creditors with regard to their loans to Korean banks. The first wave of capital outflows began as foreign creditors attempted to reduce their credit lines or reject new loan requests from Korean banks. Table 10.3 shows the trend of rollover ratios for Korean banks, according to which the runs on the Korean banks were evident from October 1997.

Clearly, the runs on Korean banks and financial institutions by foreign creditors, particularly by Japanese banks, were one of the important causes of the 1997 currency crisis. From the beginning of 1997, the Japanese banks had already started to reduce their credit lines

Table 10.2 *Foreign currency liquidity ratio (%)*[1]

	1992	1993	1994	1995	1996	1997
Commercial banks	83.2	87.9	80.6	77.5	77.7	93.4
Merchant banking corporations	3.6	4.0	3.0	3.1	6.3	14.7

Note 1: Measured by the ratio of short-term use in foreign currency over short-term borrowing in foreign currency.
Source: Moon (2000).

Table 10.3 *Rollover ratios of short-term external debts*

	December 1996	January 1997	April 1997	July 1997	October 1997	December 1997
A group	109	100	100	90	70	50
B group	100	100	90	70	10	0
C group	100	90	50	20	10	0

Note: The A group refers to the banks with the highest credit ratings, such as the government banks (KDB and Exim banks). The B group is the banks with medium credit ratings, including most of the commercial banks, while the C group is the banks with the lowest credit ratings including merchant banking corporations and two commercial banks, the Korea First Bank and the Seoul Bank.
Source: Lee (2011).

to Korean banks, reflecting the deteriorating confidence in the Japanese economy. The credit lines to Korean banks were maintained until August 1997. On 23 October 1997, eight Japanese financial institutions went bankrupt amid the collapse of the Hong Kong stock market. These were the final killer blows to the Korean economy because Hong Kong and Japan, which were major lenders to the Korean banks, had to stop all new lending to Korea. Table 10.4 shows that Japan withdrew the largest short-term loans worth US$13 billion during 1997.

The runs by foreign creditors on the merchant banking corporations had a particularly devastating impact on the FX market. As they could not roll over their maturing short-term foreign debts, they were obliged to rush into the FX market to buy US dollars in order to repay their short-term foreign currency debts. This accelerated the shortage of US dollars in the already fragile domestic FX market, resulting in the exchange rate of the Korean *won* skyrocketing against the US dollar. The decision to let these merchant banking corporations continue to buy the US dollar in the domestic FX market amid the rapidly dwindling foreign reserves was clearly the worst mistake committed by the Korean government. The value of the due foreign currency debt of the merchant banking corporations amounted to US$4.9 billion in November, accounting for around one-fourth of the trade volume in Korea's FX market. Eventually almost all merchant banking corporations were liquidated.

Table 10.4 *The trend in external debts of Korean banks (US$ billions)*

	End of 1996	End of 1997	Change
Short-term debt	62.9	25.3	–37.5
-Japan	21.8	8.8	–13.0
-US	5.6	3.4	–2.1
-Europe	17.3	9.6	–7.6
-Others	10.7	2.8	–7.8
-Commercial paper	7.4	0.6	–6.7
Long-term debt	31.5	37.5	5.9
Total debt	94.5	62.9	-31.6

Source: Moon (2000).

10.2.3 *Wrong Macroeconomic Policy Responses*

What were the most serious mistakes that the Korean government committed during the 1997 currency crisis? The biggest mistake seems to be the wrong policy responses to the crisis, which can be traced back to the fact that Korea received the emergency liquidity support subject to the 'conditionality' imposed by the IMF. The Korean government, under its standby agreement with the IMF, set a priority on stabilising the exchange rate of the Korean *won* and narrowing the current account deficits. To this end, the government implemented contractionary monetary and fiscal policies, which, combined with the financial and corporate sector restructuring programmes, led to a doom loop between credit crunch and corporate defaults. Figure 10.8 shows these monetary and fiscal policy responses.

First, the wrong monetary policy amplified the devastation of the Korean economy. The BoK had to contract liquidity supply and adopt high interest rate policies. The call rate, which was 12 per cent on 1 December 1997, increased to 31 per cent and the yield on commercial paper (CP) at ninety-one days climbed as high as 40 per cent by the end of the year. In retrospect, this monetary policy tightening only aggravated the currency crisis, transforming it into a generalised banking and economic crisis. The high interest rate policy recommended by the IMF was supposed to stem the hoarding of US dollars and to induce capital inflows from abroad. However, this expected effect turned out to be insignificant and the policy ended up wrecking the long-run viability of Korean companies, many of which went bankrupt, as they were unable to borrow even at exorbitantly high interest rates. The rising default risk of the Korean companies further aggravated the credit crunch.

Second, a tight fiscal policy was adopted to alleviate the burden on monetary policy and to consolidate budget deficits. The central government budget in 1998 was planned to record a small surplus (0.25 per cent of GDP), and, to this end, various measures to increase taxes and reduce spending were taken. For instance, the pay of civil servants was cut by 10–20 per cent and administrative expenditure was reduced, while value added tax and corporate tax were increased. Amid rapidly deteriorating economic growth, however, the collected tax fell short of the expected tax revenue, leading the Korean government to run a slight budget deficit. It is noteworthy that this deficit was not the result of a counter-cyclical fiscal policy, which would have seen an increase in public expenditure during a recession. On the contrary, the deficit was a direct consequence of the recession. The IMF did not allow the Korean government to conduct expansionary fiscal policies until the recession had developed into a severe depression and the surge in unemployment threatened political stability. Fiscal programmes to strengthen the social safety net were introduced belatedly and social expenditure increased thereafter. Nevertheless, in terms of the general government budget, the balance was still positive.

Furthermore, the Korean government resorted to massive financial and corporate sector restructuring. Making its top priority the earliest possible resolution of unsound financial institutions, in 1998, the government closed five banks whose capital adequacy ratios were below 8 per cent and merged three banks with other banks. In the case of non-bank financial institutions, by 1998, sixteen merchant banking corporations, two securities companies, four investment trust companies, and five insurance companies had all been closed down. Furthermore, many financial companies specialising in the small- and medium-sized company sector, such as credit unions and mutual savings and finance companies, were liquidated. This financial restructuring continued in 1999. Table 10.5 summarises the progress of the restructuring programme, which was completed in 1998–1999.

Amid the persistent credit crunch, corporate defaults ensued, creating a vicious cycle between banking and corporate crises. As financial market distress prevented the corporate sector from having access to credit, the recession deepened and corporate defaults increased, which, in turn, worsened the credit crunch. Many leading Korean business conglomerates

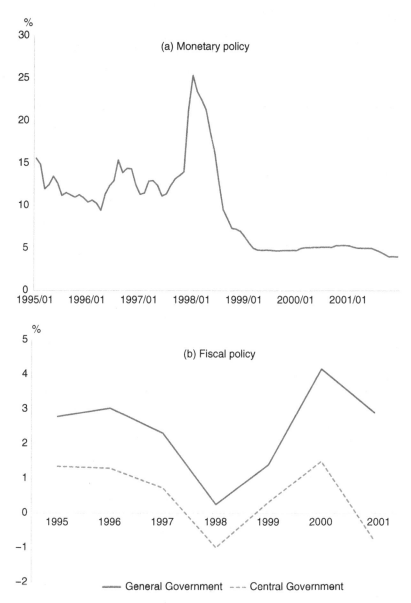

Figure 10.8 Monetary and fiscal policies during the 1997 currency crisis
Source: ECOS, BoK.

Table 10.5 *Financial restructuring in Korea (number of firms)*

Financial Sector	End of 1997	End of 1998	End of 1999
Banks	33	25	23
Merchant Banking Corporations	30	14	10
Securities Companies	36	34	32(1)
Insurance Companies	50	45	45
Investment Trust Companies	31	27	24
Mutual Savings and Finance Companies	231	211	186(1)
Credit Unions	1,666	1,592	1,444
Lease Companies	25	21	20
Total	2,102	1,969	1,784

Note: The figure includes one newly established securities company and six mutual savings and finance companies.
Source: Lee (2011).

named *chaebols* dissolved. Out of the thirty largest business groups in 1996, fourteen had gone bankrupt or entered restructuring programmes by the end of 1999. In this regard, controversy arose over whether this restructuring, which was not within the remit of the IMF, should have been implemented along with the IMF's contractionary monetary and fiscal policies. As a precondition to obtaining the IMF stand-by credit, the Korean government had submitted a very comprehensive restructuring and reform programme to the IMF, ranging from banking and corporate restructuring policies to labour-market reform. It is true that such restructuring might be helpful to the Korean economy in the long run, but the decision regarding the timing of such restructuring was another matter. Broad-ranging restructuring programmes were hurriedly implemented in the country amid a rapidly contracting economy and increasing unemployment, which might, arguably, have ended up making the short-term costs of macroeconomic adjustment far outweigh the long-term benefits of restructuring. Most probably, the government would have wanted to cover up its policy mistakes and look for scapegoats among the private *chaebol* companies (see Box 10.1).[2]

---

[2] For many government officials, the culprits of the 1997 currency crisis were the *chaebols* and their high debt levels, although no such causation has ever been proven. The debt ratio of Korean companies had been higher in earlier periods, but no such currency crisis occurred.

Box 10.1 Corporate Restructuring and the Daewoo Bankruptcy

With the outbreak of the COVID-19 crisis, many Korean companies hit by the pandemic were saved by the financial support provided by the government. However, in the wake of the 1997 currency crisis, it looked as if the priority of the Korean government's policy was to liquidate as many companies as possible, which culminated with the liquidation of Daewoo, the second largest *chaebol* (conglomerate) group in Korea, in July 1999. This liquidation, unprecedented in the history of the Korean economy because of its size, has been justified by many Korean government officials as an inevitable and timely decision to save the Korean economy, but, in retrospect, it may have been the biggest mistake ever committed by the Korean government. It is now timely to reassess how Daewoo went into liquidation.

First, there was a conflict between Woo-choong Kim, then the chairman of Daewoo, and government officials, concerning the cause of the crisis and how to overcome it. Many Korean government officials claimed that the Korean *chaebol*s, in particular, because of their large amount of debt, were responsible for the crisis. For them, corporate restructuring was thus an essential step to overcome the crisis. Against this backdrop, the government introduced guidelines to reduce the debt ratios of Korean companies below 200 per cent when the 1997 average debt ratios of Korean companies and the thirty largest *chaebols* were at 360 per cent and 512 per cent, respectively. Kim counter-argued that the crisis was just a liquidity crisis of the banks. With greater exports, Kim argued, Korea could attain a current account surplus of US$50 billion (in 1996, Korea had a current account deficit of US$24 billion, 5 per cent of GDP), and, if Korea could maintain the surplus for three years, it would have accumulated foreign reserves of US$100 billion. Thus, according to him, what the government should have done was to help Korean companies to increase exports and create a business environment favourable for exports. Indeed, Korea recorded a current account surplus of US$41 billion in 1998, which approximately matched Kim's forecast. Kim also opposed corporate restructuring through massive labour shedding, a policy which was relentlessly pushed by government officials.

Massive restructuring by big companies can destabilise the country, giving rise to too much unemployment. Big companies should refrain from layoffs during recessions. Lay-offs should be done during economic booms, not during recessions. (Shin 2014)[3]

The most important disagreements concerned the cause and size of the debt incurred by Daewoo. According to K. S. Lee, the minister of economy and finance at the time, Daewoo had to be liquidated because of its reckless and unsustainable investment.

Unlike other companies which decided to reduce their investment, Daewoo, under the flag of 'global management', did not stop investing and continued to export recklessly, financing its working capital through receivables ... despite a large increase in sales, cash flow deteriorated due to the corresponding increase in uncollected receivables ... in the case of Daewoo Corporation, which saw its sales jump to KRW13 trillion in 1998, around 75 per cent of these sales (KRW9 trillion) were in the form of uncollected receivables from overseas business units. (Lee, 2011)

However, according to Kim, these debts had to do with the malfunctioning Korean financial system. First, these debts were related to the absence of auto-financing in Korea until 1997. The establishment of an instalment finance company for Daewoo Motors, a core member of the Daewoo group, was authorised only in 1996. Thus, in contrast to the advanced economies, an individual buying a car could not get credit from instalment finance companies. Instead, the car company provided the car purchase credit to the buyer by borrowing from the banks. Thus, the more cars the company sold, the more indebted it became. Second, export financing ceased functioning in Korea. Given that Korean banks were subject to restructuring with high levels of bad loans, they could not provide even the essential services of export financing such as the purchase and discounting of bills of exchange. Again, the increase in exports led to the increase in the number of bills held. As Kim said, 'classifying Daewoo's export as reckless exports was complete nonsense. If these exports were reckless, there should have been large inventories left over in Daewoo's foreign subsidiaries, but there was no such evidence of recklessness, as an accounting

---

[3] All citations listed here are translations from Korean into English by the author.

firm later confirmed that these bills of exchange were collectable safe assets'. (Shin, 2014)

Thus, Daewoo was not insolvent. Its debt level was not particularly high compared to other *chaebols*, either. The company suffered a liquidity squeeze, in particular, due to a series of government measures that appeared to be targeting Daewoo alone[4]. In July 1998, the Korean government decided to set a ceiling on the issue of CPs by *chaebol* groups, and even before this measure was introduced, Daewoo's issue of CPs already exceeded the ceiling. Daewoo therefore had to rely on corporate bonds for finance, but, once again, the government introduced a ceiling on the corporate bonds issued by Daewoo. Most importantly, unlike the liquidation of other *chaebols*, which occurred mostly during the 1997–1998 period, the liquidation of Daewoo was decided on in mid-1999, when the impact of the currency crisis was almost over. In this regard, it seems that Daewoo was not just *allowed* to go bankrupt but was *forced* into bankruptcy by the government.

10.3 The 2008 and 2020 Crises and Policy Responses

The financial crisis that originated in the sub-prime mortgage market of the United States in the summer of 2007 quickly turned into a global financial crisis after the collapse of Lehman Brothers in the third quarter of 2008. The consequent financial crisis in the advanced economies had a far-reaching impact on Korea and on emerging market economies as the crisis spread worldwide.

The Korean economy saw its economic activity shrink sharply as the private credit supply was squeezed because of global de-leveraging. The global financial crisis hit savings banks especially hard. Many of them went bankrupt like the merchant banking corporations, a repetition of the 1997 currency crisis. The absence of supervision and transparent governance structures were again the main reasons behind their bankruptcies. Of the 105 savings banks in Korea, 26 savings banks failed or merged with other saving banks.

Notwithstanding this, when compared to the 1997 currency crisis, the 2008 global financial crisis had only a limited effect on the

---

[4] For the details, see Shin (2014).

Korean economy. There are several reasons for this. First, financial markets in Korea were relatively less exposed to the fallout from the sub-prime mortgage crisis. Second, trade liberalisation policy, especially the conclusion of the FTA with the EU and United States, was able to offset any slowdown due to the decline in global trade and exports. Furthermore, Korea obtained US$30 billion liquidity from a swap agreement with the FRS, which did not have any of the conditionality imposed by the IMF for its stand-by credits. But most of all, the Korean government could address the crisis properly, mobilising all the possible fiscal and monetary stimulus packages. Conversely, in 1997, the government had adopted a strict monetary and fiscal austerity policy which ended up amplifying the fluctuations of the real economy rather than stabilising the economy. Furthermore, the government did not undertake any important restructuring programmes in the mid of the 2008 crisis.

Figure 10.9 summarises the monetary and fiscal policy responses taken by the Korean government and the BoK to mitigate the impact of the 2008 global financial crisis. During this period, the BoK quickly proceeded to lower interest rates and to pump the necessary liquidity into the Korean economy. The policy interest rate was lowered to 2 per cent, less than half of the pre-crisis rate of 5.25 per cent, in response to the crisis. There is no doubt that monetary easing in 2008 was crucial to guarding the domestic economy from the external storm. More interesting than the policy effects, however, were the international economic policy responses that led to the easing of monetary policy. The United States and other advanced economies aggressively lowered their interest rates to cope with the crises in 2008, contrary to what Korea and other Asian countries had been obliged to do in 1997. This proves again that the tight monetary policy that Korea had to adopt with the interest rate hike during the 1997 Asian crisis was neither economically nor politically appropriate.

Furthermore, the Korean government adopted a pre-emptive fiscal policy, announcing an increase in public expenditure as soon as the recession appeared. The size of the fiscal stimulus package reached about KRW59.8 trillion during the period 2008–2010, which amounted to 5.1 per cent of the 2010 GDP. Around half of this increase came from spending (KRW30.5 trillion) and the other half from tax cuts, including tax exemptions and reductions (KRW29.3 trillion).

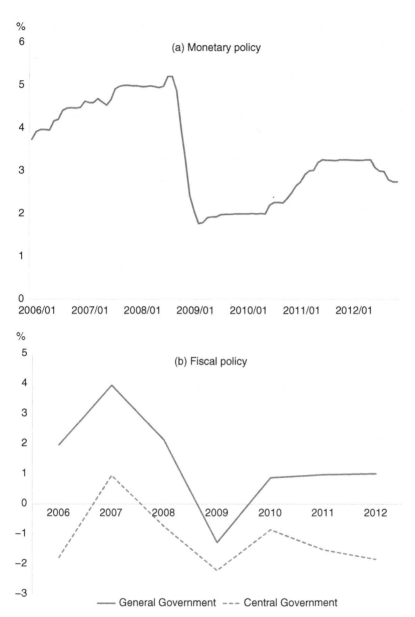

Figure 10.9 Monetary and fiscal policies during the 2008 global financial crisis
Source: ECOS, BoK.

This expansionary fiscal policy was effective in the quick recovery of the Korean economy (Hur and Kim, 2012).

Similarly, the government and the BoK responded by active monetary and fiscal stimulus packages when the COVID-19 pandemic hit the economy. First, the BoK held a special meeting on 16 March 2020 and decided to cut its base rate by 50 basis points, from 1.25 per cent to 0.75 per cent. Again, at the regular meeting in May, the BoK cut the base rate by 25 base points to a historic low of 0.5 per cent. Furthermore, to support the SMEs affected by COVID-19 in particular, the BoK raised the ceiling on its Intermediated Lending Support Facility by KRW18 trillion, from KRW25 trillion to KRW43 trillion, and encouraged commercial banks to increase their loans to the companies affected. It is now clear that the consequences of the COVID-19 pandemic will have a longer duration than was foreseen when the BoK decided to cut its base rates. Monetary policy cannot be very effective unless the COVID-19 pandemic is also addressed. The goal of monetary policy should not just be to stem the recession by pre-emptive monetary actions but also to lessen the burden and hardships of borrowers suffering from the economic consequences of the COVID-19 pandemic. The Korean government also reacted to the negative economic shock with unprecedented increases in fiscal spending, although the damage caused by the COVID-19 crisis was milder in Korea than in other advanced economies. The fiscal support provided to date has been much larger than the fiscal support response to the 2008 global financial crisis. Thus, the government deficit increased to KRW84 trillion (4.4 per cent of GDP), while the government debt increased by 6.3 percentage points to 44 per cent of GDP in 2020. In contrast, in 2009, the budget deficit was just KRW17.6 trillion (1.5 per cent of GDP) and government debt increased only by 3.0 percentage points. With the outbreak of COVID-19 pandemic, the fiscal laxity of the Korean government has deepened.

11 | *Macro-prudential Regulation and Supervision*

Although ensuring the stability of Korea's financial system was traditionally an important goal of the BoK, it has recently been eclipsed by the goals of price or output stability. The competence for maintaining financial stability through the appropriate micro-prudential measures has, however, always rested with the government and thus the BoK was not able to implement a financial stability policy separately. In the wake of the 2008 global financial crisis, however, this situation was no longer regarded as appropriate and led to the adoption and development of macro-prudential policies by the BoK, which were ready to be pre-emptively deployed in order to stem systemic crises. Against this backdrop, the Bank of Korea Act was revised to include financial stability as another of its mandates. This chapter looks at how macro-prudential policy is implemented in Korea.

11.1 Regulation and Supervision in Korea

11.1.1 Organisational Structure

Until the outbreak of the currency crisis in 1997, financial institutions in Korea were under the extensive regulatory control of the MOF, and there was no explicit division of responsibilities between financial regulation, which refers to making the laws and setting the rules for financial institutions, and supervision, which involves the enforcement of these rules.

Given its highly arbitrary exercise of regulatory power over financial institutions and markets, the MOF (which was expanded into the MoFE in 1994) seemed to regard financial supervision as being only of secondary importance. Furthermore, as the number of government officials that could take charge of the supervision was insufficient, the government delegated the enforcement of the rules to various agencies, which were compartmentalised into the supervision of banks, securities companies, insurance firms, and other non-banking firms. For instance, in the early years of economic development, when virtually all financial institutions were banks, financial supervision was largely undertaken by the Office of Bank Supervision, established as an internal organ of the BoK. The Office of Bank Supervision had a supervisory authority over a wide range of banking activities, including authorising the expansion of banking activities and enforcing regulations, undertaking investigations, and imposing sanctions in relation to the financial and management soundness of banks. The Office of Bank Supervision was officially under the auspices of the MPB, but, in practice, it was under the control of the MOF, because the BoK was not independent, and the MPB had no independent voice. From the 1970s, the securities and insurance markets expanded greatly and numerous non-bank financial institutions, such as merchant banking corporations and mutual savings and finance companies, were established. As a result, the MOF established the Securities Supervisory Committee, the Insurance Supervisory Committee, and the Credit Management Fund, respectively, to supervise them. In addition, the MOF established the KDIC in 1996. The KDIC can conduct joint examinations of insured financial institutions together with the government.

The MOF was an overarching regulator and supervisor. However, it appears that it was largely interested in creating new agencies and institutions to increase its influence, but not in the due implementation of the regulations associated with them. Furthermore, the supervision of the financial system remained fragmented between the different delegated agencies. Figure 11.1 summarises the compartmentalised financial supervisory system that prevailed in Korea until the currency crisis in 1997.

It is important to note that this fragmentation prevented unified financial supervision, thereby rendering exchange of information between the different agencies difficult. They had little reason to coordinate their policies or to collaborate with each other, given that they were not sufficiently autonomous institutions, and were only hierarchically accountable to the MOF. Furthermore, despite its overarching power, the supervision within the MOF was also extremely fragmented and uncoordinated. For instance, the activities of the merchant banking corporations, which were ultimately considered to be the principal culprits of the currency crisis, were separately regulated by diverse laws including the Banking Law, the Short-term Finance Company

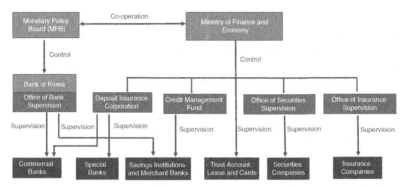

Figure 11.1 Structure of the financial regulatory and supervisory system before the 1997 currency crisis

Law, the Merchant Banking Corporation Law, the Securities and Investment Trust Law, the Foreign Exchange Management Law, and so forth. Furthermore, the co-ordination between the different departments of the MOF was too dispersed to prevent conflicts of regulations and supervisory loopholes. The compartmentalisation of the supervisory system led to supervisory negligence, which contributed to the outbreak of the 1997 currency crisis, as already outlined in Chapter 10.

Against this backdrop, the Korean government decided to unify its regulatory and supervisory system. This implied that the government would take over the Office of Bank Supervision from the BoK. Faced with strong resistance from the BoK, however, this attempt could not be realised until the IMF intervened after the onset of the currency crisis. On 29 December 1997, at a special session of the National Assembly following the Stand-by Arrangement between the Korean government and the IMF that stipulated financial sector restructuring, the reform bills were eventually enacted, which resulted in the establishment of the Financial Supervisory Commission (later renamed as the FSC) and the FSS. Together, they act as a unified regulatory and supervisory authority and thus Korea runs a two-tier regulatory and supervisory system.

The Financial Supervisory Commission, just like the MPB, was originally designed as an autonomous administrative agency with statutory authority over financial supervisory policy under the jurisdiction of the prime minister. The Financial Supervisory Commission was thus the highest decision-making body with regard to financial supervisory policy, and its chairman was automatically the chairman of the

FSS. Then, in 2008, as part of government reorganisation, the Financial Supervisory Commission consolidated the Financial Policy Bureau under the MoFE and became the FSC. As a result, it assumed both the supervisory functions of the Financial Supervisory Commission and the law-making and regulatory functions of the MoFE. Currently, the MoFE (which was renamed the MOEF in 2008) retains authority over financial policies at macroeconomic level, FX policies, and the preparation of financial-related legislation.

At the same time, the FSS was established as an executive organ of the FSC, consolidating the various financial supervisory agencies for banks, securities firms, insurance companies, and other non-bank financial firms into a unified institution. It is noteworthy that the Office of Bank Supervision, which was under the control of the BoK, was merged into this new institution. The FSS is responsible for examining, inspecting, and sanctioning financial institutions under the direction of the FSC. Thus, while the FSC assumes the primary responsibility for rule-making and licensing, the FSS conducts oversight and enforcement activities, as delegated or charged by the FSC.

Basically, the FSS was set up as an institution to support the FSC. Thus, the relationship between the FSC and FSS is very similar to the one between the MPB and the BoK. But, unlike the MPB, the FSC can enforce supervisory policy on its own, although it has delegated its supervisory competences to the FSS. Amid the many overlapping activities between the FSC and FSS, the unilateral control of the FSC over the FSS as simple enforcement branch has created tensions and power struggles between them. In Korea, rule of law was yet completely established (see Box 11.1). Therefore, competition and conflict over discretion and power were particularly acute. The FSC was equipped with its own secretariat composed of government officials, while the FSS was staffed by private-sector employees who were paid largely through the supervisory fees charged to the financial institutions being examined.[1] Thus, no independent decision-making competence was allowed at all. Despite this difference, the struggle for power did result in a separate appointment of the chairman of the FSS.

---

[1] The fact that the FSS is financially supported by the financial institutions suggests that the potential for conflicts of interest between the FSS and the financial institutions is high if the FSS is a decision-making and rule-making body with large discretionary powers. Limiting it to a strict enforcement institution may be a way of minimising the risk of such a conflict occurring.

Box 11.1 Rule of Law and Rule by Law

The role of government is to protect individual freedoms and ensure economic prosperity, although, in reality, government often exercises power arbitrarily to restrict individual freedoms. Curbing this arbitrary exercise of power by government requires the application of the rule of law, defended by an independent judiciary. However, the rule of law should not be mistaken for rule *by* law. While the rule of law is aimed at protecting individual freedoms, rule *by* law uses the law to rationalise the use of power by government and to deprive people of their freedoms. In general, the rule of law is part of the value system of Western democracies, whereas rule by law has long been prevalent in authoritarian Asian societies. This was because the concept of individual freedom seldom existed in traditional Asian societies. Thus, while the law in Western societies was to preserve the freedoms of individuals by limiting arbitrary and discretionary acts on the part of rulers, the law in traditional Asian societies, in contrast, was used to control people and to limit their freedom. Although the term 'law' has been used in China for thousands of years, for instance, its original meaning was more akin to punishing, rather than protecting, people. Rule by law means rule by *any* law, which, in turn, leads to the use of law without rules. Thus, it is very important to be circumspect about enacting bills that do not have clear rules and that give powers to institutions which are highly arbitrary in enforcing the law.

Currently, in Korea, too many arbitrary and discretionary bills are enacted, restricting people's freedoms and their private property. As the OECD (2017) pointed out, the Korean Assembly is notorious for enacting too many bills without proper scrutiny. Laws in Korea are initiated either by the government (the executive body) or by the Assembly, but the share of the bills initiated by the Assembly has continued to expand. Currently, more than 90 per cent of the legislative bills in Korea are initiated by the Assembly, and these bills frequently lack rigour and quality. Figure B11.1 shows that the number of the bills approved in the Korean Assembly increases sharply each year.

As a result, Koreans suffer from excessive regulation and their rights as citizens are too often restricted. One recent example concerns housing regulations in respect of which the government and the Korean National Assembly together have introduced new bills or revised existing legislation. Regulatory changes were made twenty-five times over a three-year period from 2017. It seemed as if the goal of housing policy was to punish – specifically through legislation – people who owned houses, and to make home ownership impossible by exorbitant taxes. Similarly, the financial sector in Korea is subject to too many regulations. Regulations and forms of supervision are not often codified. The laws and regulations are also ambiguous with many loopholes and discretionary powers, which results in overarching discretionary powers in the hands of the regulatory and supervisory agents. Penalties in respect of financial institutions under investigation are often applied to individuals, rather than to the related financial institutions. When people are charged with small regulatory negligence, this can significantly affect their future career path. Thus, strict scrutiny of legislation along with the deregulation and the simplification of existing regulations is the first step towards ensuring the rule of law in the Korean financial sector.

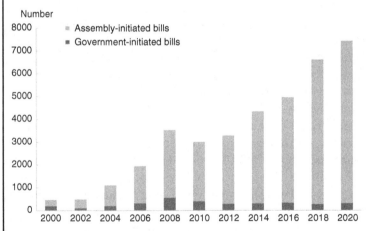

Figure B11.1 The number of bills approved in the Korean National Assembly
Source: National Assembly, Korea.

In parallel with the FSS, the BoK conducts supplementary regulatory and supervisory functions. Although the BoK is not directly responsible for the supervision to ensure the sound management of financial institutions, which is called micro-prudential supervision, it retains the right to request that the FSS conduct on-site or, in conjunction with the BoK, joint examinations of specific banks. The BoK may also request that the FSS submit the investigation results or take corrective measures against financial institutions as need be thereafter. Furthermore, when the FSC adopts financial supervisory measures directly related to monetary and credit policy, the MPB may, if it has specific objections to these measures, request that the FSC reconsiders them.

The outbreak of the global financial crisis in 2008 helped to shift the focus of financial regulation and supervision from the risk management of individual institutions to system-wide or systemic risk management and the resilience of the financial system as a whole. Against this backdrop, the Bank of Korea Act was revised, charging the BoK with responsibility for *financial* as well as *monetary* stability. This revision called for the active use of what is called macro-prudential policy by the BoK in order to ensure financial stability, although the necessary policy instruments are limited. However, during the COVID-19 crisis, the BoK's role in ensuring financial stability has become more important (see Chapter 12). Figure 11.2 summarises the current financial supervisory system in Korea.

11.1.2 Macro- and Micro-Supervisory Policy

The regulatory and supervisory policies in respect of financial stability can be divided into micro- and macro-prudential policies. While micro-prudential policy refers to ensuring the financial health of individual institutions, macro-prudential policy is defined as policy to limit systemic or system-wide financial risk by increasing the resilience of the financial system and strengthening its capacity to withstand both domestic and external shocks (IMF, 2013, 2019).

The reason why micro-prudential supervision should be supplemented with macro-prudential policy is due to the complexity of the financial market and the fallacy of composition, according to which an action which is suitable at the level of individual institutions can

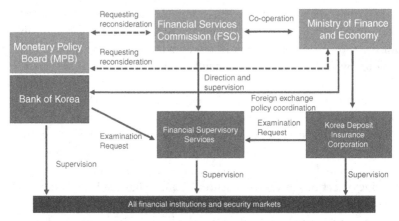

Figure 11.2 Structure of the current financial supervisory system
Note: The BoK and the MPB are legally separate, as are the FSC and the FSS, but they are administratively unified since the governor has replaced the minister of finance as the chairman of the MPB since 1998.

jeopardise the financial system as a whole. For instance, a micro-prudential measure which increases the loan losses of individual banks during an economic downturn can precipitate an economic recession by simultaneously pushing all banks to restrict their loans, thereby increasing loan losses for the whole banking system and increasing the risk of a systemic crisis.

In Korea, micro-prudential policies are principally carried out by the FSC and the FSS. One important instrument in this regard is the regulation for the entry and exit of financial institutions. Another important regulation is on the ownership structure of banks and bank-holding companies, where Korea is renowned for the strictness of its regulation. The competence for these regulations is completely in the hands of the FSC, which is staffed by the government officials, as regulatory rights in Korea are, in principle, exercised only by the government. Second, the FSS, under its delegated authority from the FSC, implements the examination and evaluation of financial institutions. In general, the FSS conducts off-site examinations of a bank's books, which is frequently followed by on-site examinations to see whether the bank is complying with the regulations. At the conclusion of its examination of the business operations and health of financial institutions, the FSS assigns a rating for each financial institution examined. In 1996, the FSS introduced the CAMELS rating system in respect of this supervisory evaluation and rating function. This system allows the FSS to assess the quality of a bank's balance sheet at a point in time, and whether it is in compliance with the regulations and restrictions in force, giving banks a rating from 1 (best) to 5 (worst) in each of the six categories represented by the acronym CAMELS: Capital adequacy, Asset quality, Management, Earnings, Liquidity and Sensitivity to market risks. After the global financial crisis in 2008, this system was replaced by the CAMEL-R system with the R referring to risk management. After evaluation and rating, the financial institutions are required to take corrective actions if they fail to meet the necessary safety and soundness standards. Prompt corrective action is a remedial measure which was introduced in this regard by the FSS in 1998 in the aftermath of the 1997 currency crisis in Korea. In cases of more serious violations of rules or compliance failures, the FSS can take stronger actions including referral to the public prosecution authorities for possible crimes, the revocation of business licences, and monetary fines (see FSS, 2020, for detailed operations).

In contrast, the competence in respect of the macro-prudential policy is shared by the MoFE, the FSC, the FSS, and the BoK. These institutions all share the responsibility for identifying the build-up of systemic risks, but only the MoEF and the FSC, which are staffed by government officials, have the competence for decision-making and legislation. However, because the MoFE and the FSC have only a small number of officials, they do not play a role in their enforcement, even though they have the legal right to do so. As pointed out in Chapter 4, the MPB originally possessed rule-making powers, but these have been deactivated since 1998. In contrast, the FSS and the BoK are, in practice, responsible for the implementation and enforcement of macro-prudential policy decisions. The staff of these two institutions are not government officials, however. Finally, only the BoK has the right and duty to submit an official report on the financial stability of Korea (the FSR) to the National Assembly.

Table 11.1 summarises the principal macro-prudential policy measures in Korea. They can be divided into measures against time-series risks, which originate from the pro-cyclicality between asset prices and credit over the financial cycle, and measures against cross-section risks, which arise through the interlinkages between financial intermediaries, especially

Table 11.1 *Principal macro-prudential policy instruments in Korea*

	Instruments introduced by the Korean government	Instruments introduced through international accords
Measures against time-series risk (pro-cyclicality)	Loan to value (LTV) Debt to Income (DTI)	Counter-cyclical capital buffer (CCyB)
Measures against cross-section risks (inter-connectivity)	FX derivatives positions regulations	Capital adequacy and liquidity regulations

when individual institutions become 'too interconnected to fail'. They are also divided into domestic measures introduced by the Korean government, and global regulations introduced through international accords (e.g., the Basel Accords).

11.2 Domestic Macro-prudential Policy

There were several domestic regulations and schemes already in use in Korea even before the notion of macro-prudential policy became popular through the financial reforms in the aftermath of the global financial crisis of 2008.[2] Among the most well-known macro-prudential policy instruments currently put in place by the Korean government are the regulatory measures that apply to the housing market and the foreign exchange markets, although such policy instruments are not available to the BoK.

11.2.1 LTV and DTI Regulations

Korean households mainly hold their assets in the form of real estate. Since the 2000s, the sizes of mortgage loans have increased due to rising house prices, expansionary monetary policy, and increased housing demand. Korean banks have led the rise in the number of mortgage loans, shifting

---

[2] For instance, the FSC and the FSS put liquidity ratio regulations and loan-to-deposit ratio regulations in place for the safety of domestic banks (Lee, 2013).

their main business from corporate loans to household loans. Mortgage loans in Korea are very safe assets with their recourse clauses. Banks also had a painful experience with the numerous corporate bankruptcies during the 1997 currency crisis, which turned their corporate loans into bad loans.

Amid soaring house prices, the government decided to limit the size of mortgage loans and to try to stop the rise in house prices. Normally, this goal would have been attained by an interest rate hike and a tight monetary policy. However, this option was not adopted given the then urgent need to stimulate the Korean economy, which was in recession. It seems that there was an implicit division of labour between the government and the BoK regarding the deployment of the optimal combination of monetary and financial stability policies. Thus, the FSC/FSS introduced the LTV regulation, placing a cap on the ratio of mortgage loans to the value of the houses put up as collateral. The LTV ratio caps varied, depending upon the loan maturity, the house price, and the location. Generally, the longer the maturity, the higher the house price, and the more speculative the location, the lower the LTV ratio cap. The LTV regulation had a limited impact on curbing the size of mortgage loans, however, because the increase in house prices helped to increase further the mortgage loan amounts by increasing the value of the mortgage collateral. As house price increase continued, further regulation had to be introduced. Consequently, the DTI regulation was introduced as a complement to the LTV regulation, and put a ceiling on the ratio of the amount of annual debt payments to the debtor's annual income. The DTI ratio caps also varied depending on borrower circumstances, such as the house price and the location of the property.

The LTV and DTI regulations were expected to reduce the pro-cyclicality of mortgage lending, but this expected outcome was, to a large extent, offset by the substitution effect. As these regulations applied only to the banking sector initially, a reduction in the size of mortgage loans by banks could be substituted by increased borrowings from non-bank financial institutions. Banks also substituted mortgage loans with other household loans which were not subject to the LTV and DTI ceilings. Thus, these regulations failed to contain the increase in overall household debts.

What is most important in respect of the LTV and DTI regulations is for the government to use them for the proper goal of financial stability only, by tightening them if mortgage loans increase, and, conversely, by relaxing them if mortgage loans decrease. After the 2008 global financial crisis, however, these prudential regulations were used by the Korean government as a means of stimulating the economy, and not for financial stability. Thus, these regulations were used to reinforce, but not to mitigate, the pro-cyclicality of the economy over the course of the business cycle. Despite the need to restrain the size of mortgage loans amid continuing interest rate cuts, for example, the Korean government relaxed these regulations to stimulate the economy in 2014. The FSC/FSS uniformly raised the ceilings for the LTV and DTI ratios up to 70 per cent and 60 per cent, respectively, even though Korea was already near to its potential growth. Thus, they were no longer macro-prudential instruments, but stimulus tools. Figure 11.3 shows how the size and growth rate of household debt in Korea have both grown rapidly along with interest rate cuts since 2014. For instance, the growth rate of household debt, which stood at about 5 to 6 per cent, rose to about 10 to 12 per cent from the latter half of 2014. As a result, the household debt ratio, as a proportion of GDP, increased from about 130 per cent in 2014 to 160 per cent in 2017.

Clearly, the interest rate cut and the wrong macro-prudential policy were two major factors that accelerated the pro-cyclicality of the

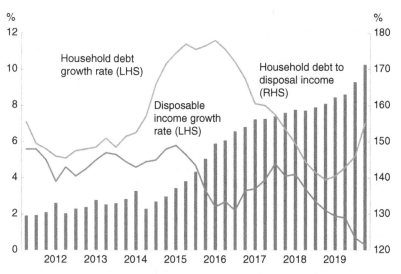

Figure 11.3 Household debt trend in Korea
Source: ECOS, BoK.

economy and caused a surge in household debt. But who was responsible for such an explosion of household debt? Was it the BoK that had cut the interest rate or the FSC/FSS that had relaxed the LTV and DTI regulations? Given that the BoK's goal was to stabilise the output and employment levels, an interest rate cut to stimulate the economy in the event of a recession would have been a natural response. However, the BoK was also responsible for financial stability. Thus, if the excessive expansion of household debt really did threaten financial stability, the BoK would not be exempt from such an accusation. Notwithstanding this, the decision to cut interest rates was basically a matter of choice under circumstances in which the goals of monetary policy and macro-prudential policy were in conflict with one another. In contrast, if macro-prudential regulatory policy was used as a means of economic stimulation, clearly this would not be consistent with the mandate of the FSC and the FSS. Thus, the primary responsibility for these decisions must lie with these regulatory institutions (see Box 11.2).

Macro-prudential policy changed again in 2017 as a new government took office. This time, to stem the rise in house prices and the consequent mortgage demand, the new government decided to lower the ceilings for the LTV and DTI ratios by 10 percentage points for households who owned second houses and to apply the DTI standard strictly. At the same time, regulations on the DSR were newly added to the existing regulatory instruments. Table 11.2 summarises the macro-prudential regulatory measures currently in use for stabilising the housing market in Korea.

Notwithstanding this, largely due to the misguided housing market policy implemented by the Ministry of Land, Infrastructure and Transportation, and along with the expected decline in the supply of houses, house prices rapidly increased and the rise in the size of mortgage loans continued unabated.

11.2.2 FX Derivatives Positions Regulations

Korea has a high degree of capital market openness. Under these circumstances, excessive capital inflows and outflows have triggered and amplified the economic crises in Korea. Given the ample global liquidity resulting from the unconventional monetary policies implemented by the central banks of the United States and other advanced economies in the aftermath of the 2008 global financial crisis, in

Table 11.2 *Evolution of housing market-related macro-prudential policy*

	Area	2012		2014	2017
		Banks and Insurance Companies	Other Non-bank Financial Companies	All Financial Companies	All Financial Companies
LTV	Seoul and Suburban Seoul	50–70%	60–85%	70%	Reduction of 10 percentage points for Second House Owners
	Other Areas	60–70%	70–85%		
DTI	Seoul	50%	50–55%	60%	Reduction of 10 percentage points for Second House Owners
	Suburban Seoul	60%	60–65%		
DSR	–	–		–	100–150% for unsecured loans 150–200% for collateralised loans

Source: BoK and author's compilation.

Box 11.2 Are Household Debts in Korea Qualitatively Improved?

If household debt is explosively increasing, the right response would be to curb the total increase in household debt.

But, as pointed out earlier, the Korean government decided to react in the opposite manner in 2014, by relaxing the LTV and DTI regulations amid an already overheated housing market. To cover up its mistake, the government implemented the so-called Quality Improvement Programme, which consisted of increasing the proportion of fixed rate and amortised loans as most Korean mortgage loans were variable-rate, non-amortised bullet loans that required a lump sum repayment at the end of the term. The government strove hard to achieve this goal.

As shown in Figure B11.2, the share of fixed-rate loans relative to all mortgage loans, which remained below 20 per cent until 2013, increased to nearly 50 per cent by 2019. The share of amortised loans has followed a similar trend, increasing from less than 20 per cent in 2013 to 55 per cent in 2019. This was particularly due to the marketing of the so-called eligible mortgage loans launched by the Korea Housing Finance Corporation, a government-owned company which was set up in 2004 to facilitate long-term housing finance and to securitise the mortgage loans. Eligible mortgage loans are long-term fixed-rate mortgages with instalment payments of the principal and the interest over a maturity period of ten years or longer. Highlighting the improvement in the quality of household debts, Korean government officials proudly declared that the programme had helped households enormously to hedge against the risk of interest rate fluctuations.

However, their self-praise that such programmes have successfully encouraged households to take on new fixed-rate mortgage loans and switch their existing variable-rate loans into fixed-rate loans with longer maturities needs to be assessed more objectively.

First of all, if household debt risk was that important, the government itself would have been more cautious about easing the LTV and the DTI regulations, which were used to stimulate the economy. More importantly, the attempt by the government to encourage Korean households to switch to fixed-rate loans was complete nonsense at a time of continuously declining interest rates from 2014 until the end of 2017. It was quite obvious to every ordinary Korean household that interest rates tended to fall over time. For example, the interest rate was cut eight consecutive times during a period of more than five years from July 2012 to November 2017. Notwithstanding this, the government officials only highlighted the risks of interest rate increases, closing their eyes to the losses to households when interest rates fell. They repeatedly promoted the fixed-rate mortgage policy despite continuous interest rate cuts. Thus, if Korean households had taken the advice of the Korean government officials, then they would have incurred extra housing costs. The main concern of the government officials seemed to be that they achieve the policy goal of increasing the share of fixed-rate mortgage loans under the assumption of unlikely rate hikes, regardless of whether Korean households would benefit from it or not.[3]

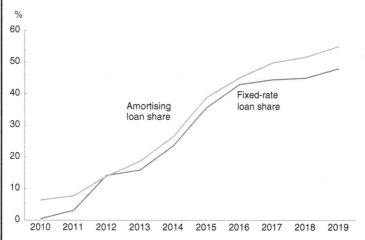

Figure B11.2 The share of fixed–rate and amortised mortgage loans
Source: BoK.

---

[3] During the four years that I served as a member of the MPB (2012–2016), interest rates were not raised once. Notwithstanding this, the government officials never stopped exaggerating the risk of interest rate increases in order to promote their programme.

Furthermore, even if the government were successful in converting the variable-rate mortgage loans into fixed-rate loans, the effect in reducing household-debt risk would be very limited because the converted fixed-rate mortgage loans were, for the most part, mixed-type loans. These mixed-type loans allow households to pay fixed interest rates at lower levels during the initial conversion period, after which they have to pay variable interest rates when the conversion period is over, leaving the overall interest rate risk of households only marginally reduced. Thus, borrowers pay interest rates at a fixed rate for the first two to three years after the conversion, but subsequently revert to variable interest rates. As a result, such fixed-rate loans cannot sufficiently protect the borrowers from the risk of interest rate rises. They are similar to 'teaser loans' that give borrowers a very favourable interest rate for a certain period of time, and thereafter charge them higher than normal interest rates. It is difficult to differentiate, to any great extent, between the mixed loans recommended by the Korean government and these fraudulent loans.

Who gained and who lost from these loans? The households that switched to fixed-rate loans, following the government's recommendation, lost money as a result. In contrast, the financial companies, who sold them these fixed-rate mortgage loans, earned increased profits from the government's policy. The financial losses of the households were matched by the increased profits of the related financial institutions (in particular, the Korea Housing Finance Corporation that borrowed funds at low variable rates and earned high fixed-rate returns). Thus, the government's programme was not in the interest of households, but rather for the benefits of the financial companies. The government should not have intervened unnecessarily in the economy. The choice about fixed- or variable-rate mortgage loans is best left to the households to decide upon, and should not be within the competence or remit of the government.

particular, there were huge capital inflows into Korea again. In these circumstances, extreme vigilance would be required to cope with potential excessive capital outflows and the consequential financial crisis. Against this backdrop, regulations on the FX derivative positions of banks were established in October 2010 by the MOEF and implemented by the BoK.

Korea's FX-related regulations were designed to address risk factors that were generated on both the demand and the supply sides. Leverage caps on banks' FX derivative positions were first introduced in October 2010, aimed at curbing increases in the short-term external debt of banks and the resulting currency and maturity mismatches occurring in the process of excessive FX forward sales by Korean companies. The leverage caps were initially set at 250 per cent of capital for foreign bank branches and 50 per cent for domestic banks, which were reduced later to 200 per cent and 40 per cent, respectively, in 2011, and further reduced to 150 per cent and 30 per cent in 2013.

In August 2011, the MSL was introduced, to curb excessive increases in the non-core liabilities of banks, which could cause systemic risk in terms of pro-cyclicality and the interconnectedness of financial institutions. The levy was imposed on the outstanding amounts of non-deposit foreign currency liabilities, with the levy rates varying from 2 to 20 basis points, depending on the maturity of the liabilities. Lower levies were applied to liabilities of longer maturity, in order to improve the maturity structure of the foreign currency liabilities of banks. These FX-stability-related measures contributed to alleviating FX market vulnerability by reducing the foreign borrowings of banks and improving their maturity structures (Kim, 2014).

11.3 Global Macro-prudential Regulations

In order to contain systemic crisis risk, the financial reforms that proceeded after the 2008 global financial crisis focused on creating a financial system in which financial institutions were better capitalised, less leveraged, held more liquid assets, and were thus better able to absorb losses and to manage liquidity risks. Significant progress was made in this direction through the Basel III process, and the implementation of the new standards is underway. The macro-prudential measures that Korea introduced through the Basel III process can be divided into those intended to reduce the inter-connectivity, and those that reduce the pro-cyclicality, of the economy.

11.3.1 *Capital Adequacy Regulations*

Capital requirement regulations are the most basic international regulations. These measures can be micro-prudential measures but strengthening the capital base of individual banks automatically protects them from the 'domino effect' and thus serves as a macroprudential instrument as well.

Following the recommendations made by the Basel Committee on Banking Supervision, the Korean government introduced a minimum capital ratio regulation, first, in 1995, which required commercial banks to hold at least 8 per cent of their risk-weighted assets in the form of capital. In the aftermath of the global financial crisis in 2008, this standard was extended to Basel III, in order to strengthen the regulations on bank capital and liquidity. The Basel III capital framework for Korean banks began in December 2013. In full compliance with the Basel Committee's stricter capital standards, Korean banks were required to hold as common equity tier 1 at least 4.5 per cent of their risk-weighted assets, and as tier 1 capital 6.0 per cent of their risk-weighted assets. Total regulatory capital, which consists of tier 1 and tier 2 capital, must be greater than 8.0 per cent of the risk-weighted assets at all times (FSS, 2020).

Basel III requires banks to build up supplementary capital buffers so as to enhance the loan loss absorption capacity of banks and to maintain their capital ratio above the minimum required ratio in times of crisis. Furthermore, for some D-SIB additional capital is required. This regulation is a typical policy tool that is intended to curb the possibility of banks being 'too interconnected to fail' and to enhance the resilience of the entire financial system.

Banks are also subject to a 3 per cent leverage ratio regulation, which was introduced to limit excessive bank leverage and thereby prevent abrupt de-leveraging in times of crisis and the resulting amplification of shocks as occurred in the 2008 global financial crisis. This ratio was initially a supplementary measure, but subsequently became an official regulatory measure in 2018.

In addition to Basel III's enhanced capital standards, banks are subject to two new regulations, the LCR and the NSFR. The LCR, defined as the ratio of the stock of high-quality liquid assets to net cash outflows for a thirty-day period, took effect in 2015, and required domestic commercial banks to meet a minimum ratio of 100 per cent. For foreign bank branches, the minimum LCR is 60 per cent. Foreign capital outflows have always been an important factor behind the currency and financial crises that Korea has experienced since 1997. Thus, although the foreign currency LCR is not a part of the Basel III requirements, the Korean government nonetheless adopted it as an official regulation in 2017. Currently, all domestic banks, with the exception of the Korea Export and Import Bank and some small regional banks, are required to maintain a minimum foreign currency LCR of 80 per cent.

Supplementing the LCR with a time horizon of one year, the NSFR is intended to improve long-term resilience by requiring banks to maintain a stable funding profile with regard to on- and off-balance sheet activities. Commercial banks are required to maintain a minimum NSFR of 100 per cent. The NSFR requirement became effective in 2019.

Table 11.3 summarises the current resilience of Korean banks based upon the Basel III capital adequacy and liquidity standards. In general, the Korean banks would seem to be sufficiently resilient as of the end of 2019. The total capital ratio of commercial banks stood at around 16 per cent and the tier 1 and common equity tier 1 capital ratios were, respectively, 13.9 per cent and 13.2 per cent. All capital ratios were in excess of the regulatory standards by a wide margin. The commercial bank leverage ratio also stood at 6 per cent, which was significantly in excess of the regulatory standard 3 per cent for all banks. The LCR and the NSFR of Korean banks stood at 110 per cent and 113 per cent, respectively. These ratios, too, are all in excess of the regulatory standard.

Currently, the FSC and the FSS handle these macro-prudential measures directly. The BoK assesses the resilience of the Korean banks to aggregate systemic shocks and communicates the results to the public. The main instrument to this end is the FSR, which it has published since 2003. In particular, in the wake of the 2008 global financial crisis, it became a biannual statutory report provided to the National Assembly, which allows the BoK to develop a strong and effective communication tool for financial stability. There are three objectives that the BoK seeks to achieve through the FSR. First, it identifies and evaluates the potential risk factors in the financial system. Second, it provides early warnings of risks to the policy authorities and market participants. In this regard, in particular, the BoK relies on a stress test, which is the principal toolkit for macro-prudential policy, hypothesising plausible stress scenarios and quantifying the potential losses from systemic

Table 11.3 Korean bank resiliency as of the end of 2019

		Basel III minimum standards			Current Korean banks
		(without capital conservation buffer)	(with 2.5% capital conservation buffer)	(with 1% for D-SIFIs)	
Capital ratio	Total capital	8%	10.5%	11.5%	15.9%
	Tier 1 capital	6%	8.5%	9.5%	13.9%
	Common equity tier 1 capital	4.5%	7%	8%	13.2%
Leverage ratio		3%			6%
LCR2		100% (for domestic currency)			110.4%
		80% (for foreign currency)			127.8%
NSFR3		100%			113.5%

Note 1: Leverage ratio = Tier 1 capital/Total assets.
Note 2: LCR = High quality liquidity asset/Net cash outflow.
Note 3: NSFR = Available stable funding/Required stable funding.
Source: FSS, BoK.

risk.[4] Third, through it, the BoK endeavours pre-emptively to curb the accumulation of systemic risk by suggesting policy alternatives when necessary. In this respect, the FSR serves as an important macro-prudential policy tool that the BoK can use. Notwithstanding this, the BoK has not made sufficient use of it, principally because of concerns about a potential conflict with the FSS, which wants to monopolise the enforcement of financial supervision. For instance, when the BoK conducts stress tests for the assessment of the resilience of financial institutions, it could also publish a rating result on the risk exposure and vulnerability of individual financial institutions. But, currently, the BoK staff are unwilling to publish these results for individual financial institutions. It reports the stress test result only for the entire financial system.[5]

11.3.2 Counter-Cyclical Capital Buffer (CCyB)

Bank lending is a typical pro-cyclical activity. Thus, Basel III requires banks to build up supplementary capital buffers so as to enhance the counter-cyclicality of the economy. In particular, banks are required to set aside ordinary equity capital for the purpose of imposing counter-cyclical capital at the 0–2.5 per cent range of risk-weighted assets during the period of credit expansion. Conversely, the downward revision of the counter-cyclical buffer capital immediately takes effect. This regulation is regarded as reducing the pro-cyclicality of bank lending behaviour as well as the interconnectedness between financial institutions.

The FSC announced its first CCyB rate for banks and bank holding companies in Korea in 2016. At present, the buffer rate is set at 0 per cent, taking into account the credit-to-GDP gap, macroeconomic conditions, co-ordination with relevant fiscal and monetary policies, and the current CCyB implementation policies of other countries. Unlike the minimum capital regulations that banks must always abide by, CCyB will only be triggered during periods of excessive credit

---

[4] The use of stress tests pre-supposes the existence of a systemic risk amplification mechanism through which shocks grow and spread across financial system. To this end, the BoK uses the 'Systemic Risk Assessment Model for Macro-prudential Policy (SAMP)' developed in 2012 (see Bank of Korea (2018) for more detail).

[5] As highlighted by Geithner (2014), stress tests for individual financial institutions can be very useful for coping with a financial crisis. In the case of Europe, stress tests for individual institutions have been intensively used as well.

expansion. Consequently, the supervisory authorities should determine when and how to increase the amount of buffer capital.

In this regard, the triggering of the CCyB by the FSC will require closer co-ordination with the monetary policy decisions by the MPB, because it should pre-announce decisions related to upgrading buffer capital levels twelve months in advance in order to give banks the time needed to put the increased buffer capital in place. Thus, macro-prudential policy cannot be much different from monetary policy, in that both policies forecast the future path of economic or financial cycles and take pre-emptive actions to stabilise these cycles. The only difference is that monetary policy actions are through changing the interest rates, while the CcyB policy actions are through regulatory changes.

Thus, the two policy decisions are inseparable. As a consequence, if the decision on the use of the CCyB is made by the FSC alone, the conflict between the two policies is seriously likely to harm their effectiveness deeply. There have been many policy conflicts between the FSC and the MPB (See Box 11.3). In 2018, for example, the FSC announced that it would amend the existing loan-to-deposit regulation, which it had introduced in 2012 in order to restrain the pro-cyclicality of bank lending, like the CCyB regulation. Assigning higher weight to household loans and lower weight to corporate loans, the new loan-to-deposit ratio was intended to curb excessive increases in the size of household loans. As all Korean banks had to meet the new loan-to-debt ratio by January 2020, it led to a decrease in the total number of loans allocated, as well as the number of household loans, amid the economic slowdown (see BoK, 2019). Thus, although it helped to mitigate the rise in the size of household loans, it contributed to the contraction of the economy, by weakening the financial intermediation function of banks. This put pressure on the MPB to stimulate the economy.

Box 11.3 Who Should Lead Macro-Prudential Policy in Korea?

It is important to decide which institution should take the leadership of macro-prudential policy, in particular, the CCyB regulations. If the FSC/FSS and the MPB/BoK are two separate organisations, and if counter-cyclical macro-prudential policy has a similar effect on the economy as monetary policy, for instance, it will be as though *two* central banks are implementing *two* different monetary policies. Clearly, such an organisational structure would lead to serious policy conflicts and harm the effectiveness of both monetary and macro-prudential policies. The reasons for this are as follows: The first reason is related to the differences in the forecasts of future economic and financial cycles between the commissioners of the FSC and the members of MPB. While the commissioners of the FSC are experienced in rule-making and legislation, the members of MPB have more expertise in economic forecasting. Thus, it is possible, for example, that, on occasion, the MPB will correctly forecast an economic downturn and thus cut interest rates, while the FSC will conversely forecast an economic upturn and require banks to put up additional capital buffers. Thus, the expansionary effect of monetary policy will be offset by contractionary effect of macro-prudential policy. As a result, the desired stimulating of the economy may fail. Second, even if the two institutions make identical economic forecasts, the financial cycle can differ from the output cycle, which can cause another conflict between monetary policy and macro-prudential policy (Shin et al., 2017). For example, the expansion phase of the financial cycle may persist even when the output cycle goes into contraction. In this case, the MPB might decide to cut interest rates, while the FSC would require banks to put up additional capital buffers to cool the overheated credit market. Their effects offset each other. Third, there is a possibility of abuse of power on the part of the FSC government officials. The FSC has sometimes used these instruments for macroeconomic stabilisation and sometimes for financial stabilisation purposes. It should not use the macro-prudential instruments for stimulating the economy, as in the case of the LTV and DTI regulations introduced in 2014. This type of behaviour would be a dereliction of duty. If the FSC uses this discretionary power in an arbitrary manner, it will even endanger the democratic principle of the division of power, by infringing upon the independence of the BoK.

Setting up an independent macro-prudential committee and creating a governance structure that can reflect the opinions and expertise of the MPB in carrying out monetary policy will greatly alleviate possible policy conflicts between different institutions. For example, in the United States, the FSOC was established to allow the chairman of the Federal Reserve Board to co-ordinate macro-prudential policy with the Treasury Secretary and other regulators. Korea also requires an equivalent co-ordination framework for macro-prudential policy.

Currently, the vice governor of the BoK is a standing member of the FSC. He is also an attendee at the Macroeconomic and Financial Stability Meetings, which were temporarily established to co-ordinate overall macro-prudential and macroeconomic policy in 2018. However, because he is not an official delegate of the MPB, he only represents the BoK, not the MPB. Thus, to state that horizontal and practical collaboration between the MPB and the FSC was actually taking place would be incorrect.

There is a strong need for closer co-operation, at least between the MPB and the FSC, either through the setting up of an independent council or through the regularisation of meetings. This will, above all, eliminate potential conflicts between the monetary policy that the BoK is responsible for, and the macro-prudential policy for which the FSC is responsible. Moreover, the BoK needs to regulate and supervise non-banking financial companies and financial markets because, under the current Bank of Korea Act, financial institutions are only defined as banking institutions. Under circumstances in which the importance of shadow banking is rapidly expanding, the traditional distinctions between banks, securities companies, investment firms, and insurance companies are no longer relevant. For macro-prudential policy, the BoK needs to focus not only on banks but also on large financial institutions including non-banking financial institutions that are systemically important. Conversely, there is also a need to reform the supervisory system in the long term, given the increasing importance of consumer financial protection. The current financial regulatory framework in Korea is charged with the function of promoting the financial industry and markets *and also* protecting consumers. This framework, which often ends up protecting financial institutions and making the financial market more monopolistic, comes into conflict with consumer financial protection, which does not appear desirable in a democratic society. This means that, while the rule-making and legislative competence of the FSC should be transferred to the MOEF, the FSS should focus on micro-prudential supervision and consumer financial protection.

12 | *Crisis Management and Lender of Last Resort*

Along with macro-prudential regulatory and supervisory policy, the BoK performs a vital role as the LOLR, providing liquidity support to individual institutions and financial markets, in order to ensure financial stability. The LOLR is originally an instrument to address financial crises *ex post*. In the wake of the global financial crisis, the LOLR has become an essential crisis management instrument of the BoK. However, the Korean government has also been active as an LOLR, because the resolution of financial crises required assisting not just *illiquid* banks but also *insolvent* ones. This chapter looks at the evolution of the BoK's role as the LOLR, focusing on the division of labour between the government and the central bank.

12.1 Who Is Responsible as the Lender of Last Resort?

In the event of a financial crisis, the central bank is the natural LOLR because it has a monopoly on the issuing of currency, which will allow it to provide unlimited liquidity in order to prevent the crisis. Providing ELA to individual financial institutions and financial markets is thus a unique function of central banks, because, even when all other economic agents suffer from liquidity shortages, central banks alone can lend them liquidity or purchase their assets with its own liquidity.

But what is the rationale for the central bank's role as an LOLR? Conventionally, the LOLR theory was developed for central banks, which should avoid incurring losses like commercial banks. Thus, according to W. Bagehot, it is important to distinguish between illiquidity and insolvency, and central banks should provide liquidity only to illiquid banks, not to insolvent ones. The objective of the LOLR is not to prevent *insolvent* banks from going bankrupt, but rather to save sound, but temporarily illiquid, banks (Bats et al., 2018).

In implementing LOLR policy, however, distinguishing between illiquidity and insolvency is not nearly as clear as Bagehot indicated

(Goodhart, 1999). Central banks automatically face a higher risk of losses in a financial crisis. First, illiquidity and insolvency are often indistinguishable when asset prices collapse and financial crisis deepens. In times of financial crisis, for example, the quality of the collateral assets that central banks hold will deteriorate over time because commercial banks that lack liquidity will undertake asset fire sales. The latter, however, can fuel further fall in asset prices, thereby creating a vicious cycle that will exacerbate the deterioration of asset quality. Furthermore, in the event of a financial crisis, common factors such as a drop in output, can simultaneously deteriorate the quality of financial assets and raise their correlation, which will raise the risk of losses for central banks providing emergency liquidity assistance. Finally, the balance sheet of the central banks expands due to the commercial banks' 'flight to quality' (Bindseil, 2014). Thus, it will be difficult for central banks to distinguish clearly between illiquidity and insolvency.

Consequently, LOLR policy should be assessed subject to whether it creates a sufficient external economy, which arises from the prevention of systemic crisis. For instance, there may be a need to bail out even insolvent financial institutions if the overall social benefit of preventing systemic crisis exceeds the cost of moral hazard. The problem is in deciding whether central banks are a legitimate LOLR or not. If a crisis is due to insolvency, the government, not the central bank, can determine the LOLR policy. This is because central banks cannot make political decisions and have no mandate for *spending* money. It is only governments in charge of fiscal policy that have such mandates. Central banks are *lending* institutions at most, not *spending* institutions. In effect, the BoK is prohibited by legislation from providing funds to financial institutions which incur losses. Furthermore, the MPB members can be indicted for any losses and can be asked to reimburse them if the BoK incurs losses arising out of its liquidity support. Thus, in practice, it is easier for the government to conduct the LOLR policy because it is less sensitive to the insolvency risk. The issuing power of the BoK does not, in itself, guarantee that the LOLR function be the exclusive role of the BoK alone. The BoK needs the collaboration of the government.

But what is the rationale for the government to assume the role of the LOLR? Blinder (2013) gives an example of why the involvement of the government is important in the implementation of LOLR policy. Let us consider the simplified balance sheet of a hypothetical bad bank, which

Table 12.1 *Changes in the balance sheet of a bad bank*

Original B/S		Mark to Market B/S	
Assets	Liabilities	Assets	Liabilities
Good loans 50	Deposits 90	Good loans 50	Deposits 90
Bad loans 50	Equity 10	Bad loans 25	Equity -15

Source: Adapted from Blinder (2013).

has KRW90 billion in deposits and KRW10 billion in equities. Let us further suppose that this bank has two types of assets, good assets worth KRW50 billion with a probability of 1, and bad assets worth KRW50 billion with a probability of 0.5. Thus, the expected value of the bad assets will be worth only KRW25 billion, a 50 per cent discount to the face value, although the book value of the bad assets is nonetheless KRW50 billion. Table 12.1 shows the changes in the bank's balance sheet positions.

The expected asset value of the bad bank is thus KRW75 billion short of its deposits, which are worth KRW90 billion and the bank is probably insolvent. Clearly, the BoK cannot bail out this bank because it could incur losses if it did so. But the government could save the bank in three different ways. Table 12.2 shows the three possible ways in which the government could support and assist the bad bank.

First, the government can simply guarantee deposit payments. This means that the government takes on the expected loss of KRW15 trillion as deposit insurance compensation. Second, the government can buy bad loans from the bank, albeit at a loss, if the social benefits exceed the cost of the bailout. The possibility of loss means that this option is available for the government alone, not for the BoK. Now, let us suppose that the government buys the bank's bad assets at book value of KRW50 billion. Then, the bank becomes solvent with an expected loss of KRW25 billion for the government. Clearly, this can lead to the criticism that this type of liquidity support is preferential. If so, the government can buy the bad assets at a reduced value of, say, KRW40 billion, which will still leave the bank solvent. By making the bank's equity holders partially responsible for losses, this will help

Table 12.2 *Three types of government liquidity support*

1. Deposit insurance		2. Asset purchases		3. Capital injection	
Assets	Liabilities	Assets	Liabilities	Assets	Liabilities
Good loans 50	Deposits 90	Good loans 50	Deposits 90	Good loans 50	Deposits 90
Bad loans 25	Equity -15	Cash 50	Equity 10	Bad loans 25	Equity 10
Cash 15	Guarantee 15			Cash 25	

Source: Adapted from Blinder (2013).

attenuate public complaints about the government bailout. However, one major practical problem for the asset purchase option is that, a priori, nobody knows exactly the true market value of bad assets. To calculate the true market value is almost impossible during a financial crisis because the value of bad assets changes constantly. Third, a simpler rescue method would be to inject equity capital into the bad bank. If, in this case, the government injects new capital worth KRW25 billion, then the government can make the bad bank solvent with much smaller liquidity support than through bank asset purchase. Currently, the BoK cannot inject capital because it is prohibited by law from owning private banks.

Therefore, the bailout of a bad bank, even if it is effective in stemming a crisis, cannot be performed by the BoK. The government alone can take the risk of insolvency losses or own private banks, and, in this respect, it is important to note that, in Korea, the government has always been a key player in the LOLR policy, substituting for the central bank.[1] The very interventionist Korean government has employed all three of these options actively whenever financial market instabilities have occurred. During the 1997 currency crisis, for example, the Korean government relied on the KDIC to guarantee bank deposits and set up the KAMCO, a government-owned restructuring company, to buy bad loans to help complete its financial restructuring programme. Furthermore, the government nationalised many Korean banks directly through capital injection. Thus, the Korean government's involvement as an LOLR was much more extensive, and, although this role is declining, it is nonetheless still an important provider of liquidity. This means that it is the *monetary authorities*, which include both the BoK and the government, that carry out LOLR policy in Korea.

12.2 The Government as the Lender of Last Resort

The MOF, which was succeeded by the FSC after 1997, had not only the necessary regulatory and supervisory powers but also full budgetary support for the enforcement of its powers. During the 1997

---

[1] This also seems the reason why the Troubled Asset Relief Program (TARP) was introduced in the United States along with the many emergency liquidity support packages provided by the FRS during the 2008 global financial crisis.

currency crisis, as outlined in Chapter 10, soaring interest rates and a credit crunch resulted in many large corporations collapsing in chain insolvencies, placing the banks and all other financial companies under severe stress. The Korean government decided to resolve this crisis by a comprehensive financial restructuring programme, which included bank closure. Five commercial banks were closed and almost all merchant banks, which were regarded as the culprits in the currency crisis, were closed as well. This resulted in around 40 per cent of bank staff losing their jobs. Along with this massive restructuring of financial companies, the Korean government injected large sums of public money, while the role of the BoK as LOLR was very limited. Not alone did the government directly recapitalise banks through cash injections from the budget, it also mobilised the necessary funds as the LOLR through two public institutions, the KDIC and the KAMCO. They respectively issued Deposit Insurance Fund Bonds and Non-performing Assets Resolution Fund Bonds, whose repayment was guaranteed by the government. Table 12.3 summarises the use of public funds as of the end of 1999. According to the table, the total amount of public funds devoted to financial restructuring stood at KRW64 trillion, out of which the KDIC used KRW21 trillion as compensation for the losses and repayment of the deposits of failed institutions. The KDIC also used KRW20.5 trillion for capital injections. Although the KDIC was not excluded from the purchase of bad assets, it was the main activity of the KAMCO. The KAMCO spent KRW20.5 trillion in the purchase of non-performing loans.

Table 12.3 *Injection of public funds as of the end of 1999 (unit: KRW trillions)*

		Banks	Non-banks	Total
Compensation for losses and Repayment of deposits	KDIC	9.6	11.4	21.0
Recapitalisation	KDIC	16.5	4.0	20.5
Purchase of assets, etc.	KDIC	1.8	0.2	2.0
	KAMCO	17.3	3.2	20.5
Total		45.2	18.8	64

Source: White Paper, Public Fund Oversight Committee (2001).

Subsequently, in 2001, the Korean government created the Public Fund Oversight Committee to ensure the efficient use of injected public funds and to facilitate their smooth redemption. Currently, the size of this Fund is around KRW160 trillion.

The eruption of the global financial crisis in 2008 again destabilised Korea's financial system. The government led the LOLR policy, setting up three new kinds of public funds.

First, with widening yield spreads on corporate bonds, it became clear that liquidity-starved companies had great difficulty in borrowing from the bond market. Financial markets in Korea had developed rapidly since the 1997 currency crisis. Thus, unlike in 1997 when indirect finance was dominant, Korean companies relied heavily on direct financial markets for their investment demand. Stabilising the bond market emerged as essential to mitigate the impact of the global financial crisis. To help resolve the liquidity shortages problem in the market, the FSC set up the Bond Market Stabilisation Fund. This was a private equity fund with a capital of KRW10 trillion to which the Korea Development Bank,[2] commercial banks, and insurance and securities companies subscribed capital contributions of KRW8 trillion, 1.5 trillion, and 0.5 trillion, respectively. The BoK committed itself to provide these financial institutions, with up to 50 per cent of the value of their subscriptions by purchasing government bonds and MSBs from them, up to a ceiling of KRW5 trillion. The Fund invested the money thus mobilised into eligible bank debentures, corporate bonds, asset-backed securities, such as PF ABCP and P-CBOs. Non-eligible bonds with lower credit ratings had funding support in the form of P-CBOs. After the launch of the Bond Market Stabilisation Fund, credit spreads between corporate and government bonds dropped substantially. For instance, the three-year credit spread between AA-grade corporate bonds and government bonds of the same maturity was nearly 8 per cent when the Fund was created in December 2008. It fell to 5 per cent in May 2009, recording around a 300 bp decrease in six months. Thus, concerns over liquidity arising from the global financial crisis could be successfully handled in Korea.

Second, the FSC set up another fund, the Bank Recapitalisation Fund, amid an intensifying global financial crisis. The Fund used its capital in

---

[2] The Korea Development Bank is a 100 per cent government-owned bank that specialises in providing loans to government projects and investment banking.

the purchase of bank shares and helped to raise their BIS capital ratios. The goal was to support banks to provide more loans, rather than to pursue financial restructuring, as in the case of the troubled banks with large non-performing loans. By enhancing the soundness of the banking sector, the Fund intended to provide a safety net to prevent bank panics, and to encourage banks to continue lending even during periods of crises. The Bank Recapitalisation Fund was planned to be set up with a capital of KRW20 trillion. Again, the BoK was committed to extending a loan of up to KRW10 trillion to the government-owned Korea Development Bank, which, when added to its own resources of KRW2 trillion, subscribed KRW12 trillion to the Fund. The Fund would then raise KRW8 trillion from institutional investors by selling preferred stocks. This scheme was designed to ease concerns over government control of private banks. By purchasing subordinated bonds (within a ceiling of KRW10 trillion) and preferred shares and hybrid bonds (within a ceiling of KRW10 trillion), the Fund supported the banks, which, upon a voluntary capital call basis, accessed it to strengthen their capital base. In order to minimise the potential stigma effect, the government assigned a ceiling *per* bank that depended on their asset sizes irrespective of their credit ratings. The Fund had purchased KRW3.9 trillion subordinated bonds and hybrid bonds from eight commercial banks by March 2009. It helped Korean banks to improve their BIS capital ratios from 10.86 per cent at the end of September 2008 to 12.92 per cent at the end of March 2009. However, amid ameliorating financial market conditions, bank reliance on the Fund declined. Furthermore, banks had strong concerns that, once they had used the Fund, the Korean government would excessively interfere in their business operations, such as cajoling them to extend loans to SMEs and to the poor households against their better assessment. As a result, the Fund ceased operation at the end of 2009.

Finally, the Korean government tried to strengthen the financial structure of banks and corporations by directly buying their non-performing assets. In May 2009, it established the Corporate Restructuring Fund with a capital of KRW40 trillion (4 per cent of GDP) to tackle bad loans. As during the 1997 crisis, the KAMCO played a leading role in purchasing non-performing assets through this Fund. By the end of 2010, the Fund had purchased non-performing loans worth KRW4.4

trillion. Most of the purchases were from banks (KRW4 trillion). The remainder was used for the purchase of physical assets and to support corporate restructuring.

In 2020, the COVID-19 pandemic broke out, generating liquidity shocks and financial market instabilities. The Korean government and the BoK had to respond to this crisis with extremely expansionary fiscal and monetary policies. To mitigate the economic damage caused by the spread of the COVID-19 pandemic and to stabilise financial markets in particular, the government held an 'Emergency Economic Council Meeting' in March 2020 and launched a KRW100 trillion liquidity support package of which KRW41.8 trillion was allocated to stabilise financial markets. Not only was the Bond Market Stabilisation Fund (within a ceiling of KRW20 trillion) re-established, but also the Stock Market Stabilisation Funds (with a ceiling of KRW10.7 trillion) were newly established.

12.3 The Bank of Korea as the Lender of Last Resort

The centrality of the three different principles underlying the LOLR policies of central banks has been raised over time (Tucker, 2014; Salter, 2016). The first important principle goes back to the 'classical doctrine' of Walter Bagehot. According to this doctrine, which was popular until the end of nineteenth century, central banks should provide as much liquidity as possible to illiquid banks at high interest rates against good quality collateral. However, by acting as LOLRs, central banks may cause a moral hazard problem by providing banks with liquidity insurance. This liquidity insurance may result in excessive risk-taking and, as such, increase the likelihood of recurrent crises. For this reason, the second principle, known as the 'Richmond Fed View', argues that central banks should provide liquidity insurance only via OMOs, accommodating demand shocks for central bank money through financial markets. According to this principle, unilateral emergency lending to individual banks is an unnecessary and objectionable function of central banks. As evidenced by the global financial crisis, the problem is that there is no guarantee that this policy alone is sufficient to stabilise financial markets. Therefore, the third principle derived from the New York Fed's response to the 2008 global financial crisis is that the proper function of the LOLR system should be a commitment to the prevention of system-wide crises. This means that the central bank should lend to anybody, be they solvent or insolvent, in order to ensure financial stability. The moral hazard problem may be more serious as a result, but the benefits from stemming a crisis can offset this cost.

These three principles can be accommodated in the three phases of the LOLR policy of the BoK. In the wake of 1997 currency crisis, the BoK followed the classical doctrine. Amid the 2008 global financial crisis, however, the BoK extended its liquidity support to financial markets. Furthermore, it supported the government initiative targeted with addressing the solvability of distressed financial institutions. The BoK accommodated the views of the Richmond Fed. Finally, along with the outbreak of the COVID-19 crisis in 2020, the BoK has become an active LOLR player, following the New York Fed's responses.

12.3.1 The 1997 Currency Crisis and LOLR according to the Classical Doctrine

Given the leadership of the Korean government in respect of active financial restructuring, the BoK had only a marginal influence on resolving the crisis as an LOLR.

During this period, the LOLR policy of the BoK was traditional, focusing on individual liquidity support. Furthermore, most of the liquidity was provided pre-emptively before the currency crisis fully unfolded. The BoK provided KRW1 trillion, respectively, to the Korea First Bank and sixteen merchant banking corporations at an interest rate of 8 per cent per annum, the average market cost of funds for commercial banks. It is noteworthy that there was no penalty charge imposed on the financial institutions bailed out, given that Korean banks had been subject to heavy government control and the crisis was more likely due to the government's regulatory and supervisory forbearances (Kane, 1994). Prior to 1997, all banks, whether private or public, were puppets of the MOF, which had never given banks freedom in respect of their activities. Furthermore, the BoK itself was not independent and liquidity support had always been at below market interest rates. The LOLR had, instead, been an instrument to provide subsidies to banks in negative profitability to refurbish their capital bases. Naturally, liquidity support availability had been always taken for granted and there was no stigma effect associated with its acceptance. Furthermore, as people could never conceive of the idea of bank failures, there was an implicit deposit guarantee even before the establishment of the KDIC. Against this backdrop, liquidity provision at market interest rates would already have been an important first step towards normalising the LOLR policy. As financial market turbulence escalated, however, the BoK had to provide a further KRW6.8 trillion in loans to fourteen banks not at market rates, but at a rate of one per cent lower than the overnight call rate. The illiquidity of Korean banks at the time would probably have deteriorated over time into insolvency and thus the need arose to increase the profitability of banks.

Furthermore, the BoK lent KRW2 trillion and KRW1 trillion at overnight call rates, respectively, to the Korea Securities Finance Corporation, which was set up to provide short-term funding for securities companies, and the Korea Credit Fund, which was in charge of the non-bank deposits insurance programme. These two financial institutions owned by the government provided KRW1.1 trillion to securities companies and KRW0.9 trillion to merchant banking corporations. This was the first time that the BoK had lent to non-bank financial companies, and, to this end, it had to invoke Clause 1, Article 80 of the Bank of Korea Act, which allowed it to lend to for-profit companies only under exceptional emergency circumstances. The Act states:

Article 80 (Credit to For-profit Enterprises)
(1) When severe impediments arise to obtaining funds from financial institutions including a severe contraction of credit or when there is a strong likelihood of their arising, the Bank of Korea may, with at least four Members concurring, render credit to any for-profit enterprise such as those engaged in the financing business other than banking institutions, the provisions of Article 79 notwithstanding.

Table 12.4 summarises the details of the loans provided by the BoK. As the financial markets began to regain stability from the latter half of 1998, the BoK progressively called in these loans. By the end of 2001, all these loans had been repaid.

12.3.2 The 2008 Global Financial Crisis and the Role of the LOLR according to the Richmond Fed View

In the wake of the 2008 global financial crisis, the BoK extended its LOLR role. In general, three different types of liquidity shortages were distinguished: (1) central bank reserve shortages due to frictional

Table 12.4 *Loans of the Bank of Korea during the 1997 currency crisis*

Type	Date	Target institutions	Reasons for assistance	Amount (Trillion KRW)	Interest charged
Traditional LOLR	1997.9	Korea First Bank	Liquidity support	1	8.0% (average market funding cost)
	1997.9	Sixteen merchant banking corporations (through the counterparty banks)	Liquidity support	1	8.0%
	1997.12	Fourteen banks	Short-term financial market crunch	6.8	Call rate – 1.0%bp
New LOLR	1998.7.6	Korean Security Finance Company	Closure of merchant banking corporations and call market crunch	1.1 (2)	Call rate
	1998.7.6	Credit Management Fund		0.9 (1)	

Note: The figures in parentheses indicate the ceilings committed to by the BoK.
Source: BoK and author's compilation.

payment shocks, (2) liquidity shortages at specific financial institutions, and, finally, (3) systemic market liquidity shortages (Bats et al., 2018). Some noteworthy developments in this regard are as follows:

First, the Intraday Overdraft Facility, which was developed in 2001, was extended to help the daily payments and settlements of financial companies. Maintaining payment and settlement systems was a unique function of the BoK. Furthermore, as already outlined in Chapter 7, standby credits and deposits were introduced in 2008, following the model of the ECB and the BoE. Though the goal of standby credits was to improve the monetary policy operation framework, it could also be used as a tool of the LOLR, which would accord with Bagehot's classical principle. The banks could use these standby credits without limit at 1 percentage point over the base rate for their daily liquidity shortages, and, if necessary, extend its maturity by up to one month. As these facilities were set up, the emergency liquidity assistance could be associated with bailing out financial firms that were insolvent, rather than illiquid, because, if their troubles were solely in respect of liquidity shortages, they could, at any time, have relied on standby credit. In fact, Korean banks rarely used this facility.

Second, no important Korean financial company went bankrupt during the 2008 global financial crisis. Thus, in contrast to the 1997 currency crisis, there was no bailing-out of individual financial companies and the primary goal of the BoK interventions was to provide market liquidity and secure the stability of the financial and foreign exchange markets, for instance, as a market-maker of last resort. Thus, OMOs began to be extensively used as the main instruments to provide market liquidity and ensure financial market stability. Through the programmes of regular and irregular RP purchases and government bond purchases, the BoK provided total liquidity of KRW18.5 trillion between September 2008 and February 2009 in the short-term and long-term financial markets, including the bank debenture and CP markets. Furthermore, it widened the scope of the collateral eligible for its open market operations and greatly increased the number of counterpart securities firms for its RP transactions. The provision of liquidity through OMOs would have been useful in order to avoid the so-called stigma effect. Thus, for the first time, the BoK fulfilled its LOLR function based upon the principle of the Richmond Fed View and OMOs have become rather important instruments for financial stability, and not simple monetary policy operational instruments. While LOLR policy based upon the Richmond Fed principle was a useful complement to address market failures, it should be temporary in nature. The BoK staff expressed continuing concern that such interventions, if frequently used, would damage a smooth monetary policy transmission channel.

Third, in collaboration with the Korean government, the BoK supplied KRW2.1 trillion to financial institutions that subscribed to the Bond Market Stabilisation Fund. Within a ceiling of KRW5 trillion, the BoK acted to provide the committed liquidity to the subscribing financial companies by purchasing government bonds and MSBs from them. However, the BoK had no direct operational involvement with the Bond Stabilisation Fund, which was completely managed under the control of the FSC. Furthermore, in March 2009, the BoK provided KRW3.3 trillion to the Bank Recapitalisation Fund, which was established by the government in order to increase the equity capital of banks to facilitate the expansion of the credit supply and the smooth implementation of corporate restructuring. The BoK was committed to lending up to KRW10 trillion to the Korea Development Bank, which would, in turn, invest it as capital in the Fund. This programme was again managed by the FSC and thus the role of the BoK was limited to lending the committed sum to the Bank Recapitalisation Fund. Clearly, the government was the principal LOLR in respect of the purchase of high-risk assets such as corporate bonds and bank capital. But it is questionable as to whether the financial markets required the BoK's money for these programmes so urgently, given the relatively meagre use of these facilities (KRW2.1 trillion out of a 10 trillion ceiling for the Bond Market Stabilisation Fund, and KRW3 trillion out of the KRW20 trillion for the Bank Recapitalisation Fund). The BoK's view of the financial market situation was different from that of government, which would explain the initial hesitation on the part of the former in collaborating with the latter. The government should have procured these sums not from the BoK but from the national budget after obtaining ratification by the National Assembly.[3]

Table 12.5 summarises the activity of the BoK as a LOLR during the global financial crisis.

12.3.3 The COVID-19 Pandemic Crisis and the LOLR according to the New York Fed View

As always, the Korean government took measures to stabilise the financial markets, reviving the idea of re-activating the Bond Market Stabilisation Fund. Notwithstanding this, the intervention of the FSC remained minimal this time, probably because the BoK was very active in addressing the COVID-19 pandemic crisis. As in the 2008 global financial crisis, the BoK expanded the supply of emergency liquidity through OMOs to secure the stability of the financial markets. It also strengthened OMOs with the expansion of eligible collateral and an increased number of counterparties. More importantly, it introduced unlimited RP transactions for providing liquidity to financial markets and a programme supporting non-bank financial companies. The financial markets in Korea have grown larger, more complex, and more interconnected than before, which requires bolder and more comprehensive interventions to stabilise them. These newer types of interventions were, to a great extent, indebted to a revision of the Bank of Korea Act in 2011, which included financial stability as an additional mandate of the BoK, as well as that of price stability.

Unprecedentedly, the COVID-19 pandemic crisis required policy measures geared towards both supply and demand shocks. Korean companies were hit hard amid concerns about reduced corporate profits and credit-rating downgrades. In particular, the shortages of liquidity were serious for companies in sectors such as the airline and travel sectors. The corporate bond credit spread widened significantly. For example, the spread between government bonds and high-rated corporate bonds (AA rated-bonds), which was at around 40 bp until the diffusion of the COVID-19 virus, increased to almost 80 bp, reflecting the increased bankruptcy risk in the corporate sectors (Bank of Korea, 2020).

---

[3] In this regard, it is worthwhile noting that the TARP in the United States was only put into practice after obtaining the approval of the US Congress.

Table 12.5 *Supply of liquidity in respect of financial stability by the BoK during the 2008 global financial crisis*

	Date	Programme	Reasons for support	Amount (Trillion KRW)
New LOLR		Intraday overdraft Standby credit	Supply of intraday credit-line and daily credit	–
New LOLR through OMO	2008.9–2009.2	RP purchase	Supply of liquidity to financial markets	16.8
	2008.10–2008.11	Outright purchase of government bonds	Supply of liquidity and diversification of transmission channel	1.7
	2008.10–2008.12	Expansion of eligible collaterals and counterparts	Supply of liquidity	–
Collaboration with the government	2008.11.24	Bond Market Stabilisation Fund	Improve the flow of funds in direct financial markets	2.1 (10)
	2009.3.26	Bank Recapitalisation Fund	Expand banks' lending capacity by enhancing their capital base	3.3 (20)

Note: The figures in parentheses indicate the ceilings committed to by the BoK.
Source: BoK and author's compilation.

Although the Korean banks are largely immune to the pandemic, corporate bankruptcies will have a negative spill-over into the financial sector, threatening its stability, which requires both the government and the BoK to support these companies as well. Thus, specifically to address this problem, the BoK has introduced two new facilities which benchmark the two facilities introduced by the FRS in the United States, namely, the Primary Market Corporate Credit Facility, and the Secondary Market Corporate Credit Facility.

The first facility is called the CBBLF, which is designed to serve as a safety net for companies, banks, and non-bank financial institutions experiencing severe difficulties in raising funds due to the prolonged impact of the COVID-19 crisis. It is operated as a standing lending facility providing banks and non-bank financial institutions, including securities companies and insurance companies, with ready access to credit from the BoK whenever they post eligible corporate bonds as collateral. Article 80 (credit to For-profit Enterprises) of the Bank of Korea Act for loans to non-bank financial institutions was invoked for the second time since the 1997 currency crisis. The ceiling for the facility was set at KRW10 trillion and the interest rate was 0.85 percentage point over the yield on MSBs (182 days).

Second, along with the Korean government, the BoK has launched a SPV loan scheme to purchase lower-rated corporate bonds and CPs. This was undertaken because of the strong credit risk aversion in the financial markets with high credit spreads and the ongoing financial difficulties for low-credit-rate companies in the wake of the COVID-19 pandemic. It seems that this would substitute for the role of the Bond Market Stabilisation Fund used by the government in 2008. Thus, in order to ensure financial market stability, a total of KRW10 trillion was directly invested in the SPV set up by government without any intermediation by banks. Purchases of corporate bonds and commercial paper would be financed through BoK's primary loans, while the Korea Development Bank, the government's bank, takes charge of subordinated loans. In particular, lower-rated corporate bonds and commercial paper were also included in the eligible instruments to be purchased to ease credit risk aversion towards non-prime bonds and to ensure stability in the credit and securities markets. Figure 12.1 illustrates the detailed operation of this new instrument.

Table 12.6 *Supply of liquidity in respect of financial stability during the COVID-19 crisis*

Type	Programme	Reasons for support	Amount (Trillion KRW)
LOLR through OMO	RP purchases	Supply of liquidity and diversification of transmission channels	19.4
	RPs from non-banks		3.5
	Outright purchase of government bonds		4.5
	Expansion of eligible collateral and number of counterparts		
New LOLR	Corporate bond-backed loan facility	Provide liquidity to companies	(10)
	SPV loans to purchase corporate bonds and CPs	Improve the flow of funds in lower-rate corporate bonds and CP markets	(8)

Note: The figures in parentheses indicate the ceilings committed to by the BoK.
Source: BoK and author's compilation.

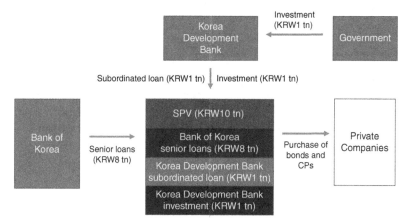

Figure 12.1 Financial structure of SPV to purchase corporate bonds and CPs

Table 12.6 summarises the crisis management measures taken by the BoK during 2020 to cope with the COVID-19 crisis. In general, these measures are assessed as being pertinent, contributing to the mitigation of the impact of the COVID-19 pandemic on the financial markets.

12.3.4 *The Bank of Korea and International Lenders of Last Resort*

The BoK has also played the role of LOLR in US dollars to domestic financial institutions via the US FRS, which, in turn, is an international LOLR to the BoK. Because the US dollar is not a legal tender that the BoK can issue freely, market perceptions about the Korean economy's solvency can suddenly deteriorate, triggering massive capital outflows. Thus, in order to stabilise FX and financial markets, the Korean government and the BoK are obliged to provide domestic financial institutions with liquidity insurance through US dollar supply, in accordance with Bagehot's classical doctrine on the LOLR.

During the 1997 currency crisis, the IMF played the role of LOLR in US dollars to Korea, providing emergency liquidity, which eventually turned out to be insufficient to quell the worries of international investors and stem the drop in the rollovers of Korean bank debt and the resulting capital outflows from Korea. More importantly, the too harsh conditionality that accompanied the borrowings from the IMF during the 1997 currency crisis generated the perception among many in the Korean public that emergency liquidity from the IMF was acceptable only after all the macroeconomic management by the government had failed (the stigma effect). Against this backdrop, the responses of the Korean government and the BoK were three-fold:

First, given the absence of reliable international LOLRs, Korea tried to self-insure its economy by desperately accumulating significant foreign reserves. But self-insurance through the accumulation of FX reserves was a sub-optimal solution. The huge amount of Korea's FX reserves was not only costly but also unsustainable. Such an option could complicate Korea's monetary and exchange rate policies, creating excess demand for the US dollar.

Second, the government wanted to protect the Korean economy from disruptive capital outflows and volatile exchange rate movements by establishing a regional and global financial safety net. This led to the establishment of the CMIM, a multilateral currency swap agreement between the ASEAN+3 countries totalling US$240 billion. Furthermore, at the G20 summit held in 2010, the Korean government argued strongly for improvements to be made to the IMF lending system, in particular relaxing the associ-ated conditionality, which prevented member countries from responding to the crisis in a timely manner. Against this backdrop, the IMF developed two new instruments, the PLL and the FCL, which attach little or no conditionality to its loans.

Third, the BoK eventually signed a currency swap agreement worth US$30 billion with the US FRS in the aftermath of the Lehman Brothers bankruptcy in 2008. The establishment of US dollar swap lines between the two central banks had a potent impact on attenuating the pressure in respect of the US dollar liquidity in the Korean FX market. The announcement of swap arrangements with the Federal Reserve alone was sufficient to bolster market confidence and stabilise the exchange rate of the Korean *won* against the US dollar. Figure 12.2 shows the contrasting reactions that the IMF borrowings and the currency swap arrangement had on the FX market in Korea.

Amid the spread of COVID-19 in early 2020, the exchange rate of Korean *won* rose to around 1,300 *won* against the US dollar, the highest level since the 2008 global financial crisis, and the swap rate between *won* and dollar plummeted. As in the 2008 global financial crisis, the BoK established a temporary bilateral currency swap arrangement with the US FRS on 19 March 2020. It signed a US$60 billion bilateral currency swap line arrangement, which was double the amount of the swap that it had concluded with the FRS during the 2008 global financial crisis. This immediately stabilised the FX market and swap market in Korea, as shown in Figure 12.3.

The currency swaps by the BoK with the FRS are also game changers in the trajectory of Asian monetary co-operation. Prior to the agreements, the main concern of the Korean government was to ensure emergency liquidity backup through swap agreements with the neighbouring Asian countries, particularly Japan and China. The goal of the Korean government and the BoK in respect of the regional arrangement was to benefit from a regional finan-cial safety net. But, after the swaps with the FRS, Korea no longer urgently needed to rely on regional arrangements, which means that the role of Korea in Asian monetary co-operation resides more in providing backup facilities to other Asian countries, than receiving them from Japan and China, the two neighbouring

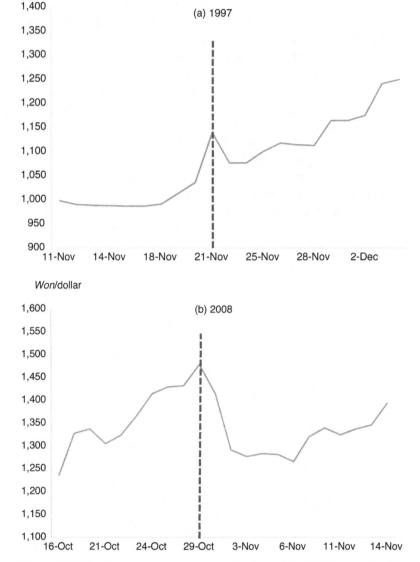

Figure 12.2 Exchange rate movement at the time of the IMF rescue funding (US$27 billion) and the Korea–US swap line (US$30 billion)
Source: ECOS, BoK.

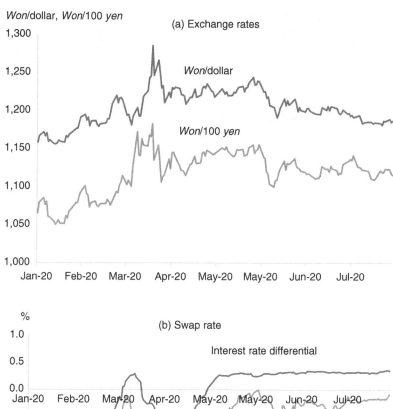

Figure 12.3 Exchange rate and swap rate movement before and after the Korea–US swap line (US$60 billion)
Source: Bank of Korea (2020).

countries which, in practice, were the only ones capable of providing Korea with emergency loans. With Korea keen on enhancing financial co-operation with the United States, its financial interest in Asian monetary co-operation, along with that of China and Japan, has started to wane.

PART V

What Will Be the Challenge for Future Monetary Policy in Korea?

13 | *Monetary Policy under Low Growth*

As Korean growth slows down and interest rates fall close to 0 per cent, the limits of the existing interest rate-based monetary policy become apparent and unconventional policy tools and instruments need to be newly developed. Against this backdrop, this chapter looks at the future challenges which will confront the BoK, and examines how the implementation of monetary policy can be improved by incorporating tools such as quantitative easing, forward guidance, and credit easing, in order to cope with the projected low growth and low inflation.

13.1 The Persistence of Low Growth

Thus far, the Korean economy has been growing successfully since the 1960s. The current growth rate of the Korean economy is, however, in rapid decline. Figure 13.1 shows the trend of the decline in the long-term growth rate of the Korean economy. For instance, the ten-year average growth rate fell from 10 per cent in the 1970s to around 7–8 per cent in the 1980s and the 1990s, and to 3–4 per cent during the first two decades of the twenty-first century. The big problem for the Korean economy is that this downward trend in the growth rate will continue in the future. According to the OECD,[1] the potential growth rate, which is currently estimated to be around 3 per cent, is expected to fall to below 2 per cent in the 2030s. Although this decline in the potential growth rate is part of the economy's maturing process, it may seriously limit the Korean economy's capacity to catch up with the advanced economies of the world, and to generate jobs.

---

[1] See the real GDP long-term forecast available at https://data.oecd.org/gdp/real-gdp-long-term-forecast.htm#indicator-chart

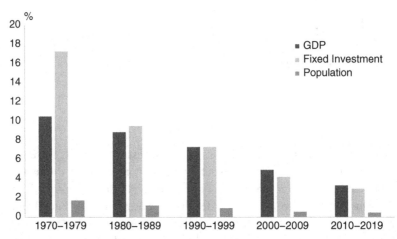

Figure 13.1 Long-term growth trend of the Korean economy (ten-year average growth rate)
Source: BoK, Statistics Korea.

Two main factors explain the projected future decline in the growth rate of the Korean economy: decline in fixed investment and population decline:

First, the current decline in fixed investment is likely to persist. Although some decline may be inevitable, reflecting the Korean economy's maturing process, Korean companies are, to a large extent, faced with an exhaustion of investment opportunities. Thus, although they have sufficient internal savings, they are reluctant to increase investment. For instance, historically, the Korean corporate sector had been the main unit of investment, while the household sector had been the main unit of savings. Consequently, the corporate sector was a deficit unit that borrowed funds from the household sector, while the household sector was a surplus unit that lent its savings to Korean companies. However, as companies cut back on their investments, retaining their profits in internal savings, their savings could eventually exceed their investment spending, transforming them into surplus units. This phenomenon has already occurred in Japan. Figure 13.2 shows the sectoral flow of funds in both Korea and Japan. Here, what distinguishes Japan from Korea, in terms of sectoral flow of funds, is that, from the second half of the 1990s,

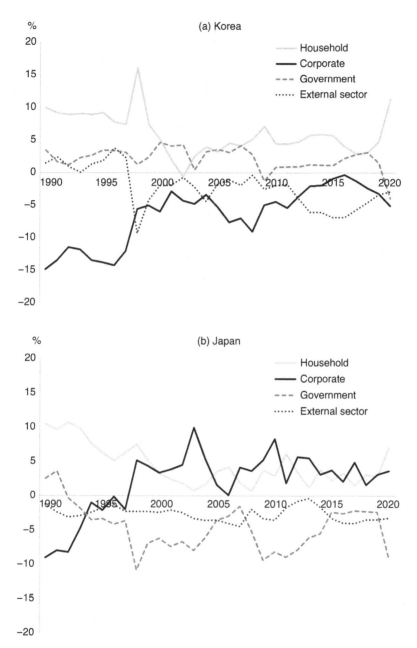

Figure 13.2 Sectoral flow of funds in Korea and Japan
Source: ECOS, BoK, and BoJ homepage.

the Japanese corporate sector acted as a savings unit, not as an investment unit, while the government sector covered for the shortage of private investment by their increases in fiscal spending. The corporate sector in Korea is currently still a deficit unit, with its investment spending exceeding its internal savings, but the trend is that it is becoming a surplus unit like its Japanese counterpart, which, along with the depletion of investment opportunities, could be called the impending 'Japanification' of the Korean economy. The shortage of investment in Korea requires not just a cyclical policy response, but also a structural remedy. It means that structural reforms to drive up potential growth rates are important, but, if these policies are not immediately possible, the government and the BoK may be induced to use fiscal and monetary policies to stimulate the economy, as in Japan. Therefore, the BoK may have to prepare a strategy to stimulate investment.

Second, Korea's population growth has fallen steadily and is expected to be in negative growth soon. A decrease in population will have a big impact on domestic demand. If exports do not increase sufficiently to offset the decline in domestic demand, the overall aggregate demand will inevitably shrink, leading to economic slowdown, as in the case of Japan. Conversely, population aging is proceeding at an unprecedented rate in Korea, which will also affect domestic demand. Unless it is addressed by an increase in productivity or technological progress, population decline and aging will affect the potential growth rate of the Korean economy. Furthermore, these trends suggest that low inflation will persist in Korea. Overall, the current low inflation is the result of a combination of factors, including a drop in commodity prices, an increase in competition due to globalisation, and the development of online and e-commerce. Nonetheless, as pointed out in Chapter 3, a change in the population structure can be an important factor in suppressing inflationary pressures.

Despite the bottleneck effect of the COVID-19 pandemic, the CPI inflation rate in Korea is expected to remain relatively low for the time being (Bank of Korea, 2021). Low inflation is not yet a concern in Korea, however. A temporary drop in the inflation rate can help to stimulate economic recovery by boosting consumption. However, the BoK may have to respond proactively in the event that low inflation causes serious deflationary expectations and consequential recession. Currently, however, the BoK has only limited capacity to handle such expectations. Despite the fact that the central banks in the advanced economies have, in the recent past, aggressively lowered interest rates to 0 per cent, and also pursued quantitative easing, it seems that these policies did not work well enough to dispel deflationary concerns completely. This raises questions about the appropriateness of the inflation-targeting framework used by the BoK and by other central banks. Unfortunately, no better alternative strategy has yet been unveiled. An inflation-targeting framework has been an important shield for the BoK to wield against all political and government interference in its decision-making, thereby ensuring its continuing independence and autonomy.

Amid this outlook of low growth and low inflation, interest rates are projected to remain low for quite a long time as well.[2] Interest rates in Korea have not yet reached 0 per cent. Nevertheless, the current level of interest rates is already unprecedently low. As in Japan during the early 2000s, an extremely expansionary monetary policy did not promote a wholehearted economic recovery and ended up only aggravating the country's asset market bubbles. It is thus necessary to devise new monetary instruments that will help to enhance the efficiency of monetary policy to stimulate the economy further and thereby raise inflationary expectations. Given the rigidity of the Korean economy, rapid increases in interest rates are unlikely. Increasing polarisation and inequality in Korean society will also make it difficult to chart an economic path forward. Furthermore, the economic damage brought about by the outbreak of the COVID-19 pandemic renders the normalisation of monetary policy even more difficult. Thus, although there is the possibility of a rise in interest rates due to the monetisation of the unprecedented increase in public deficits, interest rates may remain low until the COVID-19 pandemic has been completely overcome.

To address these challenges, the BoK faces three tasks: first, to secure a channel of influence on long-term interest rates; second, to increase the effectiveness of the credit market channel; and third, to mitigate the negative effects of international spillovers. Completing these tasks requires the BoK to incorporate many of the unconventional tools developed by other central banks of major economies into its armoury. Currently, for

---

[2] See Chapter 1 on the relationship between the potential growth rate and real neutral interest rates. The nominal neutral interest rate is the sum of the real neutral rate and inflation expectations.

instance, asset purchase programme known as quantitative easing (QE), forward guidance, credit easing, and negative interest rates are the most widely used new instruments, other than traditional short-term interest rate changes, which the BoK should continue to monitor for possible use.

13.2 Securing a Channel of Influence on Long-term Interest Rates

13.2.1 *Measures to Stimulate the Economy*

Interest rates in Korea have not yet reached zero, but, as they rapidly approach this level, the BoK needs to consider how to ensure its monetary policy has a sufficient stimulus effect. The first step it needs to take is the QE to add to its monetary policy instruments. There are two further decisions to be made in respect of a monetary policy of low or zero interest rates.

First, to the extent that the key to increase the effectiveness of monetary policy is to have the capacity to influence all segments of the yield curve, and not just its short-term ends, the BoK should envisage implementing an asset purchase programme without necessarily waiting to reach the zero-bound interest rate. This will help the BoK to flatten the yield curve without changing its policy rate. It means that the BoK can rely on two instruments to stimulate the economy further. While the short-term base rate is used for monetary policy goals, as is currently the case, the BoK can, at the same time, use QE to guide long-term interest rates to reduce the interest spread between short- and long-term interest rates.

Second, the BoK should decide on the sequencing of the use of QE. In particular, the BoK should decide on whether to use QE before or after reaching the zero interest rate bound.[3] Using QE before reaching the zero-bound interest rate seems more effective in ensuring a stimulus effect because the movement of long-term interest rates can be managed both by changes in short-term interest rates and by the asset

---

[3] In the case of the United States, for example, when this issue was first discussed among the governors of the FRS, Ben Bernanke argued that, prior to an economic crisis, these instruments could be simultaneously used along with the interest rate policy, while Alan Greenspan, then chairman of the FRS, considered that such pre-emptive action would not be necessary. In reality, the new tools and instruments were adopted in the United States only when the zero-bound interest rate was reached in the aftermath of the global financial crisis (Federal Open Market Committee Transcripts, 2003).

purchase programme. Furthermore, it has the advantage of allowing the BoK to cope more flexibly with diverse economic conditions by combining both short- and long-term interest rates (Operation Twist). Thus, the BoK should be ready to deploy QE pre-emptively, *before* interest rates fall to zero, and thereby try to secure influence on the long-term segments of the yield curve.

Figure 13.3 compares two asset purchase programmes: a conventional asset purchase programme (called QE) which is launched at zero interest rate, and a hypothetical Korean programme which is implemented while the interest rate still remains at a positive level. As shown in the top panel of Figure 13.3, the conventional asset purchase programme is a policy of lowering long-term interest rates after the short-term base rate falls to zero. The effect is summarised by a decline in the slope of the yield curve. The bottom panel of Figure 13.3 summarises the effect of the possible asset purchase programme in Korea, which consists in implementing QE before the policy rate reaches the zero bound. The effect of monetary policy is reflected by the decline in both the intercept and slope of the yield curve, which will enable the BoK to cope with the varying economic conditions more effectively.

As pointed out in Chapter 7, however, the BoK staff have traditionally been opposed to any idea of attempting to affect long-term interest rates. Figure 13.4 shows that only very small purchases of government bonds (KTBs) were made by the BoK. It is worthwhile noting that, although the BoK, in contrast to the ECB, was not forbidden from directly underwriting government bonds in the primary market, the share of government bonds held by the BoK was extremely small. This was because the open market operations of the BoK were focused on absorbing excess liquidity in the market by selling its own bonds, namely, MSBs. When recessions deepen, however, the BoK should supply liquidity to the economy and embrace open market operations for the outright purchase of government bonds, which will result in a lowering of long-term yields and a flattening of the slope of the yield curve.

It will also be crucial that the BoK ensures that long-term interest rates move in the desired direction in line with short-term interest rates. However, given that there is no guarantee of being able to manage long-term interest rates by open market operations alone, communications to change the shape of the yield curve should be

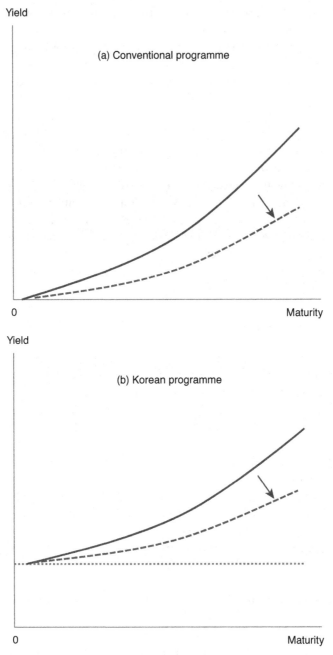

Figure 13.3 Comparison of two asset purchase programmes available in the event of a severe recession

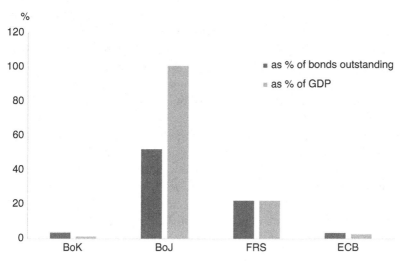

Figure 13.4 The shares of government bonds held by major central banks
Note: For the ECB, the government bonds held is based upon the public sector purchase programme.
Source: BoK, BoJ, ECB, and FRS.

used. Against this backdrop, forward guidance will be an important communication instrument that may allow the BoK to bring market expectations into closer alignment with its policy direction. To a certain extent, the BoK already provides limited forward guidance. For instance, the governor of the BoK could make an announcement that low interest rates will be maintained for an extended period or that a hike in interest rates will be delayed to a later date. However, this messaging is neither sufficiently systematic to affect long-term interest rates and generate additional stimulus effects, nor is it binding. If forward guidance can be divided into *Delphic* and *Odyssean* guidance, as Bernanke (2017) remarked, the BoK provides only Delphic guidance, which simply outlines the economic outlook as seen by the BoK, without any promises or commitments about future policy. In contrast, Odyssean guidance, which pre-commits the BoK to some contingent future policy, is completely absent, although it may be a stronger tool than Delphic guidance when it comes to affecting long-term interest rates. Notwithstanding this, this type of forward guidance is not likely to be easily introduced in Korea. Given that the government routinely intervenes in the Korean economy with infinite regulations and policy measures, pre-commitments in respect of interest rate paths could end up damaging the credibility of the BoK. Therefore, as a first step, the BoK needs to improve its Delphic guidance, by presenting the macroeconomic projections on GDP growth and CPI inflation conducted by the members of the MPB.

Direct management of long-term interest rates by yield curve control is not plausible in Korea, either. For instance, yield curve control, recently introduced by the BoJ, directly targets the yield on ten-year government bonds at zero interest rates. Given that to achieve zero interest rates would require such large-scale purchases of government bonds as to necessitate domination of the government bond market, this tool is hardly applicable to the current Korean economy.

13.2.2 The Stabilisation of Financial Markets

For the BoK, the asset purchase programme is currently used as an instrument to stabilise financial market turbulence, rather than as a tool to stimulate the economy. This is especially the case since the revision of the Bank of Korea Act in 2011, which incorporated financial stability as a supplementary mandate of the BoK in addition to price stability.

Given the absence of sufficient tools to attain the goal of financial stability, the BoK has intermittently intervened in the government bonds market in order to manage the volatility of the yield spreads, thereby stabilising the financial system. Figure 13.5 shows that long-term interest rates in Korea often show wide fluctuations even in normal times, moving quite far from the base rate determined by the BoK. For example, as Figure 13.5 shows, the long-term yield on three-year government bonds has fluctuated by more than 30 bp approximately every five months since 2005. Furthermore, long-term yields have often moved in opposite directions to short-term interest rates, damaging the smooth transmission of monetary policy. Notwithstanding this, the purchase of government bonds to this end was rare, and was carried out by the BoK staff independently of the deliberations of the MPB.

It seems that the outbreak of the COVID-19 crisis in 2020 may be a turning point in accommodating asset purchase as an official and

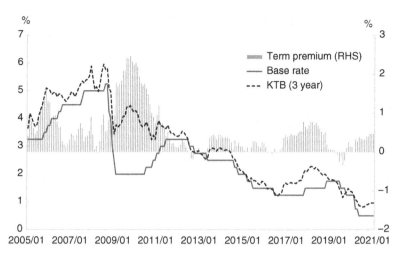

Figure 13.5 Long- and short-term interest rates and term spread
Source: ECOS, BoK.

systemic tool to achieve financial market stability.[4] For instance, faced with the rapid rise in the interest rate spread during early 2020, the BoK launched full-allotment RP purchases of an unprecedented size, reaching KRW19.4 trillion. Furthermore, the BoK conducted outright purchases of long-term Treasury bonds on seven occasions amounting to KRW11 trillion as a pre-emptive measure to stabilise the government bond market. Table 13.1 shows the outright open market purchases carried out during 2020.

Although these operations were conceived as an official measure to stabilise the volatility of long-term bond yields, in practice, they were closer to QE in stimulating the economy given their large size. However, they were not very effective in lowering long-term yields. Only one purchase out of seven slightly lowered ten-year government bond yields. This begs the question about when and how many bonds to purchase. Currently, the MPB is largely preoccupied with the setting of the base rate, while leaving market operations to the BoK staff. The MPB should also be interested in the open market operations to stabilise long-term financial markets as well. Given smaller room for changes in the policy rate, future monetary and financial policy will be more concerned about the quantity of the assets to be

---

[4] See BoK (2021) regarding the decision to incorporate the purchase of government bonds as an instrument to achieve financial market stabilisation.

Table 13.1 *Treasury bonds purchased outright during 2020*

Date	Amount (Billion KRW)	Maturity of Treasury bonds purchased (Billion KRW)				Daily changes in 10-year yields (Bp)
		3 Year	5 Year	10 Year	20 Year	
March 20	1,500	1,070	170	260		10.7
April 10	1,500		60	960	480	2.5
July 2	1,500		160	1,240	100	1.0
August 31	1,500			1,370	130	6.6
September 24	2,000		110	1,400	490	−1.3
October 28	1,500			1,090	410	3.0
November 27	1,500			1,130	370	1.8
Total	11,000	1.070	500	7,450	1,980	-

Source: BoK homepage (www.bok.or.kr/portal/main/main.do).

purchased. Close consultation between the members of the MPB and the staff of the Financial Markets Department will therefore be essential.

Meanwhile, in cases of severe financial market meltdown, it is also necessary to manage risk premiums. Figure 13.6 shows a surge in risk premiums measured by the interest rate spread between government bonds (three-year KTB) and private corporate bonds (AA-rating) during the global financial crisis and the COVID-19 pandemic. Again, along with the arrival of the COVID-19 crisis, the interest rate spread, which remained at 50 bp until the end of 2019, increased sharply by 100 bp to 150 bp.

The BoK reacted rather quickly to the crisis. The BoK expanded the scope of the assets that it recognises as eligible collateral. In addition to existing government bonds and government guaranteed bonds, for instance, bank debentures and bonds issued by public companies were included as eligible securities either for RP transactions or for outright open market operations. Furthermore, the BoK decided to apply flexible haircut ratios to those bonds taken as collateral.[5] However, given that the BoK cannot assume a credit risk in its

[5] See the policy response to COVID-19, available at: www.bok.or.kr/eng/bbs/ B0000308/list.do?menuNo=400380

Figure 13.6 Risk premiums during the global financial crisis and the COVID-19 crisis
Source: ECOS, BoK.

interventions, it faces serious hurdles managing risk premiums in conditions of exceptional financial market turmoil. Direct holding of private companies' bonds is almost impossible under the current Bank of Korea Act. This means that the BoK can only participate through collaboration with the government, which can take the credit risk, provided that it does not endanger the bank's independence.

Already the BoK has collaborated with the government through the Bond Market Stabilisation Fund. For instance, ever since the government set up the Bond Market Stabilisation Fund, it has relied on this scheme to pressure the BoK into providing funds each time there is a slight sign of financial market turmoil. Willingly or not, the BoK was forced to follow the government's decisions. During the COVID-19 pandemic, the BoK took turns in leading financial market stabilisation initiatives. Jointly with the government and the Korea Development Bank, a government-owned policy bank, the BoK established in July 2020 a SPV to invest in corporate bonds and commercial paper, including lower-rated instruments, in order to stabilise the credit securities market. If the BoK starts to participate significantly in the purchase of corporate bonds, albeit through the SPV, it will be an important monetary and financial policy decision to determine what types of securities it purchases. Quantitative easing by major central banks can make a big difference, depending on the nature of the assets purchased. For example, the US FRS invested in government and MBS bonds, while the ECB purchased covered bonds whose underlying assets were corporate bonds. In comparison, the BoJ invested not just in bonds but also in stocks, albeit indirectly through ETFs. Investments in stocks, no doubt, will have a strong effect in boosting the stock market, but, unlike investments in bonds, will be extremely difficult to taper off. In cases of bond purchase, for example, holding them until maturity automatically unwinds the QE operation, whereas, in the case of stock purchases, the normalisation of monetary policy must accompany the sale of the stocks held, thereby triggering a fall in stock prices. Again, these decisions should primarily be made by the members of the MPB, and not by the staff of the BoK.

13.3 Enhancing the Effectiveness of Credit Policy

The BoK can implement its asset purchase programme either by purchasing government bonds in the open market (QE) or expanding its credit to financial institutions (credit easing). The BILSF can be revamped as a credit-easing policy tool to cope with possible future low growth.

Unlike in the United States, in which capital markets are more developed, Europe has a relatively bank-oriented financial system. Under this system, the downward adjustment of deposit and loan interest rates is a crucial transmission channel of monetary policy in helping recovery in the European economy. Against this backdrop, the ECB launched LTROs in December 2011.[6] Then, the ECB introduced the TLTROs programme in June 2014 to encourage banks to increase their private sector loans instead of government bond purchases.

Traditionally, the BoK incentivised banks to lend more funds to companies by providing credit at rates less than the market interest rates. Similar programmes also exist for other central banks. For instance, the BoE uses the FLS, which served as a benchmark for the BoK's BILSF. Given that the BILSF provides companies with credit at lower interest rates than market rates, the BoK was afraid of losing

---

[6] The LTRO was originally an instrument for loans with a maturity of less than one year, but the ECB extended the maturity of loans to encourage banks to take out loans from the ECB for up to three years in order to ease the credit crunch caused by the euro crisis.

control of the money supply, which forced it to set a ceiling by which to limit its credits. However, as the Korean economy is maturing, with excess investment being replaced by excess savings, the goal of the BILSF is no longer to suppress inflation with less credit but to support economic recovery with more credit. Notwithstanding this, it has not yet been used as an active counter-cyclical policy tool to fight recession. Its operation and implementation need to be re-designed as follows:

First, to the extent that many of the current credits under the BILSF were used to help banks roll over their existing loans, the effect of the BILSF as a real counter-cyclical tool was limited. Thus, the BoK should focus on providing new loans, which will be more effective in stimulating the economy. Furthermore, the loans should be temporary in nature and flexible, so that they can automatically be terminated once economic recovery begins. Consideration should be given to raising the current ceiling of the BILSF so that the amount of credit easing can be flexibly adjusted.

Second, currently, the loans have been limited to small- and medium-sized companies. To work as a counter-cyclical policy tool, these loans should be extended even to big companies. However, given that a top policy priority of the Korean government is to stem the rise in household debt, it would be prudent not to extend the loans to households.

Third, there is a need to give stronger incentives to banks to increase their loans to companies and stimulate the economy. It seems that banks have little incentives to lend actively under the zero-bound interest rate. As long as its policy rate is still positive, the BoK can offer credit to banks at borrowing costs sufficiently lower than the policy rate. If the economy is in severe recession, the BoK can even offer banks negative borrowing rates, as in the TLTRO. Negative interest-rate policy cannot be effective outside the banking sector, however. Thus, it is primordial that credit easing based upon the BILSF should be launched while the policy rate is still positive. As the policy rate has been lowered to 0.5 per cent, it is important that the BoK should be careful not to misjudge the timing for the implementation of credit easing before it falls further to zero.

If the BILSF is implemented based upon these principles, it is expected to be able to support economic recovery more efficiently by allowing the BoK to act proactively, which can be called 'Korean-style real quantitative easing'.[7]

One big advantage of the BILSF is that it is an instrument for target-oriented monetary policy, because, unlike interest rate adjustments that have an undifferentiating impact on the whole economy, it can selectively affect specific sectors and target specific goals.

In Korea, the continuing low interest rates have led to a sharp rise in the number and in the size of household loans, which are very pro-cyclical. As of the end of 2020, total household loans had reached nearly KRW1,630 trillion (85 per cent of Korean GDP), among which household loans secured by residential houses are worth KRW910 trillion. Thus, there is a need to strengthen macro-prudential policy in order to contain increases in household debt which are too rapid.

In general, secured household loans in Korea are composed of two types of loans: home mortgage loans and home equity loans. Given the strong demand for home ownership, mortgage loans are likely to continue to increase. Excessively large mortgage loans raise concerns about delinquencies or defaults. So far, however, the risk exposure of banks seems relatively limited. All mortgage loans in Korea are recourse debts. Thus, they are relatively safe assets for banks. Furthermore, house prices have never witnessed any significant drop, not even during the 1997 Asian financial crisis. This explains why defaults on household loans are not likely to lead to a general banking crisis in Korea. In contrast, home equity loans were, to a substantial extent, used by self-employed business owners. They sometimes borrow as individuals, rather than as business borrowers, putting up their homes as collateral. These loans are classified as household loans, although their purpose is not for purchasing homes, but for borrowing working capital for their private businesses, instead. Thus, they

---

[7] The controversy over the so-called Korean-style quantitative easing happened in early 2016. In fact, it was nothing more than a trick to push the BoK into printing money, not to mention that it was an illegal attempt to infringe upon the independence of the BoK. The basic idea was that the BoK should print money for the restructuring of Korean companies and lend it to the Korea Development Bank, a state bank, which would use it for this goal. The idea of supporting the restructuring of insolvent companies through the issuance of BoK notes was really shocking, given that the former minister of economy and finance misled the public as its main proponent. Clearly, the restructuring of Korean companies could be realised through the National Budget, given the relatively low public debt of the Korean government. Perhaps the only reason it was proposed was that the BoK's money-printing capability could be used without obtaining the prior approval of the Korean National Assembly.

are very vulnerable to business downturns and are sometimes unable to make regular debt service payments from their precarious income sources. Alongside the outbreak of the COVID-19 pandemic, in particular, the default risk of self-employed business owners has greatly increased. Moreover, the decline in their sales revenues due to the COVID-19 pandemic is likely to persist for a long time. While current financial relief measures, such as the deferral of the loan principal and interest payments are likely to improve the liquidity conditions of self-employed business owners both temporarily and up to a point, these measures may not help solve their long-term solvability and sustainability. Therefore, while further boosting the Korean economy, the BoK should take greater responsibility for financial stability. From this perspective, the BILSF may be a far better toolkit instrument in handling the economy after the COVID-19 crisis than traditional interest rate adjustments.

13.4 Strengthening the Capacity to Mitigate International Spillover Effects

Following the liberalisation of the financial sector and the opening up of capital markets, the Korean economy has become deeply interconnected with global financial markets, particularly US financial markets. Under these circumstances, US monetary policy has close repercussions on Korean financial markets, which, in turn, leads the MPB to closely examine the decisions of the US monetary authorities and their spillover effects on the Korean economy.

Since the 1997 financial crisis, the Korean economy has been subject to repeated foreign exchange and financial market instability whenever the global financial market is turbulent. Each time, whether it be the global financial crisis, the euro crisis, or more recently the COVID-19 crisis, there were capital outflows and a subsequent surge in long-term interest rates, a repeat *déjà vu*, which ends up destabilising the foreign exchange and financial markets in Korea.[8]

Figure 13.7 shows that Korea's long-term interest rates move very closely with those of the United States and other developed countries.

---

[8] As in the case of 'Taper Tantrum' after the global financial crisis, a quick recovery of the advanced economies from the COVID-19 pandemic and consequently their quick interest rate rises are likely to trigger another big wave of capital outflow from both Korea and other emerging economies, which will suffer from slow vaccination and delayed recovery.

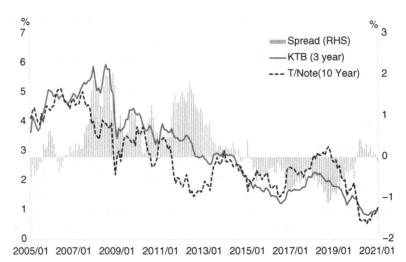

Figure 13.7 Long-term interest rate spread trend in Korea and the United States
Source: ECOS, BoK.

In fact, the interest rate correlation coefficient between Korea's three-year government bonds and US ten-year government bonds, which was only 0.5 before the global financial crisis, rose to 0.9 after the crisis (Kim, 2014).

Given the linkage between the international financial market and the domestic financial market, it is clear that the BoK should pay more attention to the movement of US long-term interest rates. In particular, the need to stabilise the spreads of yields between the United States and the domestic Korean government bonds will be strong in the event that they turn negative along with the outflow of foreign capital. The BoK should develop some strategies to prevent long-term interest rates from rising by purchasing long-term government bonds in the financial market. Conversely, in the event of foreign capital inflows, it should sell off its holdings of government bonds. In the end, the BoK could serve as a buffer institution by buying government bonds when they are cheap, and selling them when they are expensive. However, this would require that the BoK hold a sufficient amount of government bonds, which is not currently the case because it has traditionally been reluctant to do so.

More importantly, closer policy co-ordination may be needed. Clearly, US monetary policy is one of the most important

Table 13.2 *Current currency swap arrangements of the BoK*

Country	Bilateral arrangement with G7 countries and Switzerland				Other bilateral arrangements	Multilateral arrangement (CMIM)
	US	Canada	Switzerland	Japan	China and others	ASEAN+3
Size	US$60 billion	No limit	SF 10 billion	US$60 billion[1]	Equivalent to US$870 billion	US$384 billion
Date of the most recent arrangement	2020.3	2017.11	2018.2	2011	–	2014.7
Date of termination	2021.9	Permanent	2026.3	2015.2	–	Permanent

Note 1: As of 2011.
Source: Compiled by the author based upon the annual report of the BoK.

considerations in the current decision-making process of the MPB. Given capital account liberalisation, it is increasingly difficult to conduct autonomous monetary policy irrespective of the exchange rate regime deployed, as Rey (2015) emphasised.

In the long run, it will be important for Korea to strengthen its global monetary co-operation, including joining the permanent swap network that exists between the G7 countries and Switzerland. Currently, the BoK has a currency swap arrangement with the United States, Canada, and Switzerland (see Table 13.2). Against this backdrop, the internationalisation of the Korean *won* may be necessary. To this end, the government and the BoK should remove the last remaining hurdles impeding complete capital liberalisation, allowing *won* currency transactions between non-residents.

References

Adrian, Tobias and Hyun Song Shin (2009). 'Liquidity and Leverage'. *FRB of New York Staff Report*, no. 328. Available at: http://doi.org/10.2139/ssrn.1139857.

Alacevich, Michele and Pier Francesco Asso (2009). 'Money Doctoring after World War II: Arthur I. Bloomfield and the Federal Reserve Missions to South Korea'. *History of Political Economy* 41 (2): 249–270. Available at: https://doi.org/10.1215/00182702-2009-002.

Allen, Franklin and Douglas Gale (2007). *Understanding Financial Crises (Clarendon Lectures in Finance)*. Oxford: Oxford University Press.

Ambrose, Brent W. and Sunwoong Kim (2003). 'Modeling the Korean Chonsei Lease Contract'. *Real Estate Economics* 31 (1): 53–74. Available at: https://doi.org/10.1111/j.1080-8620.2003.00057.x.

Angrisani, Marco, Michael D. Hurd, and Susann Rohwedder (2015). 'The Effect of Housing and Stock Wealth Losses on Spending in the Great Recession'. *RAND Working Paper Series* WR-1101 (10 March). Available at: https://doi.org/http://dx.doi.org/10.2139/ssrn.2616945.

Axilrod, Stephen H. (2011). *Inside the Fed: Monetary Policy and Its Management: Martin through Greenspan to Bernanke*. Cambridge, MA: MIT Press.

Bank of Japan (1985). *One Hundred Year History of Bank of Japan*. Japan: Bank of Japan. Available at: www.boj.or.jp/about/outline/history/hyakunen/hyaku5.htm.

Bank of Korea (2004) Minutes of the 21st Monetary Policy Board Meeting. October 7. In Korean. Available at: www.bok.or.kr/portal/bbs/B0000245/view.do?nttId=57826&menuNo=200761&pageIndex=35.

Bank of Korea (2010). *The Bank of Korea: A Sixty-Year History*. Seoul: Bank of Korea. Available at: www.bok.or.kr/eng/cmmn/file/fileDown.do?menuNo=400231&atchFileId=ENG_0000000001007884&fileSn=1.

Bank of Korea (2013). *Monetary Policy in Korea*. In Korean. 2012 Edition. Available at: www.bok.or.kr/portal/bbs/P0000602/list.do?menuNo=200459.

Bank of Korea (2014). *Financial Stability Report (April 2014)*. Available at: www.bok.or.kr/eng/bbs/E0000737/view.do?nttId=200680&menuNo= 400042&pageIndex=2.

Bank of Korea (2016a). *Monetary Policy Report (April 2016)*. Available at: www.bok.or.kr/ucms/cmmn/file/fileDown.do?menuNo=400215&atch FileId=ENG_0000000001018614&fileSn=1.

Bank of Korea (2016b). *Foreign Exchange Institutions and Markets in Korea*, In Korean. Available at: www.bok.or.kr/portal/bbs/P0000609/view .do?nttId=215470&menuNo=200465&pageIndex=1.

Bank of Korea (2017a). *Financial Stability Report (June 2017)*. Available at: www.bok.or.kr/eng/bbs/E0000737/view.do?nttId=231178&menuNo= 400042&pageIndex=1.

Bank of Korea (2017b). *Monetary Policy Report (November 2017)*. Available at: www.bok.or.kr/eng/bbs/E0000628/view.do?nttId=233711& menuNo=400025&pageIndex=3.

Bank of Korea (2017c). *Monetary Policy in Korea*. 2017 Edition. Available at: www.bok.or.kr/eng/bbs/E0000742/view.do?nttId=234109& menuNo=400224&pageIndex=1.

Bank of Korea (2018). *Bank of Korea Act*. Available at: www.bok.or.kr/eng/ bbs/E0000824/view.do?nttId=10001380&menuNo=400261&page Index=1.

Bank of Korea (2020). *Payment and Settlement Systems Report 2019 (March)*. Available at: www.bok.or.kr/eng/bbs/E0000866/view.do?nttId= 10058511&menuNo=400047.

Bank of Korea (2021). *Monetary Policy Report (March 2021)*. Available at: www.bok.or.kr/eng/bbs/E0000628/view.do?nttId=10064115&menuNo= 400215&pageIndex=1.

Barro, Robert J. and David B. Gordon (1983). 'Rules, Discretion and Reputation in a Model of Monetary Policy'. *Journal of Monetary Economics* 12 (1): 101–121. Available at: https://doi.org/10.1016/0304-3932(83)90051-X.

Bats, Joost, Jan Willem van den End, and John Thoolen (2018). 'Revisiting the Central Bank's Lender of Last Resort Function'. *De Nederlandsche Bank Occasional Studies* 16 (4). Available at: www.dnb.nl/media/ytzjhm f0/201807_nr_4_-2018-_revisiting_the_central_bank-s_lender_of_last_ resort_function.pdf.

Bech, Morten L. and Todd Keister (2012). 'On the Liquidity Coverage Ratio and Monetary Policy Implementation'. *BIS Quarterly Review* 49 (December): 49–61. Available at: https://ssrn.com/abstract=2206362.

Belke, Ansgar and Thorsten Polleit (2009). *Monetary Economics in Globalised Financial Markets*. Cham: Springer. Available at: https://doi .org/10.1007/978-3-540-71003-5.

Bernanke, Ben S. (1993). 'Credit in the Macroeconomy'. *Quarterly Review-Federal Reserve Bank of New York* 18 (Spring): 50–70.

Bernanke, Ben S. (1999). *Japanese Monetary Policy: A Case of Self-Induced Paralysis?* Princeton, NJ: Princeton University. Available at: www.princeton.edu/~pkrugman/bernanke_paralysis.pdf.

Bernanke, Ben S. (2007). 'The Financial Accelerator and the Credit Channel'. Speech at the Credit Channel of Monetary Policy in the Twenty-First-Century Conference, Federal Reserve Bank of Atlanta, Georgia, 15 June 2007. Available at: www.federalreserve.gov/newsevents/speech/bernanke20070615a.htm.

Bernanke, Ben S. (2010). 'Central Bank Independence, Transparency, and Accountability'. Speech at the Institute for Monetary and Economic Studies International Conference, Bank of Japan, Tokyo, 25 May 2010. Available at: https://fraser.stlouisfed.org/title/statements-speeches-ben-s-bernanke-453/central-bank-independence-transparency-accountability-9072.

Bernanke, Ben S. (2012). *Monetary Policy and the State of the Economy.* Hearing Before the Committee on Financial Services, US House of Representatives. 18 July 2012. Available at: www.govinfo.gov/content/pkg/CHRG-112hhrg76116/html/CHRG-112hhrg76116.htm.

Bernanke, Ben S. (2015a). *The Courage to Act: A Memoir of a Crisis and Its Aftermath.* New York: W.W. Norton.

Bernanke, Ben S. (2015b). 'The Taylor Rule: A Benchmark for Monetary Policy'. *Brookings* (blog). 28 April 2015. Available at: www.brookings.edu/blog/ben-bernanke/2015/04/28/the-taylor-rule-a-benchmark-for-monetary-policy.

Bernanke, Ben S. (2017). 'Monetary Policy in New Era' Paper Prepared for Conference on Rethinking Macroeconomic Policy, Washington, DC: Peterson Institute, 12–13 October 2017. Available at: www.piie.com/system/files/documents/bernanke20171012paper.pdf.

Bernanke, Ben S. and Frederic S. Mishkin (1992). 'Central Bank Behavior and the Strategy of Monetary Policy: Observations from Six Industrialized Countries'. In *Monetary Policy Strategy*, edited by Frederic Mishkin, 165–206. Cambridge, MA: MIT Press, 2009.

Bernanke, Ben S. and Frederic S. Mishkin (1997). 'Inflation Targeting: A New Framework for Monetary Policy?' *Journal of Economic Perspectives* 11 (2): 97–116. Available at: https://doi.org/10.1257/jep.11.2.97.

Bernanke, Ben S., Mark Gertler, and Simon Gilchrist (1996). 'The Financial Accelerator and the Flight to Quality'. *The Review of Economics and Statistics* 78 (1): 1–15. Available at: https://doi.org/10.2307/2109844.

Beyer, Andreas, Giulio Nicoletti, Niki Papadopoulou, Patrick Papsdorf, Gerhard Rünstler, Claudia Schwarz, João Sousa, and Olivier Vergote (2017). 'The Transmission Channels of Monetary, Macro-and Microprudential Policies and Their Interrelations'. *ECB Occasional Paper No. 191 (May)*. Available at: https://doi.org/10.2866/138051.

Bikhchandani, Sushil, David Hirshleifer, and Ivo Welch (1998). 'Learning from the Behavior of Others: Conformity, Fads, and Informational Cascades'. *Journal of Economic Perspectives* 12 (3): 151–170. Available at: https://doi.org/10.1257/jep.12.3.151.

Bindseil, Ulrich (2014). *Monetary Policy Operations and the Financial System*. Oxford: Oxford University Press.

Bindseil, Ulrich and Flemming Würtz (2007). 'Open Market Operations: Their Role and Specification Today'. In *Open Market Operations and Financial Markets*, edited by David G. Mayes and Jan Toporowski, 54–79. New York: Routledge.

Bindseil, Ulrich and Jeroen Lamoot (2011). 'The Basel III Framework for Liquidity Standards and Monetary Policy'. *SFB 649 Discussion Paper* No. 2011–041. Available at: http://hdl.handle.net/10419/56679.

BIS (Bank for International Settlements) (2009). '79th Annual Report: 1 April 2008 – 31 March 2009'. *BIS Annual Report*, Bank for International Settlements. Available at: www.bis.org/publ/arpdf/ar2009e .pdf.

BIS (Bank for International Settlements) (2015). 'Digital Currencies'. Committee on Payments and Market Infrastructures, *CPMI Papers* No. 137, Bank for International Settlements. Available at: www.bis.org/ cpmi/publ/d137.pdf.

Blanchard, Olivier, Giovanni Dell'Ariccia, and Paolo Mauro (2010). 'Rethinking Macroeconomic Policy'. *IMF Staff Position Note* SPN/10/03 (February), International Monetary Policy. Available at: http://citeseerx .ist.psu.edu/viewdoc/download?doi=10.1.1.153.7293&rep=rep1&type= pdf.

Blinder, Alan S. (1997). 'Distinguished Lecture on Economics in Government: What Central Bankers could Learn from Academics–and Vice Versa'. *Journal of Economic Perspectives* 11 (2): 3–19.

Blinder, Alan S. (1999). *Central Banking in Theory and Practice*. Cambridge, MA: MIT Press.

Blinder, Alan S. (2008). 'Making Monetary Policy by Committee'. *CEPS Working Paper* No. 167 (June), Paper presented at the Bank of Canada Conference. Available at: https://gceps.princeton.edu/wp-content/uploads/ 2017/01/167blinder.pdf.

Blinder, Alan S. (2013). *After the Music Stopped: The Financial Crisis, the Response, and the Work Ahead*. Vol. 79. New York: Penguin Group USA.

Blinder, Alan S. and John Morgan (2005). 'Are Two Heads Better than One? Monetary Policy by Committee'. *Journal of Money, Credit, and Banking* 37 (5): 789–812.

Bloomfield, Arthur I. and John P. Jensen (1950). 'Recommendations regarding Central Banking Reform in Korea'. *The Architecture of the Bank of Korea Act*, vol. 2, Bank of Korea, 2015.

Boivin, Jean, Michael T. Kiley, and Frederic S. Mishkin (2010). 'How Has the Monetary Transmission Mechanism Evolved over Time?' *NBER Working Paper* No. 15879 (April). Available at: https://doi.org/10.3386/w15879.

Bordo, Michael D., Ronald MacDonald, and Michael J. Oliver (2009). 'Sterling in Crisis: 1964–1967'. *NBER Working Paper* No. 14657 (January). Available at: https://doi.org/10.3386/w14657.

Borio, Claudio (2011). 'Central Banking Post-Crisis: What Compass for Unchartered Waters?' BIS Working Papers No. 353 (September), Bank for International Settlements. Available at: www.bis.org/publ/work353.pdf.

Borio, Claudio and Piti Disyatat (2009). 'Unconventional Monetary Policies: An Appraisal'. *BIS Working Papers* No. 292 (November), Bank for International Settlements. Available at: www.bis.org/publ/work292.pdf.

Borio, Claudio, Magdalena Erdem, Andrew Filardo, and Boris Hofmann (2015). 'The Costs of Deflations: A Historical Perspective'. *BIS Quarterly Review* (March): 31–54. Available at: www.bis.org/publ/qtrpdf/r_qt1503e.htm.

Brunnermeier, Markus K. (2009). 'Deciphering the Liquidity and Credit Crunch 2007–2008'. *Journal of Economic Perspectives* 23 (1): 77–100. Available at: https://doi.org/10.1257/jep.23.1.77.

Calvo, Guillermo A. (1998). 'Capital Flows and Capital-Market Crises: The Simple Economics of Sudden Stops'. *Journal of Applied Economics* 1 (1): 35–54. Available at: https://doi.org/10.1080/15140326.1998.12040516.

Calvo, Guillermo A. and Carmen M. Reinhart (1999). 'Capital Flow Reversals, the Exchange Rate Debate, and Dollarization'. *Finance and Development* 36 (3): 13–15.

Case, Karl E., John M. Quigley, and Robert J. Shiller (2005). 'Comparing Wealth Effects: The Stock Market versus the Housing Market'. *Advances in Macroeconomics* 5 (1): 1–32. Available at: http://lps3.www.proquest.com.libproxy.snu.ac.kr/scholarly-journals/comparing-wealth-effects-stock-market-versus/docview/205029479/se-2?accountid=6802.

Cecchetti, Stephen and Kim Schoenholtz (2016). 'A Primer on Helicopter Money'. VoxEU. 19 August 2016. Available at: https://voxeu.org/article/primer-helicopter-money.

Cho, Dongchul and Younguck Kang (2013). *2012 Modularisation of Korea's Development Experience: Korea's Stabilisation Policies in the 1980s.* Korea: Ministry of Strategy and Finance. Available at: https://archives .kdischool.ac.kr/handle/11125/41955?mode=full.

Cho, Seonghoon (2020). 'Natural Interest Rate, Potential GDP Growth Rate and Long-Term Monetary Policy Stance'. *Journal of Economic Theory and Econometrics* 31 (2): 40–69. In Korean.

Chow, Hwee Kwan and Fot Chyi Wong (2020). 'Monetary Policy Implementation in Singapore'. In *Monetary Policy Implementation in East Asia*, edited by Frank Rövekamp, Moritz Bälz and Hanns Günther Hilpert, 31–42. Financial and Monetary Policy Studies, vol. 51. Cham: Springer.

Christiano, Lawrence J., Mathias Trabandt, and Karl Walentin (2010). 'DSGE Models for Monetary Policy Analysis'. In *Handbook of Monetary Economics*, vol. 3A, edited by Benjamin M. Friedman and Michael Woodford, 285–367. Amsterdam: Elsevier.

Clapham, John Harold (1944). *The Bank of England: A History.* London: Macmillan.

Clarida, Richard H., Jordi Gali, and Mark Gertler (1999). 'The Science of Monetary Policy: A New Keynesian Perspective'. *Journal of Economic Literature* 37 (4): 1661–1707. Available at: https://doi.org/10.1257/ jel.37.4.1661.

Clarida, Richard H. and Mark Gertler (1997). 'How the Bundesbank Conducts Monetary Policy'. In *Reducing Inflation: Motivation and Strategy*, edited by Christina D. Romer and David H. Romer, 363–412. Chicago IL and London: University of Chicago Press.

Coleman, Wilbur John (1996). 'Money and Output: A Test of Reverse Causation'. *American Economic Review* 86 (1): 90–111.

Demertzis, Maria, Massimiliano Marcellino, and Nicola Viegi (2010). 'Anchors for Inflation Expectations'. DNB Working Papers 229, Netherlands Central Bank.

Dewatripont, Mathias and Jean Tirole (1994). *The Prudential Regulation of Banks.* Cambridge, MA: MIT Press.

Diamond, Douglas W. (1996). 'Financial Intermediation as Delegated Monitoring: A Simple Example'. *FRB Richmond Economic Quarterly* 82 (3): 51–66.

Disyatat, Piti (2008). 'Monetary Policy Implementation: Misconceptions and Their Consequences'. *BIS Working Papers* No. 269 (December). Available at: www.bis.org/publ/work269.pdf.

Draghi, Mario (2012). Speech at the Global Investment Conference in London, 26 July 2012. Available at: www.ecb.europa.eu/press/key/date/ 2012/html/sp120726.en.html.

ECB (European Central Bank) (2012). 'Monthly Bulletin February 2012'. *Monthly Bulletin*, 81–2, European Central Bank. Available at: www.ecb .europa.eu/pub/pdf/mobu/mb201202en.pdf.

Ehrmann, Michael (2014). 'Targeting Inflation from Below-How Do Inflation Expectations Behave?' Staff Working Paper 2014–52 (December), Bank of Canada. Available at: www.bankofcanada.ca/wp-content/uploads/2014/12/wp2014-52.pdf.

Eichengreen, Barry (1996). *Globalizing Capital: A History of the International Monetary System*. Princeton NJ: Princeton University Press.

Eichengreen, Barry (2004). 'Monetary and Exchange Rate Policy in Korea: Assessments and Policy Issues'. Paper prepared for a symposium at the Bank of Korea, 25 August 2004.

Farhi, Emmanuel and Jean Tirole (2012). 'Collective Moral Hazard, Maturity Mismatch, and Systemic Bailouts'. *The American Economic Review* 102 (1): 60–93. Available at: https://doi.org/10.1257/aer.102.1.60.

Fawley, Brett W. and Christopher J. Neely (2013). 'Four Stories of Quantitative Easing'. *Federal Reserve Bank of St. Louis Review* 95 (1): 51–88. Available at: https://doi.org/10.20955/r.95.51-88.

Federal Reserve Bank of St. Louis (n.d.). 'Supervision and Regulation: An Introduction'. In *Plain English: Making Sense of the Federal Reserve*. Available at: www.stlouisfed.org/in-plain-english/introduction-to-supervision-and-regulation.

Fischer, Stanley (2017). 'Committee Decisions and Monetary Policy Rules'. Speech at the Structural Foundations of Monetary Policy, Hoover Institution Monetary Policy Conference, Stanford University, Stanford CA, 5 May 2017.

Fisher, Irving [1911] (1963). *The Purchasing Power of Money: Its Determination and Relation to Credit Interest and Crises*. New York: Macmillan. Reprint, New York: Augustus M. Kelley. Citations refer to the Kelley edition.

FOMC (Federal Open Market Committee) (1996). Federal Open Market Committee Meeting Transcript, 2–3 July 1996. Available at: www.feder alreserve.gov/monetarypolicy/files/FOMC19960703meeting.pdf.

FOMC (Federal Open Market Committee) (2009). Federal Open Market Conference Call Transcript, 16 January 2009. Available at: www.federal reserve.gov/monetarypolicy/files/FOMC20090116confcall.pdf.

FOMC (Federal Open Market Committee) (2012). *Statement on Longer-Run Goals and Monetary Policy Strategy*. Available at: www.federal reserve.gov/monetarypolicy/files/FOMC_LongerRunGoals.pdf.

Friedman, Benjamin M. and Kenneth N. Kuttner (2011). 'Implementation of Monetary Policy: How do Central Banks Set Interest Rates?' In *Handbook of Monetary Economics*, vol. 2B, edited by Benjamin M. Friedman and Michael Woodford, 1345–1438. Amsterdam: Elsevier.

Friedman, Milton [1970] (2006). 'A Counter-Revolution in Monetary Theory'. Reprinted by Kent Matthews and Philip Booth. *Issues in Monetary Policy: The Relationship between Money and the Financial Markets*, John Wiley & Sons Ltd.

FSS (Financial Supervisory Service) (2020). *Handbook 2019*. Financial Supervisory Service, Seoul, Korea. Available at: https://english.fss.or.kr/fss/eng/p/publications/fh_list.jsp?bbsid=1289364537633.

Fukuda, Shin-ichi (2017). 'The Impacts of Japan's Negative Interest Rate Policy on Asian Financial Markets'. ADBI Working Paper Series No. 707 (March), Asian Development Bank Institute. Available at: www.adb.org/sites/default/files/publication/237186/adbi-wp707.pdf.

Galbi, Douglas (2008). 'Locrian Law: Some Peculiar Legal Institutions'. *Purple motes*. Available at: www.purplemotes.net/2008/10/19/some-peculiar-legal-institutions.

Galbraith, John Kenneth (1991). *A History of Economics: The Past as the Present*. London: Penguin Books.

Geithner, Timothy F. (2014). *Stress Test: Reflections on Financial Crises*. New York: Broadway Books.

Goodfriend. Marvin (2002). 'Interest on Reserves and Monetary Policy'. *Economic Policy Review* 8 (May): 77–84. Federal Reserve Bank of New York. Available at: www.newyorkfed.org/medialibrary/media/research/epr/02v08n1/0205good.pdf.

Goodhart, Charles A. E. (1999). 'Myths About the Lender of Last Resort,' *International Finance* 2 (3): 339–360.

Goodhart, Charles A. E. (2010). 'The Changing Role of Central Banks'. BIS Working Papers No. 326 (November), Bank for International Settlements. Available at: www.bis.org/publ/work326.pdf.

Gordon, Robert J. (2013). 'The Phillips Curve is Alive and Well: Inflation and the NAIRU during the Slow Recovery'. *NBER Working Paper* No. 19390 (August). Available at: https://doi.org/10.3386/w19390.

Gordon, Robert J. (2015). 'Secular Stagnation: A Supply-Side View'. *The American Economic Review* 105 (5): 54–59. Available at: https://doi.org/10.1257/aer.p20151102.

Greenspan, Alan (2013). *The Map and the Territory: Risk, Human Nature, and the Future of Forecasting*. New York: Penguin Press.

Henning, C. Randall (1999). *The Exchange Stabilization Fund: Slush Money or War Chest?* Washington DC: Peterson Institute for International Economics.

Hofmann, Boris and Bilyana Bogdanova (2012). 'Taylor Rules and Monetary Policy: A Global "Great Deviation"?'. *BIS Quarterly Review*

(September): 37–49. Available at: www.bis.org/publ/qtrpdf/r_qt1209 .pdf.

Holston, Kathryn, Thomas Laubach, and John C. Williams (2017). 'Measuring the Natural Rate of Interest: International Trends and Determinants'. *Journal of International Economics* 108 (Supplement 1): S59-S75. Available at: https://doi.org/10.1016/j.jinteco.2017.01.004.

Hur, Seok-Kyun and Seong-Tae Kim (2012). 'Fiscal Policies of Korea through the Global Financial Crisis'. *Korea and the World Economy* 13 (3): 395–418.

IMF (International Monetary Fund) (2008). 'Financial Stress, Downturns, and Recoveries'. *World Economic Outlook Reports*, October 2008. Available at: www.imf.org/en/Publications/WEO/Issues/2016/12/31/ World-Economic-Outlook-October-2008-Financial-Stress-Downturns-and-Recoveries-22028.

IMF (International Monetary Fund) (2009a). 'From Recession to Recovery: How Soon and How Strong?' *World Economic Outlook*, April 2009, Chap. 3, 97–132. Available at: www.imf.org/-/media/Websites/IMF/ imported-full-text-pdf/external/pubs/ft/weo/2009/01/pdf/_text.ashx.

IMF (International Monetary Fund) (2009b). 'Sustaining the Recovery'. *World Economic Outlook* October 2009. Available at: www.imf.org/~/ media/Websites/IMF/imported-flagship-issues/external/pubs/ft/weo/2009/ 02/pdf/_textpdf.ashx.

IMF (International Monetary Fund) (2013). 'The Dog That Didn't Bark: Has Inflation Been Muzzled or Was It Just Sleeping?' *World Economic Outlook*, April 2013, Chap. 3. Available at: www.imf.org/en/Publications/ WEO/Issues/2016/12/31/~/media/Websites/IMF/imported-flagship-issues/ external/pubs/ft/weo/2013/01/pdf/_c3pdf.ashx.

IMF (International Monetary Fund) (2019). 'Republic of Korea: Staff Report for the 2019 Article IV Consultation'. *Country Report* No. 19/132 (May), Available at: www.imf.org/-/media/Files/Publications/CR/2019/1KORE A2019001.ashx.

IMF (International Monetary Fund) (2020). 'Republic of Korea Financial Sector Assessment Program: Technical Note-Macroprudential Policy Framework and Tools'. *Country Report* No. 20/277 (September), Available at: www .imf.org/en/Publications/CR/Issues/2020/09/18/Republic-of-Korea-Financial-Sector-Assessment-Program-Technical-Note-Macroprudential-Policy-49749.

Janis, Irving L. (1973). 'Groupthink and Group Dynamics: A Social Psychological Analysis of Defective Policy Decisions'. *Policy Studies Journal* 2 (1): 19–25.

Jo, Se Hyung et al., (2018). 'Examination of Changes in Monetary Policy Framework and Endogeneity of Money Supply'. *Bank of Korea Monthly Bulletin*. (February) In Korean.

Johnson, Roger T. (2010). *Historical Beginnings-The Federal Reserve*, Federal Reserve Bank of Boston, www.bostonfed.org/publications/ economic-education/historical-beginnings.aspx.

Kahn, George A. (2010). 'Monetary Policy under a Corridor Operating Framework'. *Economic Review* 95 (Q IV): 5–34, Federal Reserve Bank of Kansas City.

Kahneman, Daniel (2013). *Thinking, Fast and Slow*. New York: Farrar, Straus and Giroux.

Kahneman, Daniel and Amos Tversky (1974). 'Judgment under Uncertainty: Heuristics and Biases'. *Science* 185 (4157): 1124–1131. Available at: https:// doi.org/10.1126/science.185.4157.1124.

Kaldor, Nicholas (1982). *The Scourge of Monetarism*. Oxford: Oxford University Press.

Kaminsky, Graciela L., Carmen M. Reinhart, and Carlos A. Vegh (2003). 'The Unholy Trinity of Financial Contagion'. *Journal of Economic Perspectives* 17 (4): 51–74. Available at: https://doi.org/10.1257/ 089533003772034899.

Kane, Edward J. and Min-Teh Yu (1994). 'How Much Did Capital Forbearance Add to the Cost of the S&L Insurance Mess'. *NBER Working Paper* No. 4701 (April). Available at: https://doi.org/10.3386/ w4701.

Kang, Mansoo (2005). *Thirty Years of Korean Economy on the Spot*. In Korean. Seoul: Samsung Economic Research Institute.

Keynes, John Maynard [1923] (1973). 'A Tract on Monetary Reform'. In *The Collected Writings of John Maynard Keynes*, vol. IV, edited by Elizabeth Johnson and Donald Moggridge. London: Macmillan.

Keynes, John Maynard [1936] (1973). 'General Theory of Employment, Interest and Money'. In *The Collected Writings of John Maynard Keynes*, vol. VII, edited by Elizabeth Johnson and Donald Moggridge. London: Macmillan.

Kim, Jun (2014). 'The International Transmission of Monetary Policy: Korea's Experience'. *BIS Papers* No. 78 (August). Available at: www.bis .org/publ/bppdf/bispap78.pdf.

Kindleberger, Charles P. and Robert Z. Aliber (2005). *Manias, Panics and Crashes: A History of Financial Crises*. 5th ed. Hoboken NJ: John Wiley & Sons.

King, Mervyn (2005). 'Monetary Policy: Practice Ahead of Theory'. Speech at the Mais Lecture, Cass Business School, City University, London, 17 May 2005. Available at: www.bankofengland.co.uk/-/media/boe/files/ news/2005/may/monetary-policy-practice-ahead-of-theory-speech-by- mervyn-king.

King, R. and C. Plosser (1984). 'Money, Credit and Prices in a Real Business Cycle'. *The American Economic Review* 74 (3): 363–380. Available at: www.jstor.org/stable/1804013.

Kiyotaki, Nobuhiro and John Moore (1997). 'Credit Cycles'. *Journal of Political Economy* 105 (2): 211–248. Available at: https://ssrn.com/abstract=3914.

Kroeger, Alexander, John McGowan, and Asani Sarkar (2018). 'The Pre-crisis Monetary Policy Implementation Framework'. *Federal Reserve Bank of New York Staff Reports* No. 809. Available at: www.newyorkfed .org/medialibrary/media/research/staff_reports/sr809.pdf?la=en.

Krugman, Paul (1998). 'It's Baaack: Japan's Slump and the Return of the Liquidity Trap'. *Brookings Papers on Economic Activity* 2: 137–187.

Kydland, Finn E. and Edward C. Prescott. (1977). 'Rules Rather than Discretion: The Inconsistency of Optimal Plans'. *Journal of Political Economy* 85 (3): 473–491. Available at: https://doi.org/10.1086/260580.

Laeven, Luc and Fabian Valencia (2008). 'Systemic Banking Crises: A New Database'. *IMF Working Paper* No. 08/224 (September). Available at: www.imf.org/-/media/Websites/IMF/imported-full-text-pdf/external/pubs/ft/wp/2008/_wp08224.ashx.

Lall, Subir (1997). 'Speculative Attacks, Forward Market Intervention and the Classic Bear Squeeze'. *IMF Working Paper* No. 97/164 (December). Available at: www.imf.org/-/media/Websites/IMF/imported-full-text-pdf/external/pubs/ft/wp/_wp97164.ashx.

Law, John [1705] (1966). *Money and Trade Considered: With a Proposal for Supplying the Nation with Money.* Edinburgh: R. & A. Foulis. Reprint, New York: Augustus M. Kelley.

Lee, H. M. and H. Kim (2013). 'The Role of Money and Credit in the Monetary Policy of Korea'. In Korean. *BOK Economic Study* No. 2013–13, Bank of Korea. Available at: www.bok.or.kr/ucms/cmmn/file/fileDown.do?menuNo=500788&atchFileId=KO_00000000000097112&fileSn=1.

Lee, Jong Kyu (2013). 'The Operation of Macroprudential Policy Measures: The Case of Korea in the 2000s'. *BOK Working Paper* No. 2013–1, Bank of Korea. Available at: www.bok.or.kr/ucms/cmmn/file/fileDown.do?menuNo=400067&atchFileId=ENG_0000000001011771&fileSn=1.

Lee, Kyu Sung (2011). *The Korean Financial Crisis of 1997: Onset, Turnaround, and Thereafter.* The World Bank and the Korea Development Institute.

Mersch, Yves (2017). 'Central Bank Independence Revisited'. Keynote Address delivered at the *Symposium on Building the Financial System of the 21st Century: An Agenda for Europe and the United States*, 30 March 2017.

Meyer, Laurence H. (2000). 'The Politics of Monetary Policy: Balancing Independence and Accountability'. Remark delivered at the University of Wisconsin, 24 October 2000.

Mill, John Stuart [1859] (2015). *On Liberty*. London: John W. Parker and Son. Reprint, Dover Publications.

Mishkin, Frederic S. (2001). 'Monetary Policy Strategies for Latin America,' In *Monetary Policy Strategy*, edited by F. Mishkin, 279–308. Cambridge, MA: MIT Press.

Mishkin, Frederic S. (2002). 'The Role of Output Stabilization in the Conduct of Monetary Policy'. In *Monetary Policy Strategy*, edited by Frederic Mishkin, 75–88. Cambridge, MA: MIT Press, 2009.

Mishkin, Frederic S. (2009). *Monetary Policy Strategy*. Cambridge, MA: MIT Press.

Mishkin, Frederic S. (2011). *The Economics of Money, Banking, and Financial Markets*. Canadian ed. Toronto: Pearson Addison-Wesley.

Moon, Woosik (2000). 'The Causes of the Korean Currency Crisis: Policy Mistakes Re-examined'. *Korea Review of Applied Economics* 2 (June): 93–118.

Moon, Woosik (2017). 'A Coinless Society as a Bridge to a Cashless Society: A Korean Experiment'. In *Cash in East Asia*, edited by Frank Rövekamp, Moritz Bälz, and Hanns Günther Hilpert, 101–115. Financial and Monetary Policy Studies, vol. 44. Switzerland:Springer.

Moon, Woosik (2018). *A Study on Monetary Policy*. In Korean. Seoul: Yulgok Books.

Moon, Woosik (2020). 'Inflation Targeting in Korea'. In *Monetary Policy Implementation in East Asia*, edited by Frank Rövekamp, Moritz Bälz, and Hanns Günther Hilpert, 31–42. Financial and Monetary Policy Studies, vol. 51. Cham: Springer.

Moon, Woosik and Yeongseop Rhee (2000). 'Foreign Exchange Market Liberalization Policies in Korea: Past Assessment and Future Options'. *Journal of International and Area Studies* 7 (1): 59–79.

Moon, Woosik and Yeongseop Rhee (2006). 'Spot and Forward Market Intervention during the 1997 Korean Currency Crisis'. *Banca Nazionale del Lavoro Quarterly Review* 59 (238): 243–268.

Moon, Woosik and Yeongseop Rhee (2012). *Asian Monetary Integration: Coping with a New Monetary Order after the Global Crisis*. Cheltenham: Edward Elgar.

Morris, Stephen and Hyun Song Shin (1998). 'Unique Equilibrium in a Model of Self-Fulfilling Currency Attacks'. *American Economic Review* 88 (3): 587–597. Available at: www.jstor.org/stable/116850.

Moutot, Philippe, Alexander Jung, and Francesco Paolo Mongelli (2008). 'The Working of the Eurosystem: Monetary Policy Preparations and

Decision-Making – Selected Issues'. *ECB Occasional Paper* No. 79 (January). Available at: www.ecb.europa.eu/pub/pdf/scpops/ecbocp79 .pdf?f0cb48fbc23bd2e23be1c22ca4ccae0f.

Nam, Sang-woo (1984). 'Korea's Stabilization Efforts since the Late 1970s'. *KDI Working Paper* No. 8405 (March).

National Assembly (1999). 'Special Investigation Commission Report on the Causes of Economic and Currency Crisis'. In Korean. National Assembly Special Investigation Commission, Korea.

Orphanides, Athanasios (2007). 'Taylor Rules'. *Finance and Economics Discussion Series* 2007–18 (May), Federal Reserve Board. Available at: www.federalreserve.gov/pubs/feds/2007/200718/200718pap.pdf.

Ortiz, Guillermo (2009). *Issues in the Governance of Central Banks: A Report from the Central Bank Governance Group*. Bank for International Settlements. Available at: www.bis.org/publ/othp04.pdf.

Park, Kyounghoon, Hyun Joon Lim, and Kyung Seo Noh (2020). 'Results of Bank of Korea Macro-Econometric Model (BOK20) Construction'. *Bank of Korea Quarterly Bulletin*, September 52 (3): 15–41. Available at: www.bok .or.kr/eng/bbs/E0000829/view.do?nttId=10061505&menuNo=400216& pageIndex=1.

Poole, William (1968). 'Commercial Bank Reserve Management in a Stochastic Model: Implications for Monetary Policy'. *The Journal of Finance* 23 (5): 769–791. Available at: https://doi.org/10.1111/j.1540-6261 .1968.tb00316.x.

Poole, William (1970). 'Optimal Choice of Monetary Policy Instruments in a Simple Stochastic Macro Model'. *Quarterly Journal of Economics* 84 (2): 192–216.

Poole, William (1971). 'Rule of Thumb for Guiding Monetary Policy'. *Open Market Policies and Operating Procedures-Staff Studies* (July), Board of Governors of the Federal Reserve System.

Radcliffe Committee (Committee on the Working of the Monetary System, and Cyril John Radcliffe) (1959). *Report: Committee on the Working of the Monetary System*. Chancellor of the Exchequer. London: H.M. Stationery Office.

Reifschneider, David, Robert Tetlow, and John Williams (1999). 'Aggregate Disturbances, Monetary Policy, and the Macroeconomy: The FRB/US Perspective'. *Federal Reserve Bulletin*, Board of Governors of the Federal Reserve System, January. Available at: www.federalreserve.gov/pubs/ bulletin/1999/0199lead.pdf.

Reinhart, Carmen M. and Kenneth S. Rogoff (2008). 'Is the 2007 U.S. Sub-Prime Financial Crisis so Different? An International Historical Comparison'. *NBER Working Paper* No.13761 (January). Available at: https://doi.org/10.3386/w13761.

Rey, Hélène (2015). 'International Channels of Transmission of Monetary Policy and the Mundellian Trilemma'. Paper presented at the 15th Jacques Polak Annual Research Conference, International Monetary Fund, Washington DC, 13–14 November 2014. Available at: www.imf.org/external/np/res/seminars/2014/arc/pdf/Rey.pdf.

Rhee, Gwang-Ju and Eun Mo Lee (2005). 'Foreign Exchange Intervention and Foreign Exchange Market Development in Korea'. *BIS Papers* No. 24: 196–208. Available at: www.bis.org/publ/bppdf/bispap24q.pdf.

Rhee, Yeongseop and Chi-Young Song (1996). 'Exchange Rate Policy and Effectiveness of Intervention: The Case of Korea'. Paper presented at the International Conference on Exchange Rate Policies in Emerging Asian Countries: Domestic and International Aspects, Seoul, Korea, 15–16 November 1996.

Ricardo, David (1824). *Plan for the Establishment of a National Bank*. London: John Murray. Reprinted as *The Works and Correspondence of David Ricardo*, vol. 4, edited by Piero Sraffa with the collaboration of M. H. Dobb, Indianapolis, IN: Liberty Fund, 1984.

Rist, Charles [1940] (1966). *History of Monetary and Credit Theory: From John Law to the Present Day*. Macmillan. Reprint, translated by Jane Degras, New York: Augustus M. Kelley. Citations refer to the Kelley edition.

Rodrik, Dani and Andres Velasco (1999). 'Short-Term Capital Flows'. *NBER Working Paper* No. 7364 (September). Available at: https://doi.org/10.3386/w7364.

Rowe, J. Z. (1965). *The Public-Private Character of United States Central Banking*. New Brunswick, NJ: Rutgers University Press.

Ryoo, Sangdai, Taeyong Kwon, and Hyejin Lee (2013). 'Foreign Exchange Market Developments and Intervention in Korea'. *BIS Papers* No.73: 205–213. Available at: www.bis.org/publ/bppdf/bispap73o.pdf.

Salter, Alexander William (2016). 'Robust Political Economy and the Lender of Last Resort'. *Journal of Financial Services Research* 50: 1–27.

Santor, Eric and Lena Suchanek (2016). 'A New Era of Central Banking: Unconventional Monetary Policies'. *Bank of Canada Review* 2016 (Spring): 29–42. Available at: www.bankofcanada.ca/wp-content/uploads/2016/05/boc-review-spring16-santor.pdf.

Sargent, Thomas J. (1982). 'The Ends of Four Big Inflations'. In *Inflation: Causes and Effects*, edited by Robert E. Hall, 41–98. Chicago, IL: University of Chicago Press.

Schmittmann, Jochen M. and Chua Han Teng (2020). 'Offshore Currency Markets: Non-Deliverable Forwards (NDFs) in Asia'. *IMF Working Paper*

WP/20/179 (September) Available at: www.imf.org/en/Publications/WP/Issues/2020/09/04/Offshore-Currency-Markets-Non-Deliverable-Forwards-NDFs-in-Asia-49712.

Seong, Byung Hee and Tae Soo Kang (2011). *Developments and Characteristics of the Korean Chonsei Rental System*. BOK-IMF Workshop on Managing Real Estate Booms and Busts. Seoul: Bank of Korea.

Shin, Ho Soon, Jungyeuon Lee and Jungmin Park (2017). 'Macroprudential Frameworks, Implementation and Relationship with Other Policies in Korea'. *BIS Papers* No. 94 (December). Available at: www.bis.org/publ/bppdf/bispap94.pdf.

Shin, Jang-sup (2014). 'Dialogue with Kim Woo-choong: The World Is Still Wide and There Are Many Things to Do'. In Korean. Seoul: Bookscope.

Shirai, Sayuri (2017). *Mission Complete: Reflating Japan's Economy*. Tokyo, Japan: Asian Development Bank Institute. Available at: http://hdl.handle.net/11540/8313.

Shirakawa, Masaaki (2012). 'Demographic Changes and Macroeconomic Performance: Japanese Experiences'. Opening remark at 2012 BOJ-IMES Conference, Bank of Japan, 30 May 2012.

Shirakawa, Masaaki (2018). *Central Bank: The 39-Year Experience of a Central Banker*. In Japanese. Tokyo: Toyo Keizai Shinpōsha.

Sibert, Anne (2006). 'Central Banking by Committee'. *International Finance* 9 (2): 145–168. Available at: https://doi.org/10.1111/j.1468-2362.2006.00180.x/.

Smith, Adam [1776] (2014). *The Wealth of Nations*. Shine Classics.

Summers, Larry (2014). 'U.S. Economic Prospects: Secular Stagnation, Hysteresis, and the Zero Lower Bound'. *Business Economics* 49 (2): 65–73.

Summers, Lawrence H., David Wissel, and John David Murray (2018). *Rethinking the Fed's 2 Percent Inflation Target*. Washington, DC: Brookings Institution, June. Available at: www.brookings.edu/wp-content/uploads/2018/06/ES_20180607_Hutchins-FedInflationTarget.pdf.

Surowiecki, James (2004). *The Wisdom of Crowds: Why the Many are Smarter than the Few and How Collective Wisdom Shapes Business, Economies, Societies and Nations*. New York: Anchor Books.

Svensson, Lars E. O. (2011). 'Inflation Targeting'. Chap. 22 in *Handbook of Monetary Economics*, vol. 3B, edited by Benjamin M. Friedman and Michael Woodford, 1237–1302. Amsterdam: Elsevier.

Svensson, Lars E. O. (2013). 'Some Lessons from Six Years of Practical Inflation Targeting'. *Sveriges Riksbank Economic Review* 2013 (3): 29–80. Available at: http://archive.riksbank.se/Documents/Rapporter/POV/2013/2013_3/rap_pov_131122_eng.pdf.

Svensson, Lars E. O. (2020). 'Monetary Policy Strategies for the Federal Reserve'. *International Journal of Central Banking* 16 (1): 133–193. Available at: www.ijcb.org/journal/ijcb2002_3.pdf.

Sveriges Riksbank (2014). 'The Riksbank's Operational Framework for the Implementation of Monetary Policy – A Review'. *Riksbank Studies*, March 2014. Available at: http://archive.riksbank.se/Documents/Rapporter/ Riksbanksstudie/2014/rap_riksbanksstudie_140326_eng.pdf.

Tanzi, Vito (1997). 'The Changing Role of the State in the Economy: A Historical Perspective'. *IMF Working Paper* No. 97/114 (September). Available at: www.imf.org/-/media/Websites/IMF/imported-full-text-pdf/ external/pubs/ft/wp/_wp97114.ashx.

Taylor, John B. (1993). 'Discretion versus Policy Rules in Practice'. *Carnegie-Rochester Conference Series on Public Policy* 39 (December): 195–214. Available at: https://doi.org/10.1016/0167-2231(93)90009-L.

Taylor, John B. (1995). 'Stabilization Policy and Long-Term Economic Growth'. In *The Mosaic of Economic Growth*, edited by Ralph Landau, Timothy Taylor, and Gavin Wright, 129–149. Stanford, CA: Stanford University Press.

Taylor, John B. (2018). 'Rules versus Discretion: Assessing the Debate over the Conduct of Monetary Policy'. *Stanford Institute for Economic Policy Research Working Paper* No. 17–045 (January). Available at: https://siepr .stanford.edu/sites/default/files/publications/17-045.pdf.

Tetlock, Philip E. and Dan Gardner (2015). *Superforecasting: The Art and Science of Prediction*. New York: Broadway Books.

Thornton, Daniel L. (2004). 'The Fed and Short-Term Rates: Is It Open Market Operations, Open Mouth Operations or Interest Rate Smoothing?' *Journal of Banking & Finance* 28 (3): 475–498. Available at: https://doi.org/10.1016/S0378-4266(02)00409-0.

Tucker, Paul (2014). 'The Lender of Last Resort and Modern Central Banking: Principles and Reconstruction'. *BIS Papers* No 79 (September): 10–42. Available at: www.bis.org/publ/bppdf/bispap79.pdf.

Wicksell, Knut [1898] (1965). *Interest and Prices*. Jena: Gustav Fischer. Translated by R. F. Kahn, New York: Augustus M. Kelly.

Wicksell, Knut [1901] (1967). *Lectures on Political Economy, Volume II: Money*. Translated by E. Classen, London: Routledge & Kegan Paul.

Woodford, Michael (1995). 'Price-Level Determinacy without Control of a Monetary Aggregate'. *Carnegie-Rochester Conference Series on Public Policy* 43 (December): 1–46. Available at: https://doi.org/10.1016/0167-2231(95)90033-0.

Woodford, Michael (2001). 'Monetary Policy in the Information Economy'. In *Economic Policy for the Information Economy*, A Symposium

Sponsored by Federal Reserve Bank of Kansas City. Federal Reserve Bank of Kansas City.

Woodford, Michael (2005). 'Central-Bank Communication and Policy Effectiveness'. Paper presented at the Federal Reserve Bank of Kansas City Symposium, The Greenspan Era: Lessons for the Future, Jackson Hole, Wyoming, 25–27 August 2005. Available at: www.columbia.edu/ ~mw2230/JHole05.pdf.

Woodford, Michael (2011). 'Optimal Monetary Stabilization Policy'. In *Handbook of Monetary Economics*, vol. 3B, edited by Benjamin M. Friedman and Michael Woodford, 723–828. San Diego, CA: North-Holland.

Woolley, Anita Williams, Christopher F. Chabris, Alex Pentland, Nada Hashmi, and Thomas W. Malone (2010). 'Evidence for a Collective Intelligence Factor in the Performance of Human Groups'. *Science* 330 (6004): 686–688. Available at: https://doi.org/10.1126/ science.1193147.

World Bank (1993). *The East Asian Miracle: Economic Growth and Public Policy*. A World Bank Policy Research Report. New York: Oxford University Press.

Yellen, Janet (2017). 'The Economic Outlook and the Conduct of Monetary Policy'. Remarks made at the Stanford Institute for Economic Policy Research, Stanford, CA: Stanford University, 19 January 2017.

Index

Printed in the United States
by Baker & Taylor Publisher Services